SPEAKING RELATIONALLY

THE GUILFORD SERIES
ON PERSONAL RELATIONSHIPS

Steve Duck, *Editor*
Department of Communication Studies, The University of Iowa

SPEAKING RELATIONALLY

Culture, Communication, and Interpersonal Connection

KRISTINE L. FITCH

THE GUILFORD PRESS
New York   London

©1998 The Guilford Press
A Division of Guilford Publications, Inc.
72 Spring Street, New York, NY 10012
http://www.guilford.com

Printed in the United States of America

This book is printed on acid-free paper.

Last digit is print number: 9 8 7 6 5 4 3 2 1

Library of Congress Cataloging-in-Publication Data

Fitch, Kristine L.
    Speaking relationally: culture, communication, and
interpersonal connection / Kristine L. Fitch.
        p.   cm. — (The Guilford series on personal
relationships)
    Includes bibliographical references.
    ISBN 1-57230-277-1 (hardcover). —
ISBN 1-57230-305-0 (pbk.)
    1. Interpersonal relations—Colombia.
    2. Interpersonal communication—Colombia.
    3. Culture—Social aspects. 4. Colombia—
Social life and customs.   I. Title.   II. Series.
HM132.F576   1998
302'.09861—dc21
                                        97-41159
                                            CIP

A la memoria de
Aurelio Muñoz Hoyos
un gran colombiano
1941–1993

ACKNOWLEDGMENTS

For any work that gestates as long and transforms as often and completely as this one has, indebtedness has a way of piling up exceedingly high. The Fulbright Foundation and a Faculty Fellowship from the University of Colorado provided generous support for fieldwork, and an Old Gold Fellowship from the University of Iowa enabled me to spend the summer of 1995 writing. The Fulbright Commission in Colombia facilitated data collection in numerous ways and put me in contact with numerous Colombians willing to discuss the preliminary version of many of the ideas presented here. The list of Colombians who worked with me in a variety of ways, from allowing me access to their organizations and relationships, to transcribing interviews, to reading drafts of chapters, extends endlessly. Appreciation is especially due to Gabriel Lara, Leonor Galindo, Clemencia Garzon, María Eugenia Cerón, Angela Hernández, José Gabriel Muñoz, Dioselina de Lozano, Alberto Melo, and Miriam de Melo. I also owe profound thanks to my in-laws for opening their home, their lives, and their hearts to me as I pursued objectives that could only have seemed incredibly odd to them.

The network of friends, colleagues, and helpful critics in the United States and beyond who gave generously of their time to read, comment on drafts, and offer crucial encouragement to persist in the face of despair is similarly far-flung. Donal Carbaugh, Bob Craig, Jerry Hauser, Wendy Leeds-Hurwitz, Stuart Sigman, and Graham Allan are due profound thanks in this regard.

I have been blessed with exceptional teachers along the way. I took my first Spanish class solely because Kathy Hamm was teaching it; that act changed my life forever, and continues to enrich it daily. In very great measure she made this book possible. Robert Hopper is largely responsible for my having undertaken scholarly examination of social life in the first place, and his teaching continues to enlighten my best efforts to do so. Gerry Philipsen provided sure, insightful guidance throughout the dissertation process in which this project first took shape. His invaluable advice and endless support have stimulated and informed each of the varied forms through which the project has evolved. The two of them are exemplars of what mentoring can be, and I consider myself incredibly fortunate to have encountered them both.

Karen Tracy and Daena Goldsmith, constant intellectual companions through all these years, gave incisive feedback on various partial drafts of this manuscript and helped enormously as I struggled to refine my understandings of discourse and culture. They would be wealthy people had I in fact paid them the quarter I sometimes promised for every idea they contributed or clarified in this project, and both are friends that make life worth living as well as studying. Leslie Baxter and Steve Duck read various versions of the full manuscript and provided more detailed and useful feedback on them than any junior colleague could rightly hope for or deserve. Their support during the final stages of this project was only part of what they have done to make Iowa ("Is this *heaven?*") home. Nina Molinaro, *colegamiga del alma*, was a further source of inspiration, perseverance, and humor. Robert Sanders has contributed steady assistance throughout the process, has taught me to argue, and has been a razor-sharp intellect to hone my ideas on. My respect and admiration for him are as deep as my gratitude.

Finally, Jairo Muñoz provided my original motivation to try to understand Colombians in personal relationships, and the delight of his companionship remains the primary reward for those efforts. Without his strength and countless sacrifices this work would never have been possible.

CONTENTS

SPEAKING RELATIONALLY

INTRODUCTION

Hillary Rodham Clinton's 1996 book, *It Takes a Village*, focused on the importance of community involvement in the socially crucial task of raising children. Her argument about the significance of social context for parent–child interaction is a highly public parallel to a conceptual shift during the past few years that emphasizes the social nature of personal relationships. Just as it takes a village to raise a child, similarly "it takes a community" to form a friendship, to negotiate a work relationship, to dance (or muddle) through a courtship, to muddle (or churn) through a divorce. Although the fact that people need people is well understood, this new attention to social context additionally suggests that human agency—traditionally the focus of individualist perspectives on interpersonal communication (cf. Allan, 1993, and Lannaman, 1991, among many others)—has been overemphasized, and the influence of social structures largely overlooked, in relationships research.

Although the call for increasing attention to the social aspects of personal relationships has not been controversial, neither has it been answered with empirical research. Despite a number of conceptual moves to investigate relationship processes in social contexts (e.g., Baxter, 1992, 1993; Duck, 1993; Duck, West, & Acitelli, 1997; Montgomery, 1992; Werner, Brown, Altman, & Staples, 1992), studies of personal relationships that attend to the symbolic webs of culture, history, and class in which those processes unfold remain scarce. In this book I address that scarcity by way of an ethnographic study of certain speaking practices among urban, largely middle-class Colombians that shape how they understand and enact personal relationships. I explore the embeddedness of relational practices in cultural practices, and thus suggest that culture and relationships are not separate (i.e., relationships cannot be enacted outside of a cultural context, and culture is created and sustained in the course of particular relationships).

Culture is typically represented as a pervasive, generally invisible system of symbolic resources and shared beliefs arising from the shared experiences of a group of people, that stands outside but still shapes their understanding of how the world works. For some time culture has also been recognized as a powerful current running through the daily lives and experiences of human beings, not simply ritual occasions they take part in from time to time. In this book I connect these two ideas to show how daily practices constitute, affirm, and sometimes challenge cultural understanding.

It is usually clearer to us that *another* culture has invisible shared beliefs than that our own does. Yet cultural values and norms have been offered with increasing frequency as explanations for people's actions, from greeting sequences to arranged marriage, and for the way people interpret the actions of others. For this reason, cultural differences and the impact they have on interaction have been scrutinized with concern that has risen in proportion to the frequency of contact between members of distinctive cultural groups (usually construed at the international level). Efforts to understand how culture influences perception and behavior, and how different cultures view the world, have been signs of hope in the face of intergroup conflict. Those efforts have extended into other areas of communication research, as scholars have started to theorize about culture independent of its connection to nationhood. In this book

I take a somewhat different path, examining daily interactional practices as cultural practices.

Yet the road between cultural beliefs and interpersonal relationships has not been a well-traveled one to date, at least in the sense of detailed consideration of culture as a system of symbolic resources with which people construct their relationships throughout their lives. Certainly, there are side roads with plenty of traffic: ethnographies of speaking that address interpersonal relationships as those are demonstrated in the broader cultural code (e.g., Carbaugh, 1988; Katriel, 1986, 1992; Kondo, 1990; Varenne, 1986), cross-cultural studies that compare patterns of interaction and relationships in different groups in order to highlight the contrasts between two or more systems (e.g., Heath, 1983; Kochman, 1981), and studies that examine intercultural contact and emphasize the impact of cultural differences on communication (Gudykunst & Kim, 1992; Kim, 1988; Ting-Toomey, 1988). Where the last type of analysis has fallen short is in not providing enough detailed exploration of interactive practices and their symbolic content, tending to focus instead on macrolevel patterns of communication identified as characteristic of particular groups in contact with one another.

This book is an attempt to deepen understanding of interpersonal relationship processes by exploring the patterns of interaction through which members of a particular culture construct and maintain their relationships. Integral to this exploration is attention to the premises about personhood, relationships, and communication that lend symbolic coherence to these interpersonal practices. As an ethnography of speaking, it takes a perspective on communication and personal relationships that focuses on the distinctiveness of speaking practices and relationships across communities. Of primary concern in this approach are the communal resources, both communicative and symbolic, that people utilize to construct meaning in everyday activities.

In taking this approach, the book does not fall neatly into categories of related work, despite aspects of it that are similar to each of them. Whereas the book has obvious connections to explorations of culture, it is also intended to enrich, and perhaps redirect to some degree, current approaches to interpersonal communication. Chapters 1 and 6 show that, by framing interaction and relationships as processes inescapably enacted in culture, we can gain a detailed point of reference from which to examine the constitutive role of culture in social life. By showing how communicative resources are utilized in culturally structured ways and exploring how people employ the implicit assumptions of their particular interpersonal ideology to engage in interpersonal tasks, the book has something to say about a language/culture-based framework for interpersonal communication more generally.

To make this broader contribution, the book takes an ethnographic case study as its starting point. All the same, its focus is not exclusively on exposition of the distinctive cultural beliefs and practices of urban Colombian professionals. Rather, it examines more generally the connections among speech patterns, relationships, and cultural systems of symbolic resources and values. Still, there is enough ethnographic detail that the book, particularly Chapters 2–6, could be read as a case study. The communicative resources described in those chapters are language practices each of which is a substantially developed area of inquiry in the ethnography of speaking in its own right. The focus of Chapter 2, for example, is personal address, acknowledged in various social science disciplines as one of the linguistic structures that most distinctly encodes the social structure of communities. Directives, as discussed in Chapter 3, and narratives, as discussed in Chapter 4, have similar grounding in research concerned with illuminating the cultural bases of meaning.

By illustrating the broader questions of relationships and culture through a case study, the book describes a culture primarily on its own terms rather than as a point of contrast to another group, as is customary in much previous cross-cultural and intercultural literature. Nonetheless, comparison to U.S. culture is inevitably touched on throughout the book as a consequence of my own point of reference as a North American researcher working within a distinctive cultural setting. Additionally, Chapter 7 offers further comparisons of Colombian cultural patterns and values to those of other cultural groups. These comparisons thus situate this work within the realm of intercultural communication.

The significance of the trend toward identifying interpersonal communication practices more closely with culture is threefold. First, by developing a cultural approach to interpersonal communication, the book will facilitate research and theory building whose scope extends beyond the taken-for-granted assumptions of Euro-American, late-twentieth-century culture. Second, the elaboration of speaking practices and the symbolic system that makes them a coherent basis for personal relationships of a speech community brings the hidden assumptions of that view into stark relief. Because these assumptions are characterized by vastly different understandings of such matters as compared to those primarily represented in current research (based primarily on the U.S. white middle class), the contrast illuminates the pervasive and largely implicit influence of those understandings. Third, the study employs a research strategy that is attuned to the rich complexity of interpersonal processes, thus exposing the dynamics of the cultural context in which they are enacted. It provides a starting point for further empirical work that integrates relational practices and their cultural context much more fully than existing research.

Finally, there is inherent value in careful study of a culture about which numerous stereotypes exist in public discourse. It may seem paradoxical to study interpersonal relationships, let alone cultural values, in a society characterized as chaotic at best, and murderously dysfunctional at worst. Colombia is, after all, the country with the highest noncombat homicide rate in the world. It is the country where a star soccer player was gunned down after his miscue in a World Cup game cost his team the championship. In Colombia a drug kingpin walked away from a supposedly maximum-security prison, then, after years on the run, he died in a hail of police bullets—only to be mourned at his funeral by throngs of sobbing people. Colombia is the country where both the winner and loser of the most recent presidential election stand accused of financing their campaigns with drug money. The investigation of those contributions has generated widespread debate over whether, if the president were found guilty, the offense would be serious enough to demand his resignation. The ever present potential for violence, the power of interpersonal connections to transcend law or regulation, and the precarious capacity of institutions to control the behavior of fellow citizens were thus pervasive elements of these Colombians' talk about the nature of social life as they lived and sought to understand it.

Nonetheless, although nearly every person in Colombia is affected to some degree by the pervasive violence and corresponding mistrust and fear that it generates, there is a distinctive system of interpersonal relationships that centers around connectedness. Despite the effects of more than half a century of first political then social upheaval, that interpersonal ideology of connectedness generates a tremendous human warmth. A goal of this book, beyond its theoretical and methodological aims, is to show another side of Colombia: an interpersonal system that counters, and acts as a way of dealing with, the harsh social, political and economic realities that are already quite well known.

DATA COLLECTION AND ANALYSIS

Data were collected for this study in two phases. For 10 months of 1987 and 3 months in 1992, I lived in Bogotá with my in-laws, a middle-class, middle-aged Colombian couple. Being included in their daily lives as a family member provided access to Colombians from a wide range of occupational and regional backgrounds, as well as a certain degree of social class variation. Sponsorship from the Fulbright Foundation and involvement with the Instituto

Caro y Cuervo, a linguistics research and teaching institution, provided a wider network for participating in and studying Colombian culture.

Both phases of the research centered around (1) ethnographic observation, (2) interviews (both individual and focus group), (3) tape recording and transcription of conversations, and (4) analysis of written documents of various kinds. The research was conducted in a wide variety of interactional settings: schools, a printing plant, a free legal aid clinic, a family and couples counseling service, several business organizations, and numerous social functions. Six Colombian research assistants, recruited from the Instituto Caro y Cuervo and a masters program in social psychology, were involved in the later phase and provided me greater access to naturalistic interactions among their own families and friends.

A later series of interviews revolved around four kinds of personal relationships: friendship, marriage, family, and work relationships. The Colombian research assistants recruited the respondents from among their own personal relationship networks. The respondents in these interviews ranged in age from 10 to 70, with the median age about 27. None had participated in other phases of the study. Eight were students at the time of the interview, two were working-class, six were professionals, and there was one artist, one writer, and one housewife (one interview was conducted with two sisters, making a total of 19 respondents in 18 interviews). Interviews lasted from half an hour to three hours and were audiotaped and transcribed by the research assistants.[1]

---

1. By asking natives directly to formulate their understanding of relational ideals, I hoped to hear the values, beliefs, and premises specific to those relationships put in natives' own words. Nonetheless, eliciting information within a structured interview naturally presents certain limitations. As Mishler (1986) and others have noted, interviews are a speech activity in which interviewers and respondents adjust their questions and answers to each other. Despite this mutual adjustment, a power imbalance is inherent in interviews, given that one partici-

Data analysis in each phase of the study followed the theoretical framework set forth by Hymes (1962, 1972).[2] More concretely, Spradley's Developmental Research Sequence (1979, 1980) was the basis for the principal analytic

---

pant shapes and controls the responses of the other. Those responses are formulated under the pressure of being "cooperative" with the interviewer and with the knowledge that answers deemed inadequate or unhelpful may be discarded.

Further, interviews are in a sense artificial: talk *about* an event or a relationship is clearly not the same as talk *during* an event or *within* a relationship. The connection between interview data and communication practice is, therefore, open to question (Sanders & Sigman, 1994). Nonetheless, given that the meaning of communicative practice is generally left unsaid, particularly those aspects of meaning derived from taken-for-granted understandings, analysis of meaning necessarily goes outside of interaction itself to other locations of the knowledge brought to bear on it (Hodge & Kress, 1993). In the context of this case study, these interview data are presented as complementary to observational data presented earlier. The consistency of responses in interviews with inferences made from other data sources lends support to those claims.

2. The initial formulation of the ethnography of speaking (Hymes, 1962) included a framework for describing the particularities of ways of speaking in diverse speech communities. It was designed to provide an emic/etic framework: an acontextual format for discovering, describing, and comparing cases. That original framework, as a result of application and testing in fieldwork, was revised extensively (Hymes, 1972). Important extensions included further development of the social units of description proposed in the original scheme; a typology for characterizing societies as to the quantitative and qualitative importance of speaking; formalized procedures for rule discovery and rule statement; and expansion of the number of factors in speech events. Sixteen components comprised the resulting descriptive framework, grouped into eight main entries, to be remembered by way of the mnemonic device SPEAKING: S (situation: setting and scene); P (participants: speaker/sender, addressor, hearer/receiver/audience, addressee); E (ends: outcomes, goals); A (act sequence: message form and content); K (key); I (instrumentalities: channel, forms of speech); N (norms: of interaction and of interpretation); G (genres). The framework provides an initial set of questions and descriptive possibilities in the study of ways of

moves in each case: (1) categorize patterns of language use (i.e., terms of personal address and directive performance [requests and commands]); (2) identify exceptions to common patterns of use; (3) collect native terms that categorize talk, particularly those applied to personal address and directive performance; and (4) pinpoint cultural premises about the kinds of talk, the kinds of persons, or the kinds and states of relationships that are revealed in or inferrable from interaction. Sometimes these premises are evident in metacommunication about the meanings of language use and particular instances of it. For example:

> Male, 24, commenting on the custom of addressing unmarried older women with a diminutive form of their first name: You can't just call them by their first name—to a 60-year-old woman that would be disrespectful! On the other hand, you can't call them *doña* anything, because they haven't been married, and you don't want to forever say *señorita* so-and-so, reminding them all the time of their bad luck [in being single].

> Taxi driver to passenger: Look, I'm giving you some advice. You have to be less trusting.

Because the underlying premises are largely left unspoken, however, they were often inferred from patterns or instances of language use. The function of the interviews was largely to examine and, where possible, expand upon the premises inferred from other kinds of data. The ontological nature of premises as a central aspect of culture is discussed further in Chapter 7.

Partial results of the research conducted between 1987 and 1992 have been presented elsewhere (Fitch, 1991a, 1991b, 1994). For this book, I reanalyzed the data from both phases of the study to explore cultural themes that had

---

speaking in particular communities. It also provides a format for comparison across communities, a set of categories for the discovery of similarities and differences.

emerged when the two forms of language use were considered separately. I also drew upon data collected in both phases of the study to examine larger interactional genres, one of which, **palanca** narratives, is presented in this volume. Finally, during the lengthy process of writing this book, I relied on two electronic sources both to stay abreast of ongoing events in Colombia and occasionally to try out a claim I had formulated. One was a hotline named "Colext," an abbreviated form of reference to **Colombianos en el exterior,** or Colombians Abroad. For a time the hotline had more than 400 members, often generating 5 to 15 messages per day, consisting of discussion among Colombians living both inside and outside of Colombia and other interested parties of many nationalities. The subject matter ranged from passionate commentary on soccer matches, to humor appealing to a variety of tastes, to extended debate on world events. The second source was a news service called **Noticol,** which, until its demise in 1997, posted almost daily summaries of news, features, and sports appearing in two major Bogotá newspapers (**El Espectador** and **El Tiempo**) and a monthly national magazine, **Cambio 16.**

OVERVIEW OF THE BOOK

The case study and its extension into broader issues of interpersonal ideology proceed as follows. Chapter 1 begins by examining personal relationships in this urban Colombian speech community in terms of abstract relational ideals. Chapters 2, 3, and 4 each focus on a specific linguistic phenomenon that is both ubiquitous in everyday talk and revelatory of interpersonal ideology. In Chapter 2, personal address practices are shown to be an index of one's connections to relevant others as much as, or more than, a marker of individual identity. Examination of the personal address system in this community focused on the naming and referring practices that functioned as indices of identity and relationships. The patterns and meanings of personal address revealed the most meaningful dimensions of personhood to be connections *between* people, particularly with regard to their position in a social structure centered around class and gender.

Chapter 3 explores the use of directives as definers of interpersonal interconnectedness. The use of directives to build and reinforce relationships, as well as to accomplish particular tasks, is described in some detail. Directive performance was a ubiquitous resource for coordinating social actions. In compelling, cajoling, inspiring, and forbidding the actions of others, these Colombians both accomplished specific tasks and created and sustained connections with others.

Chapter 4 examines **palanca** (literally, a lever) as a phenomenon that is at once a form of interpersonal relationship, a ubiquitous explanatory narrative, and a cultural myth of how the social world of the urban Colombian professional works. Like directive performance, establishing, exercising, and acting as a **palanca** (a connection through which objectives are pursued) is a communicative practice that revolves around interpersonal connectedness. The shared understanding of **palanca** is that it is an interpersonal connection through which rules, laws, and scarcity are transcended. **Palanca** further constitutes a cultural myth that underscores the importance of interpersonal connections, revolving around the notion that almost any goal may be accomplished by way of strong relationships with appropriately powerful others. In the stories they told of achieving personal objectives and overcoming life's obstacles by connecting with others, these Colombians paid homage to the transcendent importance of interpersonal bonds.

Chapters 5 and 6 each present a different kind of synthesis of the preceding chapters. Chapter 5 presents a detailed case study of a 20-year relationship between two women to show how the communication resources described earlier are brought to bear on everyday conversation and the negotiation of a multifaceted personal relationship. Chapter 6 summarizes and elaborates on the interpersonal ideology of connectedness that is developed in Chapters 2–5. In this community, connectedness between individuals is a central premise for interpersonal communication and relationships. Valued ways of speaking that reveal that premise are ones that create, acknowledge, and strengthen particular connections and deny, block, and limit certain others. Those conceptual resources that cohere and warrant social interaction are referred to here as "interpersonal ideology," defined as *a set of premises about personhood, relationships, and communication around which people formulate lines of action toward others, and interpret others' actions*. Interpersonal ideology, then, is that subset of cultural premises related most specifically to interpersonal relationships, as opposed to (for example) beliefs about wellness and illness, pedagogical concerns, economic and religious perspectives, and so forth. The distinctiveness of this Colombian interpersonal ideology, and the applicability of interpersonal ideology as a lens through which to view personal relationships, is then highlighted through contrast to ideologies from other speech communities.

CHAPTER ONE

A BROAD VIEW OF PERSONAL RELATIONSHIPS

Relational Ideals

"You have to understand, this is a collectivist culture. For Colombians, a person is a set of bonds to others."
—Raúl, 40, economist

Communal life is a pervasively symbolic, inescapable basis for personal relationships. Without workplaces, classrooms, street corners, and front porches, how would friendships or romances ever be formed? Without meetings, parties, chance encounters, and recurrent path crossings of various kinds, how could sparks ever fly or a grin ever bring on shared warmth? By the same token, friendships, mateships, work relationships, families, networks, and licit and illicit partnerships are pervasively important interactional sites for construction of communal meaning. Some meanings are specific to the shared experiences of dyads or groups. Many others, however, are more widely accessible to (because they are drawn from) the speech community(-ies) in which the relationship is enacted.

Fundamental to both communal life and personal relationships are communication practices. People construct relationships by arguing, making small talk, insulting, praising, negotiating, flirting, complaining, proposing, and so forth. They learn how and when to engage in all of these communicative activities through observing and engaging in social interaction with others. They also learn, by virtue of membership in a particular community with specific understandings of such matters, what kinds of talk count as each of those activities, and what certain speech events mean in the context of particular relationships. The terms for talk themselves form part of a communal code that endows ways of speaking with symbolic meaning (cf. Carbaugh, 1989).

Ordinarily, however, personal relationship researchers are only peripherally (and only fairly recently) concerned with the culturally situated symbolic resources through which people construct meaning in relationships. Although scholars in the area of personal relationships acknowledge the influence of culture in general ways—for example, that culture legitimates certain relational forms and practices while ignoring or decrying others (Weeden, 1987; Wood, 1993), or that different cultures have different assumptions about relationships that affect definitions and enactments of relational forms (e.g., Gudykunst & Ting-Toomey, 1988; Ting-Toomey, 1991)—the power of cultural premises to shape personal relationships has necessarily been sketched in broad strokes. Emphasis in that literature largely has been on the private aspects of personal relationships, such as how specific personalities mesh into partnerships (or, alternatively, may doom them).

The position taken in this book is that personal relationships are, like speaking more generally, culturally situated processes. Thus, I focus primarily on describing certain speaking practices among urban, largely middle-class Colombians that are consequential for the way they understand and enact personal relationships, as an empirical basis for elaborating an interpersonal ideology of connectedness that links those practices into a coherent symbolic system.

As such, this study is rooted in the theoretical tradition of the ethnography of speaking.

AN ETHNOGRAPHIC APPROACH
TO PERSONAL RELATIONSHIPS

Culture may be represented in various ways, most easily and superficially as that of a "nation" and more subtly as a collection of conceptual resources that answers universal questions of what exists in the world, and why, for a particular group of people. The approach in this book of building communication theory from detailed study of talk practices in a particular culture is rooted in the Hymesian tradition (Hymes, 1962, 1972, 1986) of ethnographies of speaking. This approach takes as its starting point a view of culture as a system of symbols and meanings (Schneider, 1976) and then focuses on how that system is expressed and enacted in ways of speaking. Essentially, then, this view of culture is that the conceptual resources are both *constructed through talk practices and reflected in them,* such that the connection between talk and culture is indivisible.[1]

The object of study within this tradition is situated discourse: how speaking is organized and conceptualized within a given community. Thus, this vein of ethnography is concerned with describing ways of speaking as they construct and reflect social life within particular speech communities. This approach assumes that talking is not driven by some abstract system of beliefs. Rather, talk constitutes and enacts the culture. In that sense, such an approach is concerned further with developing cross-culturally valid

1. This point may need some clarification in light of recent interest in social science theory about the bidirectional relationship between talk and social structure (e.g., Boden & Zimmerman, 1991). On one hand, talk is taken as productive of social realities in an ongoing, in-the-moment sense of construction of understanding; on the other, certain social realities become standardized and self-sustaining over time and are implicitly reflected in talk.

concepts and theories for interpreting and explaining the interaction of language and social life rather than seeking to describe differences in cultural practice for their own sake.

Methodologically, ethnography refers to fieldwork (supplemented by techniques developed in other areas of study, notably conversation analysis, history, and pragmatics) that produces a written description of the way of life of a group of people. Its focus is on the observed patterns of speaking and the symbols and meanings, premises, and rules applied to speaking within a given community.

A foundational assumption of the ethnography of speaking is that societies differ as to the communicative resources available to their members in terms of languages, dialects, registers, routines, genres, artistic formulae, and so forth. Societies also differ in the patterns of distribution for the resources in use, in the work done (and doable) by and through speech and other communicative means, and in the evaluation of speaking as an instrument of social action. Ethnographies of speaking thus begin as case studies of the particulars of a speech community, with comparison across case studies as the basis for many of the central theoretical insights. Such comparisons may be made on several levels of analysis: *speech events,* locally defined contexts for speaking, each of which has an internal structure that differentiates it from other events in a community, revealed in native terms for talk (cf. Carbaugh, 1989); *speech communities,* in which ways of speaking and language codes are definitive of social group boundaries (e.g., Katriel, 1986, 1992; Philipsen, 1992); community-specific *patterns and meanings* of universal communicative resources such as personal address (e.g., Philipsen, 1992; Scotton & Zhu, 1983), directives, and so forth.

It is important to recognize that the ethnographic approach does not rest on unitary perception and consensus but rather focuses on ways of constructing meaning and pursuing interpersonal objectives that allow for diverse subgroups to live out social histories in richly connected ways. This is particularly significant in a study of Colombia, given that the culture is a complex mix of different practices based on commonalities across significantly different groups of people. A brief description of some of those differences, and some idea of the common sense constructed from them, may be useful at this point.

The Setting: A Profile of Colombia

From the first time I arrived in Colombia in December 1983, with the idea of someday doing research there, I was struck by the sheer intensity of life as Colombians live it. Noise levels were higher, social class divisions were deeper and wider, and the effort expended to carry out even simple tasks, and to form even transitory relationships, was greater than anything I had experienced while growing up in the United States, or during extended stays in Mexico and Spain. Much of that response, especially on my first trip there, might be attributed to culture shock and to the fact that I spent most of my time in Bogotá. Even after repeated visits, however—for 10 months in 1987, 1 month in 1989, 3 months in 1992—and countless conversations with Colombians, that impression has been repeatedly confirmed. Everyday life presents incredible obstacles in Colombia: traffic, economic and political uncertainty, the ever present threat of violent crime, social unease, competing demands from countless relational ties, byzantine institutional constraints on virtually every public act, and an urban infrastructure (roads, facilities, services) subject to the usual strains of dense populations in developing countries everywhere.

Yet the beauty of Colombia was then, and remains, as stunning as the continuous struggle. There is breathtaking scenery—as diverse as in any geographical region in the world—from beaches to mountains to jungles to desert. There is abundant personal wit, and a delight in verbal agility, enacted differently but valued highly across the social spectrum. There is, most pervasively, an involvement in peoples' lives that makes a richly woven fabric of social life. That involvement sustains families and friendships with a firmness that is enviable by U.S. standards, and often extends its warmth and support to strangers and foreigners.

This study was conducted in and around Bogotá, the capital city of Colombia. Bogotá is, in many ways, the Colombian equivalent of New York City, although its residents include a much smaller percentage of non-Colombians than New York has non-U.S.-born residents. It encompasses the full range of educational and socioeconomic classes and the full spectrum of political variations observable within the country as a whole. It is also diverse in the regional background of its inhabitants, as Colombians from other parts of the country are drawn to the capital city by the greater availability of lifestyle conveniences. As a slice of Colombian life more generally, it is worth noting that Bogotá is both blessed and plagued with the usual assortment of big-city paradoxes: sophisticated educational and technological facilities located in a milieu pervaded by widespread crime and fear of violence; a heightened sense of artistic and commercial significance, coupled with a lessened sense of neighborly closeness and belonging.

A central theme of this book is that an interpersonal ideology of connectedness to people is a powerful symbolic resource for dealing with these difficulties. To survive in the complexity that is Bogotá—indeed, to be truly a "person" in the Colombian sense of the word—interpersonal bonds *must* be accorded primordial importance. Above and beyond individual hard work, luck, persistence, and the intervention of deities required to thrive in this environment, human existence itself depends crucially on durable connections to other people.

The connections—especially, the types of connections accorded importance—are also influenced by the historical, political, and topographical forces that have formed the culture itself. Geographically, the country is split into four separate regions by three imposing mountain ranges. The natives of the different regions are as distinctive from one another as the terrain, differences that are remarked on by Colombians as reflected in personality, dialect, and characteristic styles of speaking. In more general terms, the

Colombian understanding of both personhood and speaking is also responsive to these forces.

Of those perceived differences, dialectal variation is most immediately evident. Only isolated indigenous tribes still speak anything other than Spanish, although some dialects incorporate loan words from two prominent indigenous languages, Chibcha and Quechua. Dialect regions—Bogotá and environs, Tolima-Cauca, Nariño (*pastuso*), Antioquia-Caldas (*paisa*), and both coasts (*costeño*)—reflect waves of settlement from different parts of Spain and decades of subsequent isolation that maintained the original differences (Canfield, 1981). Regional dialectal characteristics are a frequent theme for good-natured teasing, less congenial mockery, and sincere though perhaps stereotyped inferences about personal habits and abilities.

Beyond the legacy of Spanish conquest and domination evident in language, present-day social class divisions plainly have their roots in colonial classifications of people. Generally speaking, the more closely descended from Spaniards a Colombian is, the higher in the social order he or she is likely to be. The more pronounced the indigenous heritage, the lower one's station is likely to be. A third prominent ethnic influence is drawn from descendants of African slaves brought by the Spaniards, originally concentrated along the coasts and in the coffee-growing regions of central Colombia, within which there are wider economic disparities. The vast majority of the population is a mixture of two or more of these ethnic groups, and the range of combinations is evident in the diverse blendings of skin and eye color, facial features, height, and textures of hair. For this reason, identification with a particular ethnic heritage, or discrimination on a purely racial basis, is rare.

There clearly is, however, a correlation between race and social class, and social class status is a pervasive index of identity, relationships, and expectations for life. The rigid distinction between "mental" and "manual" labor extends into an elaborate code of class-defined behavior: upper-class people (and, where possible, the middle classes) do not clean their own houses, do their own laundry, or send their children to public schools. In turn, the system perpetuates itself by way of access to educational and occupational opportunities that are extensively controlled by way of personal connections, most of whom are within close range of one's own social status.

Politically, Colombia's two-party democratic system is usually described as more stable than its Latin American neighbors'. That stability, however, is often more apparent than real. Colombia has a history of violent partisan politics, the stakes raised higher by a patronage system in which government jobs at every level were traditionally controlled by whichever party won the presidency. Until a reform movement in 1954, law enforcement was handed over to the victorious party as well. Officials belonging to one party selectively applied the law to members of the other party, including seizing their lands, denying them access to basic services and preventing them from voting in elections. Violent resolution of political disputes spread to all manner of personal grudge settling that the state was largely powerless to control. Although affiliations to political parties have decreased in importance, and the extent of governmental power that can be applied capriciously based on such affiliations has been drastically reduced since its peak in the 1940s, a mistrust of the police and the military (as truly neutral) continues to this day. There is little faith in the government's ability to control disruptive forces in society or to provide for the needs of its citizens. Colombians do not necessarily call the police when a crime has been committed, nor do they see the actions of the military as necessarily reflective of either the will of the people or the orders of the president. In contrast to the situation in the United States, lawsuits are rarely used to address interpersonal or organizational grievances. There is, nonetheless, a belief in the ideals of democracy, and because of that no single revolutionary group has found much public support during this century.

A counterpoint to Colombians' lack of faith in their government is that government's distrust of citizens' honesty, evident in the labyrinths of paper and bureaucracy that turn seemingly simple governmental and business transactions into Faustian ordeals. Opening a personal checking account or renewing a car's license plates, for example, requires sworn affidavits and piles of notarized documents with myriad seals and signatures correctly affixed. Having everything in order the first time is never a certainty, and even under the best of circumstances such tasks may occupy a day or longer.

Colombia is a society that has gone from primarily rural and agrarian to primarily urban in one generation. Large cities, particularly Bogotá, show the strains of burgeoning population density. The crime rate is staggering, creating a pervasive fear of burglary and robbery. That fear is evidenced by the bars on every window, multiple locks and chains on every door, car alarms that swoop through the other noises of the city with numbing regularity, and the bodyguards around every judge, politician, and businessperson of even moderate influence. Hastily constructed apartment complexes spread Bogotá's sprawling urbanization further into the countryside with each passing year.

Yet, there are nostalgic reminders of Colombia's recent agrarian past as well. *Zorros*—wooden carts hauled by horses or mules—clatter down major thoroughfares of Bogotá, sometimes at rush hour, and the animals graze peacefully in the Parque Nacional near downtown. Although electrical appliances are abundant, there often seems to be little faith in their effectiveness. Refrigerators may stand nearly empty because of a distrust of leftovers. Washing machines may be proudly acquired as a symbol of middle-class identity, yet be used only occasionally in the belief that only washing by hand gets clothes really clean.

Concern for public order has naturally been exacerbated by the social and political upheavals occasioned by drug trafficking. The importance of the drug trade to the economy is difficult to estimate, though it is clearly a major employer in some regions of the country. Most drug money is in the hands of a few people, but its influence is felt throughout the economy. It jeopardizes financial institutions through penetration and/or control of legitimate private corporations, diverts large sums of government funds to suppress growing and trafficking, and contributes to tax evasion (Craig, 1981). It also further undermines the confidence of Colombians in their government and fosters a collective resentment of the stereotypes of Colombia that have arisen from negative international attention focused on drug-related violence. This resentment is often directed specifically at U.S. drug users, who are perceived as the real cause of the myriad woes in Colombian society associated with drug trafficking.

Such stereotypes overlook an intellectual richness that is abundantly evident in Bogotá. Although acknowledging their technological limitations, Colombians cherish the educational institutions and the vibrant artistic life that make Bogotá "the Athens of South America." A similar shared understanding that is frequently voiced is that Colombians speak the "most correct" variety of Spanish in existence today. Despite the class-based disparities in access to education and the association of "educated" speech with "correctness" (not to mention the regional dialect differences mentioned earlier), that perception is one echoed by many non-Colombian speakers of Spanish, including many Spaniards.

A final area of Colombian discursive life that contributes to understanding is the spiritual arena, in which a great deal of mental and verbal energy finds its basis for expression in everyday interaction. The Catholic Church, a further legacy of Spanish colonialism, is of course a pervasive presence in social, educational, and political activity. Beyond the formalities of that tradition, however, extends a wide range of folk religion, from **curanderos** (which may be translated as anything from "faith healers" to "witch doctors," depending on whether one approves of them), to palm readers, to herbalists in health stores who include chants and charms along with their nutritional goods. Boundaries blur between the Catholicism imposed by the Spaniards and indigenous beliefs and practices. Staunch Catholics "pay promises" to a saint or the Virgin Mary that involve relics and rituals evocative of an animistic, earth-centered past.

Curanderos include "Hail Marys" and "Our Fathers" along with more mystical incantations. Lively discussion of the relative merits of different avenues for addressing life's problems, from unemployment to marital discord to a rebellious child, often include spiritual routes: a visit to a palm reader who can both tell the future and prescribe a "cure" for the problem, or prayers to a particular saint at a particular shrine at a particular time and day.

The vividness and variety of spiritual expression are perhaps testament to the idea that life is never easy for Colombians, though the difficulties faced in the capital city will logically be quite distinct from those faced in rural areas or in resort towns along the coast. In all of these places, and nowhere more than in Bogotá, a person needs connections to other people to continue the struggle in the face of pervasive violence, the vagaries of personal fortune inevitably shaped by social categories, and the inefficiencies and impotence of the government.

The Speech Community:
Urban Colombian *Profesionales*

At first sight, given this complexity, it may seem paradoxical to describe such a diversity as a single "speech community." Dell Hymes originally defined a *speech community* as an analytic unit, as "a community sharing rules for the conduct and interpretation of speech, and rules for the interpretation of at least one linguistic variety" (1972, p. 54). This definition has been construed in at least two ways. One is that a speech community is an interacting group in which most members know and have chances to interact with one another (e.g., Scollon & Scollon, 1981; Sequeira, 1993, 1994). Alternatively, larger and less tightly connected groups, and even heterogeneous societies, have been defined as speech communities on the basis of shared ways of speaking that cut across subgroups. This view suggests that the relationship of persons to a speech community is a matter that may be empirically established by familiarity with those ways of speaking rather than personal acquaintance with most or all members of the group:

> To know the local parlance, but be unwilling to use it, or feel not permitted to use it, or to feel that using it would insinuate oneself somewhere that one does not belong, reveals a relationship, perceived or real, that places one at some distance from the group. . . . These patterns of use and nonuse have expressive import for the individual and the audiences to which they are revealed and addressed, because they are intricately woven into the texture of lives and societies. (Philipsen, 1992, p. 14)

This perspective offers a way of defining the boundaries of a speech community that echoes Hymes's original emphasis on ways of speaking that are used rhetorically (1) to show that one is a member of a group or (2) to show that one does not presume or deign to be a member of a group. In approaching Bogotá as *a* speech community, therefore, I did not presume consensus among disparate, often competing, groups.[2] Where patterned ways of speaking differed among subgroups, and where symbolic meanings were disputed, I have discussed those differences.

Nonetheless, I have struggled to find a descriptive term that captures accurately the commonalities and differences among the Colombians who were included in this study, and to place the limited subset of people I worked with or observed (perhaps one thousand in all) in the broader spectrum of "Colombians" as a designation of citizenship and residence. The speech community I observed can be described as urban Colombian professionals, with an under-

---

2. Fiske (1991) claims that ethnographies of speaking conducted in the Hymesian mode privilege consensus in their emphasis on discovering a common code that cuts across groups that may, in fact, compete with (or oppress) one another. The point is ably disputed by Carbaugh (1996), who argues that common codes underlie conflict as well as consensus. This thread will be developed further in the discussion of ideology in Chapter 7.

standing that the term has a particular meaning among the natives that is not equivalent to its English cognates. ***Profesional*** is a designation of social status that is most closely related to educational level: technically, it is anyone with a college degree. More to the point, ***profesional*** is an identity that is constructed through engaging in some relationships and activities and avoiding others (e.g., socializing primarily with, marrying, and enabling one's children to become ***profesionales***; avoiding manual labor of any kind, even at home; and so forth). It is not a designation of income, and the people I worked with most closely in this study were not *upper* middle class by any means. In most cases, they were first- or second-generation ***profesionales*** who struggled, at times, to maintain that position and identity. It was a crucial and somewhat fragile social identity constructed through talk and relationships.

Because that identity is indispensably achieved through connections to other people, it is fair to say that the ideology of connectedness pervasive in Colombian society more generally is described here in an instantiation that is very closely linked to the worldview of urban, middle class professionals. This is not to say that professionals were the only people who were observed or interviewed. The sample of settings and informants was constructed to include as broad a cross section of Bogotá's population as possible in terms of social class, regional origin, age, and gender. Shared expectations of differences in language use along all those lines were among the findings of the study. Far more pervasive than those differences, however, were uses of shared symbolic terms and interpretations of actions related to the defining force of connections between people, as central to the social activities of constructing identities and relationships.

RELATIONAL IDEALS

It seemed logical to explore shared understandings about personal relationships in this speech community as directly as possible, by asking urban Colombians to talk about what they consider "ideal" relationships within readily defined types. To the extent that common themes appeared when informants described desirable and undesirable instances of friendship, marriage, workmates, and families, cultural premises relevant to constructing and maintaining relationships in those areas could be discerned. By stimulating talk about relationships that people were involved in or had observed, as well as talk about more abstract notions of desirable and undesirable relational forms, those premises could be verbalized by the participants themselves instead of being inferred from other kinds of talk.

In these interviews, Colombians articulated many of the same ideals for relational types that U.S. respondents have expressed (cf. Davis & Todd, 1985; Rawlins, 1992; Weiss & Lowenthal, 1975) but also invoked some substantial differences. Both similarities and differences were particularly evident in their discussions of friendship.

> Carlos, 21, student: A good friendship more than anything is one where there's sincerity, where you have the tranquility to say to your friend, "This is what's happening to me, I have this problem." Clearly that's a good friendship, where both parties are sincere with one another.

> Miriam, 14, student: A good friend would never talk behind your back, would never get into those silly things, "look how her shoes are never shined," none of that. . . . A good friendship is one with lots of mutual understanding, lots of **confianza** (trust) and, more than anything, sincerity. I think sincerity is what most influences a good friendship.

> Elena, 29, painter: A good friend is a person that you encounter along the way, and that person accompanies you for a while. . . . You share things and create ties that, that are mutually respected, respect for the individual that you are, for all of your world.

> Ricardo, 27, writer: A good friendship is when you can make rude jokes with each other and everyone understands it's not really an insult.

In Colombia as in the United States, an ideal friend gives assistance when needed, is someone to be confided in and trusted, shares activities, accepts the friend as s/he is, does not dominate the other, and is there for the bad times as well as the good. Nonetheless, one distinctive aspect of Colombian relationships is revealed in the term ***confianza.*** Its equivalent in English (trust; closeness) is only partly accurate.[3] The term was pervasively mentioned both as a characteristic of close friendship and as a likely site for violation.

> Mauricio, 31, professional: A good friendship is where there is respect for individuality, understanding. . . . I have to be understanding of my friend's ways of being, don't I? Respect him. A bad friendship is where the same ***confianza*** that makes people friends makes people lose respect. . . . Certain individualities are violated, and there ceases to be real friendship.

> Ricardo, 27, writer: When there's a great deal of ***confianza*** you can say things that ordinarily would be ***confianzudos*** (too chummy), that would seem insulting, but if you and I are good friends I'll know—maybe you're even reproaching me, but I'll know you don't mean to start something

3. Rheingold (1988), drawing from Pacificon Productions (1981), puts the case strongly, defining ***confianza*** as "a combination of utterly eternal, unshakable reliance, trust, confidence, and unconditional social support. . . . ***Confianza*** goes down to the spiritual marrow" (p. 28). In tracing the word to Spain, where ***confianza*** characterized long-term friendships and especially solid family relationships, Rheingold suggests the distinctiveness of the term lies in cultural patterns of relationships: "This sort of trust doesn't come about automatically in an era where your best friend might be someone you've known for only a few years" (1988, pp. 28–29). Although his definition probably overstates the absolute profundity of ***confianza***—as we shall see in Chapter 2, it exists in degrees—Rheingold's observation about differences in friendship patterns in the United States and in Colombia, and the impact of those patterns on the nature of friendship itself, seems generally accurate.

with me, but if we have a bad relationship I'll hear it entirely differently.

Certainly there are echoes of an independence/connection dialectic in Mauricio's comment, noted as a central theme in friendship in the United States (Rawlins, 1992). Yet to invoke "respect" as what may be lost or violated in a bad friendship locates ***confianza*** in a symbolic web of interpersonal forces centered around a code of "proper conduct" in which the risk of acting too informally (being ***confianzudo***) is ever present. Among good friends, as Ricardo notes, the risk is minimized through relaxation of usual expectations/standards for proper conduct; generally speaking, however, it is rarely entirely absent. Chapter 2 will explore further the notion of ***confianza*** as a defining feature of personal relationships, and Chapter 6 will elaborate further on its connections to symbolic clusters of hierarchy and formality as definitive of proper conduct.

Given these similarities and differences in ideals of friendship, some prominent themes in two other categories of relational ideals are worth mentioning.

Descriptions of what constituted good family relationships revolved overwhelmingly around the premise that families should be ***unidas*** (literally, united; a more accurate translation is "together"). Vivid examples were offered both of families that enacted the ideal and some that blatantly violated it.

María Luz, 12, student: My grandparents in Fusa, no? They have four children, and what a lovely family that is. They've had their fights and everything but nothing so bad the children would leave home over it, right? All of them but my dad live right there in Fusa, and we all go to visit, we stay for weeks there, everyone together. It's a very united family (***una familia muy unida***), everyone helps everyone else. Everyone gives each other good presents.

Alfonso, 40, doorman: There are six children in that family, all married now, but they all live together, it's quite a union between them. They're all one family, there's never been any separation. The daughters in law, the sons in law all just moved in and became part of the family.

Tomasa, 48, factory worker: I know some very blessed families, one for example that has 13 children, and all of them are so united (***esa gente es muy unida***), they all get together, they all help each other, and whatever the mother says, that's what's done (smiles).

Enactments of unity involved some material signs of connectedness such as helping one another and "giving good presents." More importantly, unity was enacted through togetherness: living together in the same town or house, visiting for weeks or months, getting together frequently despite conflicts. In times of difficulty, the premise that being **unida** required physical presence was carried further, as in this excerpt from my field notes:

When Aurelio was killed, everyone in the family went immediately to his house, to be with (***acompañar***) his wife Libia and their two grown sons. Aurelio was one of 11 children, Libia was one of 10; and less than 24 hours after his death every single sibling, their spouses, and most of their children were there in the house, along with assorted cousins, his mother, and so forth. The numbers boggled my mind—what if the widow, who was in the car with him when he was murdered, wanted to be alone to deal with her grief? Everyone assured me the *last* thing anyone could possibly want under the circumstances was to be alone. No one asked her, of course; it was simply unthinkable that she could want solitude. I wondered how all of these people got fed. To bring a covered dish, as you might in the States, would cast a negative light on the hospitality of the bereaved. (And hospitality and providing for guests were expectations that apparently were not suspended, despite the terrible shock, and despite the fact that they were all family.) When I asked about it, people told me that there was a lot of ordering out, a number of quick trips to the store, and Libia of course stayed very busy attending to all these people who were there to "help" her through her grief.

The ideal of unity was further supported in the negative, in that descriptions of "bad" families often centered around the lack of involvement family members had in one another's lives.

> Miriam, 15, student: These people we know . . . they're always fighting. The mother never asks her daughter, "How are you doing?"—you know, like, "What's going on in your life?" She never asks, "Do you have a boyfriend, do you have a best friend, how did you do in that class, I want to see your grades." She acts like nothing's going on, she has no control. The whole family is out of control, everyone going their own way.

> Ricardo, 27, writer, describing the family of a friend: The dad and mom sleep in separate rooms, all the children detest the father, apparently. I was amazed—I was over there once when the father got home, and no one even said hello to him. . . . He said hello to me, but neither the wife nor the daughter even looked up. When he talked they ignored him; when he asked if dinner was ready they said, "Yeah, it's in the pots," and no one went to get him any; he had to do everything for himself.

These two descriptions of "bad families" further suggest that a family fulfills the cultural ideal of being unified to the extent that its members are involved and interested in one another's lives, as shown by asking detailed questions and offering guidance instead of "everyone going their own way." Similarly, to say "dinner's on the stove" (i.e., help yourself) instead of serving a latecomer is as damning to the image of a "good family" as sleeping in separate rooms. The prototypical "good family" in this culture is, in many ways, a paradigmatic case of the ideology of interpersonal connectedness, which pervades other contexts and relational types as well.

To live in accordance with this idea of involved, intertwined lives requires (or, at least in the urban Colombian case, seems to entail) significant coordination of action. In addition, intervention in the lives of family members and close friends was described (as above) as a hallmark of a "good" family relationship. Chapter 3 will elaborate on the ways in which directive performance enacts these ideals. A further dimension of directive performance, as it relates to ideals of hierarchical relationships, is also discussed in Chapter 3.

Finally, the possibility that relationships ideally based on sincerity and mutual understanding might be based on self-interest instead was a frequent theme in talk about friendship. For U.S. Americans, friendships and instrumental connections are ordinarily separate categories of relationships. For these Colombians, however, emotional ties seemed to be inextricably tied to possibilities of instrumental need:

> Marco, 45, professional: A bad friendship is when there's some [self]-interest in the middle. Then there's no sincerity. . . . Once they have used me, I've been a ***palanca*** for their interests—goodbye to the friend, right? I've had that happen so many times.

Palanca literally means a "lever" but in this context refers to personal influence exercised on one's behalf by friends or relatives. Its closest equivalent in English is a personal connection used to obtain some objective, such as a job, entry into a university, contacts with other important people, and so forth. To bring up such connections in the context of ideals of friendship seems a little strange, even as a negative instance.

Despite its apparent linguistic equivalent in English and seeming similarity to a relational type in U.S. American culture, the term ***palanca*** in Colombian culture indexes a galaxy of meaning (Schneider, 1976) organized around a notion of connectedness as both fundamental to human existence and problematic in its enactments, and thus requires a chapter of its own (Chapter 4).

The existence of these relational ideals, and the fact that interviewees elucidated many of them with some degree of consistency, suggests that before particular individuals ever get together to form a friendship, engage in a work relationship, or form a family, cultural understandings of personhood and relationships constitute a general framework of expectations and interpretations that fundamentally shape the process of relating. Social contexts are created from symbolic resources and shared understandings of the nature of personhood and relationships, and the kinds of experiences that lead individuals to define themselves as a relational unit. Development of personal relationships occurs as people attach meanings to actions and events, drawing upon communal symbolic resources to do so. Each relationship is unique to some degree, as partners adapt communal forms and symbolic meanings to create a relational code based on their unique history. Chapter 5 will explore the evolution of relational codes from cultural systems of meaning by way of a detailed case study of a 20-year close relationship. It will show how relational codes are the basis for the intimacy and cohesion that make personal relationships significant contexts for experience, whether as a refuge from the storm of social life or as a promontory where the winds blow even harder and colder.

Although people interviewed in this part of the larger ethnographic study gave specific examples of relationships that illustrated the ideals they articulated, abstractions such as these leave unexplored much of the landscape of personal relationships among urban Colombians. Illuminating the interpersonal ideology that underlies these relational ideals, and showing the broader applicability of interpersonal ideology to the study of personal relationships more generally, is the ultimate goal of this book. First, however, it is necessary to move from the broad orienting premises about these relational types sketched here to elaborate the patterns and specific meanings of the communication resources from which such ideals were created. Chapters 2–5 detail the interactional materials with which such ideals are invoked, approached, denied, thwarted, questioned, defied, and so forth. They attempt to capture the flavor of the messy and often self-contradictory stream of events, actions, and interpretations that constitute social life and personal relationships. The first of these communication resources to be described, the system of personal address, is the most pervasive, an inescapable index of identity and relationship invoked each time one person speaks to or about a specific other.

CHAPTER TWO

PERSONAL ADDRESS

Personal address terms are a useful starting point for learning about a speech community's shared understandings about personhood and communication—in that they are a ubiquitous linguistic feature through which speakers conduct interpersonal business. Although personal address behavior has an obvious referential function (it points to one person or another), it simultaneously performs interpersonal functions as well. Considerable research into personal address, conducted in a number of cultures (Philipsen & Huspek, 1985, give an overview and list nearly 200 studies) suggests that, in the act of addressing others, speakers evoke personal identities and create and define relationships. The personal address resources that exist, and the patterns and meanings of their uses, are culture-specific: they reflect communal understandings of the aspects of personhood that are important enough to draw attention in a particular social structure. They also reflect the nature of the relationship between the speaker and the hearer, locating particular relationships on relevant dimensions (such as close/distant, personal/professional, peers/rank-differentiated, and so forth) along which relational types are distinguished within shared understandings of the community. Personal address is a fundamental aspect of interpersonal communication, then, in the sense that it reveals the basic symbolic categories that reference personhood and relationships within a community. Further, interpretations and evaluations of personal address behavior reveal expectations, and meanings attached to violations of expectations, that extend into other areas of social life.

The cultural perspective on interpersonal communication presented in this book thus takes personal address as a starting point because of its pervasiveness in everyday language, its intrinsic connection to relationships and communication, and its well-documented link to cultural meaning. This chapter briefly describes the five kinds of address terms and related terms of reference observed in use by and reported by the Colombians who were the focus of this study. Several native categories of intentions, interpretations, and evaluations associated with personal address are then listed as another kind of symbolic resource (described here as speech events with names) through which identities and relationships were constructed. Finally, several cultural premises reflected in patterns of address term use, and in the named categories of intention and interpretation through which specific personal address acts were understood, are presented. Taken together, these resources reveal the salient characteristics of personhood, relationships, and evaluations of behavior related to identity and relational status. Further, they detail a linguistically constituted system of premises centered around interpersonal connectedness among these urban Colombians.

FIVE CATEGORIES OF ADDRESS TERMS

Second-Person Pronouns

This class of terms consists of all the ways of directly addressing one or more persons as "you" (see Table 2.1).

Second-person pronoun choices have traditionally been singled out for particular attention in address term research (Brown & Gilman, 1960; Friedrich, 1972). In languages that utilize more than one form of second-person address (e.g.,

TABLE 2.1. Second-Person Pronouns

Term	Literal translation	Grammatical function
tú	you	informal, singular
usted	you	formal, singular
vos	you	informal, singular
su merced	your mercy	formal, singular, affectionate
su mercedcita	your little mercy	formal, diminutive, affectionate
su persona	your person	formal, singular, affectionate
su personita	your little person	formal, diminutive, affectionate
ustedes	you	formal, plural
vosotros	you	informal, plural

Spanish, French, German, Italian, Swedish, and Russian), a pronoun must at least be implied every time a verb refers to an addressee. Beyond their necessarily frequent uses, second-person pronouns are significant because of co-occurrence rules (Ervin-Tripp, 1972) that connect them to other categories of terms in a personal address system. Co-occurrence rules are regularities of usage that link selections among linguistic alternatives in ways that reveal relational expectations. Formal titles such as **Doctor** would ordinarily co-occur with **usted** (the formal pronoun) rather than **tú** (the informal pronoun), for example, and the combination generally signals a relatively formal, distant relationship (although this simplest paradigm case is subject to a wide variety of complications, as we shall see). Although most other terms (proper names, titles, nicknames, and so forth) often can be avoided through some kind of "no-name" option, second-person pronoun choices generally cannot.

Further, because they are limited in number—Colombian Spanish includes three singular and two plural second-person pronouns—the meanings of each term are necessarily complex. Each must serve as a vehicle to enact varied interpersonal intentions, despite the practice in Spanish grammar texts to label pronouns as either "formal" or "informal." Although the linguistic resource of second-person pronoun choices is common to all dialects of Spanish, the patterns of use and the range of intentions and interpretations attributed to those uses are situated within particular speech communities of Spanish speakers. Similarities will inevitably exist between urban Colombian pronoun choices and those of other communities, but the differences are substantial as well. The specific patterns and meanings associated with second-person pronouns, their co-occurences with other address term uses, and the interpersonal dynamics enacted through manipulation and negotiation of pronoun choices will be examined later in this chapter.

Proper Names

The number of specific items in this category is virtually limitless. Summarized in Table 2.2 are the forms of proper names that occur in address term acts, examples of each form, and the combinations that are frequently heard.

TABLE 2.2. **Proper Name Combinations**

Term	Examples
first name (FN)	Pedro, Juan, Walter, Nancy, Tomasa, Beatriz
first name (diminutive)	Pedrito, Juancito, Pacho, Pepe, Beto
last name (LN)	Gómez, Pérez, Torres, Cerón, Garzón, Cáceres
last name (diminutive)	Correita, Gomecillo, Muñocito
FN + second name (2N)	José Luis, María Bernarda, María del Pilar
2N	Claver, Gabriel, Eugenia, Carmen, Pilar
FN de (husband's LN)	Bertha de Lozano, Lola viuda de Perez

Almost all first names have diminutive forms. Some are conventionalized shortened forms of the names that reflect the pronunciation of small children, for example, Pepe for José and Pacho for Francisco (much like the use of Peggy for Margaret in English). Others involve addition of the diminutive particle *-ito* or *-ita* to the name, for example, Juancito for Juan, Lilita for Lilia, and so forth.

The most common woman's name, María, is given as both a first and a second name. Often, several girls in the same family will all have María as one of their names: María Teresa, Luz María, and María Ximena might be sisters, for example. Yet there is no equivalent abundance of male names using José. Although José is a common name, it is given with no more frequency than other important male saints' names such as Pedro and Juan.

Children receive both parents' surnames at birth, with the father's always first. Children of unmarried women receive only their mother's last name, and having only one last name is interpreted as a sign that the father has not "recognized" (i.e., taken legal responsibility for) the child. Nonetheless, common law marriage is relatively common (although stigmatized in the middle classes and up), and the offspring of such marriages often carry both parents' names. If a parent remarries after divorce or widowhood, the children retain their biological father's or mother's last name, regardless of how close a relationship they may develop with their stepparent.

Women generally retain their father's last name and drop their mother's last name for "de" plus their husband's last name upon marriage. "De" translates to "of," and is a particle indicating ownership. Teresa Pérez López would thus become Teresa Pérez de Torres (wife of Torres) upon marrying Juan Torres. When identifying herself or signing her name, however, she could choose to do so as either Teresa Pérez or Teresa de Torres. In recent years, the oppressive connotations of "belonging" to a husband have generated some discussion, particularly among well-educated urban dwellers, and some women have chosen not to change their names upon marriage. Such choices are less publicly visible than in the United States, however (and, perhaps for that reason, less fraught with symbolic tension; see Carbaugh, 1996; Hamblen, 1979; and others for explorations of the cultural meanings of married women's names in the States) because of general expectations that wives' surnames usually will differ from their husbands' anyway.

Kinship Terms

The kinship category includes terms that suggest biological relationship, used both literally (***Mamá*** to one's mother, ***primo*** to a cousin) and metaphorically (see Table 2.3).

Evident from this list is the fact that some kinship terms are the basis for a number of variations, such as ***padre*** (seven forms) and ***madre*** (ten forms), while others are not (two forms of ***hermano*** [brother], three forms of ***abuelo*** [grandfather]). The number of terms available for mothers and fathers reflects their relational importance, as compared to siblings and grandparents. Additionally, the metaphorical extensions of parent terms, particularly ***madre*** terms, index the symbolic meanings attached to such figures (a point I have expanded on elsewhere; see Fitch, 1991a).

Kin terms are metaphorically extended in other ways as well. ***'Mano*** (brother) is a common form of address among adult males, roughly equivalent to "buddy" in English. ***Hermana*** (sister) is not shortened and is rarely used in this way. ***Mijo*** and ***mija,*** (my son/daughter), and their diminutives ***mijito/mijita*** are heard frequently between family members and friends.

Titles

The category of titles is made up of terms that reflect a non-kinship-related status or position. Those positions designated by use of titles generally referred to organizational, educational, or social status achieved by or ascribed to an individual. Because such titles were numerous, even when re-

TABLE 2.3. Kinship Terms

Term	Literal translation	Gloss(es)
Padre	father	male parent or priest
Other forms: Padre + name; papá; papito; papi; padrecito; mi papá		
Madre	mother	female parent or mother superior in a convent
Other forms: Madre + name; mamá; mamita; mami; madrecita; mamacita; mamasota; mi mamá; mi mami; mi madre		
Hermano/a	brother/sister	biological sibling or member of a religious order (nun or brother)
Other form: 'mano		
Hijo/a	son/daughter	biological offspring
Other forms: hijo mío/hija mía; mijo/a; mijito/a		
Abuelo/a	grandfather/ grandmother	biological parent's parent
Other forms: abuelito/a; papá + name, mamá + name		
Tio/a	uncle/aunt	parent's sibling
Other form: Tio/a + name		
Primo/a	cousin (male/female)	cousin
Comadre/compadre	co-mother, -father	godparent to biological parent
Ahijado/a	godson/goddaughter	godchild
Madrina/padrino	godmother/godfather	godmother/father
Esposo/a	husband/wife	conjugal partner
Other forms: marido/mujer		

stricted to those actually used as address terms (thus excluding those that would exist on an organizational chart, for example, but would never be used in interaction), only a few examples need be discussed.

Doctor/a, denoting male and female forms of "doctor," traditionally designated any person with a college degree. Nowadays, it is extended to any adult of middle to high social status, especially by members of the working class. *Doctor/a* may be combined with either first name or last name, when those are known. Teachers below college level are generally addressed as *profesor/a* or simply *profe* ("teach"), or by their clerical titles when they are members of religious orders. College teachers are addressed as *doctor/a, profesor/a, profe,* and occasionally by first name.

Patrón/a and *jefe/a,* all equivalent to "boss," are used to address supervisors and employers, often in a lighthearted tone when the speaker is a white collar employee. Parents, particularly fathers, are also sometimes addressed in this way. Generally speaking, *patrón* is more closely associated with blue collar workers and service employees, because of the lordly image it evokes of wealthy ranch owners and their servants.

Señor/a and *don/doña* are alternative forms to denote Mr. and Mrs. Each may be used with a first name or last name, alone, or with a possessive pronoun (*mi señora, mi don*) to show affection. *Don/doña* was originally a term of considerable formality that designated nobility. It has taken on much more informal overtones in the New World and is used frequently as a middle ground between the more formal *señor/a* plus last name and the extremely informal first name alone, in that it is used as a title but is ordinarily combined with the first name. It is also described as more affectionate than *señor/a.*

Señorita (Miss), as a designation for a young, unmarried female, has no male equivalent and is itself rarely used. As quoted in the Introduction, one informant commented on the address term quandary posed by elderly unmarried women:

You can't just call them by their first name—to a 60-year-old woman that would be disrespectful! On the other hand you can't call them **doña** anything, because they haven't been married, and you don't want to forever say **señorita** so-and-so, reminding them all the time of their bad luck [in being single].

The customary solution to the social identity of an unmarried older woman, culturally defined as problematic for speakers and tragic for the woman who leads her life this way, is to address her by the diminutive of her first name (e.g., Sarita, Rosita, Merceditas). The connotation of childlike status conveyed by use of the diminutive is not seen as disrespectful, although the use of the first name alone is.

Nicknames and Adjectival Terms

Nicknames may be of two kinds (1) derivatives of first or last names or (2) references to such characteristics as one's personality, ability, or physical appearance. This category also includes those address terms that were, roughly speaking, adjectival terms. Nicknames are another resource in which nearly infinite variation is possible, so only a few of the most common forms will be discussed here (a longer list is included in the Appendix).

A class of nicknames heard very frequently were those that referred, loosely, to color of skin, hair, and eyes. People with dark skin and hair, both male and female, were often addressed as **negro/a** (black one), **moreno/a** (brown one) and their diminutives, **negrito/a** and **morenito/a.** Those with lighter hair and skin, especially with blue or green eyes, were addressed as **mono/a, monito/a** (blond one). The pervasiveness of nicknames referring to color is quite likely connected to the racial heritage of Colombians discussed in the Introduction. Dark hair and eyes were features common to African slaves, Spanish conquerors, and indigenous tribes, yet there were distinctive textures and shades that characterized each group. Pale skin, fair hair, and light-colored eyes were remarkable as relatively unusual features in a population where most came from darker stock.

Nonetheless, given the status differences among racial groups and the evaluative ranking of Spanish heritage as most prestigious, indigenous origin least so, and African heritage somewhere in the middle, it is surprising that all of these nicknames were generally used affectionately. For example, *mi Negrito* was a common nickname for taxis, back when they were black (a city ordinance has since mandated that they be painted yellow to increase their visibility), and informants commented on this pattern as signifying—beyond the car itself—the profound love a taxi driver felt toward his or her source of livelihood. *Mono, Negro,* and *Morena* were all common terms of endearment between romantic partners and from parents to their children (though not vice versa). One possible explanation is that, in a society where racial mixing was commonplace despite the fact that racial origin was crucially tied to social status (itself an intriguing juxtaposition, quite different from the caste system of India, for example), physical indicators of racial background took on universal importance, encoded in the personal address system through a number of terms describing those physical features. Because of the importance of color as a characteristic, family members engaged in the (probably universal) effort to establish who each child "took after" based on skin, hair, and eye color (rather than, for example, shape of nose, mouth, or eyes, as seems to be more common in some Anglo speech communities). The connection of the child to a previous generation is thus celebrated through affectionate reference to color.

Other personal characteristics that seem negative in their literal meaning were often used with evident affection. *Gordito* (fatso) and *viejo* or *cucho* (old one), for example, were frequently used to address men, especially by their wives. Neither term was ordinarily directed at females, suggesting a more negative connotation for women of both excess weight and advanced age.

A number of terms denoting stupidity were commonly heard: **boludo, huevón, pelotudo** (all of which designate a large-testicled male), **bruto/a, imbécil,** and **tonto/a** are some examples. Although these terms of address were primarily directed at strangers (such as inconsiderate drivers), they also occurred during arguments and were even used playfully among friends.

The wide variation in uses of many of these terms illustrates just how impossible (and unproductive) it would be to try to classify any particular term as inherently insulting, descriptive, or complimentary. On the basis of observed variations in use and meaning (e.g., terms of insult were used with affectionate tones and responded to with laughter on some occasions, hurled with venom and responded to with anger on other occasions), it is evident that most address terms have no fixed, singular meaning. The formal second-person pronoun **usted** was used to show both respect and, on other occasions, anger. A kinship term such as **madre** could be used both literally and in a multitude of metaphorical ways. Nicknames and adjectival terms could be used in both insulting and playful ways.

Yet there was obviously a system of meaning that made these different uses coherent. That system was evident in patterns of use, reactions to address term usage that marked certain events as violations, and natives' spontaneous reflections on their own and others' personal address behavior. Contextual factors (such as topic, setting, and dialect), aspects of relationships between users and hearers of address terms (status, intimacy, kinship), and pragmatic factors (literal/figurative uses of language, conversational expectations, and so forth) were obvious parameters for the uses and meanings of address terms. As a colleague and I have argued elsewhere in detail, however (Fitch & Sanders, 1994), social factors of this type make sense only against a culture-specific backdrop of premises about personhood and relationships. Elaborating those cultural premises requires an examination of an intermediate level of the system of meaning embedded in native terms for speech events involving personal address.

SPEECH EVENTS WITH NAMES

From very early in this study, I heard a number of native terms used to comment on address term use. Some uses of those terms sounded neutral and descriptive (e.g., ***Como le tengo bastante confianza, siempre le tuteo***—Because we have a great deal of ***confianza*** [i.e., we're very close], I always speak to him as ***tú***). Other uses seemed to encode either praise or blame of some kind (e.g., ***Esa grosera, ¡diciéndole Tula a mi mama! ¡Tula! ¡Qué falta de respeto!*** —That vulgar woman, saying Tula [nickname] to my mother! Tula! What a lack of respect!). The fact that such terms were used spontaneously and frequently, as Colombians talked about interpersonal actions and relationships, made the categories of intention and interpretation they referred to publicly available for observation and analysis. It seemed reasonable to include these terms for talk as part of the resources of the personal address system, especially in light of the documented importance of such terms in many other cultural systems (see Carbaugh, 1989). Thus, terms for talk that were heard in everyday conversation were recorded in field notes, along with address term occurrences, and later were explored in more detail in interviews. These native terms denote speech events in Hymes's (1972) sense: they are categories for speech action that encompass the patterned uses of terms, the symbolic dimensions of the patterns, and strategic/creative deviations from those patterns.

Personal address was not the only (or in some cases, the most important) communicative mode in which the speech events described below were realized. A useful aspect of the terms used to identify and distinguish between the speech events associated with personal address, in fact, is that they encompassed a wide range of other interpersonal actions and other associations with identities and relationships. Personal address was thus an index to many other aspects of the system of meaning underlying interpersonal communication in this speech community.

The principal speech events associated with personal address are listed below, grouped loosely into constellations of terms related to three symbolic fields: connections from birth, hierarchy, and relationships. The enactment of these speech events in personal address, and their connections within and across these symbolic fields, are represented in Figure 2.1 and then explored more fully in the next section, which focuses on the underlying cultural premises. Grouping these 23 specific speech event names into three broad categories suggests which dimensions of personhood and relationships were most consistently invoked as informants explained and described the uses of both address terms themselves and these local terms for talk (see Table 2.4).

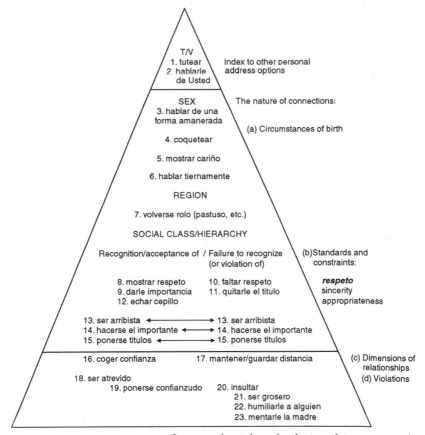

FIGURE 2.1. Dimensions of personhood and relationships enacted through speech events 1–23 (see Table 2.4).

TABLE 2.4. Twenty-Three Speech Events (Terms for Talk)

1. *tutear:* to speak using the informal pronoun *tú*.
2. *hablar de usted:* to speak using the formal pronoun *usted*.
3. *hablar de una forma amanerada:* to talk like a "sissy."
4. *coquetear:* to "sweet-talk" someone in order to obtain some favor.
5. *mostrar cariño:* to show affection, for example, through use of *tú*, a diminutive form of a name, or a nickname.
6. *hablar tiernamente:* to speak tenderly, again referring to some uses of *tú*, nicknames, diminutives, and other affectionate terms.
7. *volverse rolo (pastuso, costeno, etc.):* to turn into a *rolo* (*Bogotano*), and so on, particularly by speaking in ways associated with the region mentioned.
8. *mostrar respeto:* to show respect, for example, through use of a title or the formal pronoun *usted*.
9. *dar importancia a la persona:* to "give importance" to the person, that is, to show that someone is important to the speaker, either because of hierarchical status or because of the *confianza* that exists between them.
10. *faltar respeto:* to fail to show proper respect, for example, through use of informal or derogatory forms of address. To fail to show respect is a more serious transgression than to "get too chummy" (see #19) because it violates norms of hierarchy rather than personal closeness. An included term is:
11. *quitarle el título a alguien:* to take someone's title away, for example, to address them as *tú* rather than *usted*, or by first name rather than a title. To take someone's title away is one way to *faltar respeto*.
12. *echar cepillo:* to "run a brush," to curry favor with someone because s/he is in a position to do important favors.
13. *ser arribista:* to be a pretender or "social climber;" to act as though one were wealthy or well educated when such is not really the case.
14. *hacerse la (el) importante:* to "put on airs," that is, to presume a personal importance that may not be representative of one's true status.
15. *ponerse títulos:* to "put titles" on oneself, to insist on being addressed with a title that designates high status or position. Although the claim to high status may be legitimate, *ponerse títulos* suggests an inappropriate insistence on formality and rank. "Putting titles" on oneself is one way to *hacerse la (el) importante*.

(continued)

TABLE 2.4. (cont.)

16. *coger confianza:* to create or "catch" trust, that is, to establish a relationship based on trust, affection, and connection to another person.

17. *mantener/guardar distancia:* to keep/guard one's (interpersonal) distance. The opposite of creating *confianza,* this was accomplished through use of *usted* and formal titles. *Distancia* may be horizontal, as between peers who know one another and interact with some frequency but never establish any interpersonal trust or connection. It may also be vertical, in which a status difference is treated as relevant to interaction.

18. *ser atrevido:* to be daring; to take the chance, usually in joking or flirtation, of violating expectations for interpersonal conduct associated with the level of *confianza* and the status differences obtaining within a given relationship.

19. *ponerse confianzudo:* to act as though more *confianza* exists than is actually the case; to get too chummy.

20. *insultar:* to insult someone. Included terms that designate insults accomplished through personal address are:

21. *ser grosero:* to be vulgar.

22. *humillarle a alguien:* to humiliate someone.

23. *mentarle la madre:* to "mention the mother," that is, to call someone *hijueputa* (sonofabitch). This is the most specific and emotionally charged of these speech terms; it is limited to a single term of address and had the strongest potential to escalate conflict to a violent level. *Hijueputa,* as an especially virulent insult, was almost never used playfully.

The two speech events at the top of Figure 2.1 represent choices between second-person pronouns, mentioned earlier as the basis (through co-occurrence rules) for most personal address behavior in this speech community. Rather than constituting an exclusively relational index, as is sometimes suggested in Spanish textbooks (i.e., that use of **tú** designates familiarity and/or intimacy whereas **usted** connotes formality and/or distance), these two address terms and their close derivatives (**su merced, su persona,** and **vos**) invoked connections to social categories reflective of certain circumstances of birth: sex, regional origin, and social class. Those circumstances were described as ones that exerted enduring influences on personality, perception, and action, and that, for that reason, constituted fundamental bases for relationships. The act of selecting between these two pervasive forms of address functioned to create and display such connections.

Sex

Traditional standards that has maintained a sharp separation between males and females in Colombia have been relaxed somewhat in recent years, particularly in urban areas such as Bogotá. Nonetheless, single-sex educational institutions are common through high school, particularly in private schools (which are largely the province of middle and upper classes). Cross-sex friendships are rare; close nonromantic relationships between males and females are largely restricted to the extended family. Strong, enduring, and influential relationships were expected to obtain primarily among people of the same sex, both because of fundamental differences between men and women and because of gender expectations that affected their experiences in life.

Reflecting those distinctive experiences, there were observable gender differences in the use of *tú*. Men used *tú* much less than women, particularly when speaking to other men. One man in his mid-thirties commented that, although he was very close to his younger brother, he never addressed him as *tú*: *"Le muestro respeto como hombre con hablarle de usted"* (I show him respect as a man by calling him *usted*).

When address terms observably carry different meanings according to the context in which they are used—respectful distance in some cases, angry distance in others[1]—other accompanying cues help hearers to distinguish between

---

1. Silverstein (1976) identifies linguistic terms whose meanings change in this way as "shifters."

potential meanings. These variations in meaning are demonstrated more fully in Chapter 5 by showing address term
uses (e.g., *tú, culicagada paseadora esa,* etc.) in their
full conversational and relational surroundings, including
tone of voice, responses from onlookers as well as participants, and so forth.

For an adult male to *tutear* other men runs the risk of
an undesirable evaluation invoked in speech event #3:
hablar de una forma delicada (amanerada)—to talk
like a "sissy." A man in his mid-40s commented on his teenaged son:

> *Por lo general le hablo de usted, como mis papás me*
> *hablaban a mí. A veces me habla de tú, pero me ha*
> *dicho que jamás les hablaría de tú a sus compañeros*
> *en el colegio. Es un colegio masculino, y él dice que*
> *tutear dentro del colegio es ya quedar tachado de*
> *marica.* (For the most part I address him as *usted,* as my
> parents did me. Sometimes he calls me *tú,* but he told me
> he would never use *tú* with his schoolmates. He goes to
> an all-boys school, and he says that *tutear* in school is to
> be tagged right away as gay.)[2]

Another speech event that indexed gender was #4,
coquetear, to "sweet-talk" someone. It was used to describe a quasi-flirtatious speech style to obtain some favor,
usually (though not always) by a female speaking to a male.
Coquetear included address terms such as *mi amor* (my
love) and *cariño* (darling), and was distinguished from
real flirting in that the objective was plainly obtaining a
favor of the moment rather than developing even a short-
term relationship. A sincere use of affectionate forms of

2. Interestingly, a contemporary award-winning Colombian novel
(Molano, 1992) revolved around two gay teenaged boys who spoke to
one another always as *usted,* even in private, intimate moments. The
desire to talk in appropriately masculine ways extended, apparently,
to exploration of sexuality normally associated with use of the intimate
term of address.

address, including *tú* in some circumstances, was referred to as #5, ***mostrarles cariño*** (to show someone affection), or #6, ***hablarles tiernamente*** (to speak to someone tenderly). Both of those speech events generally referred to ways of speaking to women, small children, and close relatives regardless of their age.

These gender expectations for personal address suggest that, in this community, women were discursively associated with tenderness and affection in a way that was extended to small children. Women were also associated with persuasive strategies that relied on manipulation and insincere manifestation of affection. Men, on the other hand, avoided address term behavior that linked them too closely to expectations of feminine behavior out of fear that they would be seen as inadequately masculine. The valued way for men to speak to other men was with ***usted,*** to "show them respect" as a man. The valued way of speaking to women was to "show them affection." Nonetheless, a woman may be ***verraca*** (tough), in the sense of determined to get her way, as long as she is not vulgar or unfeminine in the process. Insistent "sweet-talking" is an acceptable feminine way for women to achieve desired ends, because it invokes a connotation of persuasion through nonserious sexual attraction. Indirect criticism of others' behavior is consistent with females' natural "tenderness," because taken literally it is either not critical (i.e., merely an observation) or not addressed to the person being criticized (e.g., the utterance is phrased as a hypothetical statement or as though intended for a hearer other than the person criticized—though the target may well be within hearing range).

Similarly, men who "speak tenderly" (***hablarles tiernamente/alcahuetearles***) to women and children have performed a morally approvable act. Being on tender and affectionate terms with women and children is a desirable interpersonal state. Serious flirting with any and all women, on the other hand, is not desirable in the connotations of disrespect it carries, both to the women themselves and (more significantly) to the other males who are connected to them (whether boyfriends, husbands, brothers, or fathers).

Speaking tenderly to other males, by contrast, invokes a connotation of homosexuality, which constitutes a deficient "manhood" and is thus included in a separate, negatively evaluated category of speech: **ser delicado en una forma de hablar** (to talk like a sissy). Morally "good" men are supportive to male friends by going drinking with them, by listening to their complaints about their wives, and by sharing activities outside the home with them such as sporting events. "Typically male" speech such as vulgarity, joking insults, and formal pronoun use draws an effective distinction between natural male closeness and sexual deviance.

Region

Another very common attribution offered, often spontaneously, for patterns of personal address was regional origin. Related orientations toward interpersonal relationships were also described as reflected in those distinctive patterns.

> Omar, age 35, in an impromptu discussion of a classmate: **Y todos los costeños, son mucho más abiertos y le hablan a todo el mundo de tú.** (And all the **costeños** [people from the coast] are much more open [informal] and they talk to everyone as **tú**.

> Julia: **¡Hasta las muchachas les hablan de tú a las señoras de la casa! Y se supone que eso es muy grosero, ¡hablar al jefe de uno de tú!** (Even the maids call their employers **tú** [in the coastal region]! And one supposes that's very vulgar, to talk to your boss as **tú!**)

> Alicia, 28, in a focus group interview: **Es que aquí en el interior es cosa de costumbre mantener como más distancia con la gente. Por eso casi no se usa el tú. Ahora el usar tú es más bien influencia de la gente que ha venido desde otras regiones.** (Here in the interior [i.e., Bogotá and environs] it's customary to maintain more distance from people. Because of that **tú** is almost

never used. Nowadays I think the use of *tú* is more the influence of people who have come here from other regions [of Colombia].

German, 22, in individual interview: ***En Nariño casi no hablamos de tú. Debe ser nuestra herencia realista*** (laughs) ***que somos muuuuy respetuosos.*** (In Nariño we almost never use *tú.* Probably it's our royalist heritage [laughs]—that's why we're verrrry respectful.)

Cupertino, a man in his thirties who had lived on the Atlantic coast until he was 13 and then moved to Bogotá, commented that he was in some ways "a typical ***costeño***": he loved parties, felt a kinship to the ocean and the sun, and didn't stand on ceremony. In other ways he considered himself "atypical": he viewed himself as very shy, he read a lot, and thought about the world a lot "instead of living from one minute to the next." I asked during an individual interview if there were different expectations for behavior in Bogotá, and he emphatically said yes, there were. Along the coast, parents encouraged their children to use *tú* with almost everyone they knew even slightly, and their use of ***usted*** was corrected as "unfriendly." ***Señó*** was an affectionate alternative to most titles, particularly ***señor*** and ***señora. Usted*** was potentially derogatory, indicating a respect based "merely" on an official role, rather than being part of a wide inner circle of people accorded genuine affection and respect.

A speech event that highlighted these regional patterns of address term use was ***volverse rolo*** (to turn into a ***rolo,*** or Bogotano). Other regional designations are substitutable but are less frequently heard. Because other characteristics and habits beyond personal address were imputed to the region of origin (frugality and religious nature to ***paisas,*** stupidity to ***pastusos,*** quickness to anger and tendency to violence to ***boyacenses,*** and so forth), claims that someone was acting out of character for her or his region of origin might have been tied to behaviors other than address term use. In practice, the speech event was largely used as a comment on unexpected uses of *tú*.[3] The perception that homeland (*tierra*) had significant impact on personality and behavior was expressed in interpretations of persons' actions and relationships. *Costeños* were widely understood to be an extreme case in this regard: their characteristics as a group sharply distinguished them from other Colombians. *Costeño* as a descriptive term was metaphorically extended to anything loud, flamboyant, or inappropriately casual, consistent with perceptions of the dress and behavior of natives of that region. *Costeños* in Bogotá routinely face discrimination in hiring and promotion for professional jobs in the government and in corporations where they are a minority (and favoritism under those same circumstances when the decision-makers are fellow *costeños*).

Social Class

A third aspect of personal identity keyed by pronoun choice was social class. A tendency for upper class people to *tutear* more than members of the middle and working classes was consistently asserted by informants from all levels, and this claim was supported in observations. *Tutear* was characteristic of wealthy and powerful individuals, and they ex-

---

3. To associate "going Bogotano" with uses of *tú* is potentially contradictory to the statement earlier in this chapter that "here in the interior people tend to maintain more distance from each other and don't use *tú* very much." Two explanations are possible: by "here in the interior" the focus group participant might not have meant to include Bogotá, since the capital city is viewed as exceptional in some significant ways. Alternatively, there may in fact be contradictory perceptions of address term use coexisting in this speech community: People in the interior, including Bogotanos, maintain more distance; and (by contrast) a characteristic of *rolo* speech is to *tutear* frequently. Bilmes (1976), Rosaldo (1989), and others have pointed out that contradictions and dilemmas are at the heart of culture, so that these contradictory beliefs substantiate their claim.

pected and received the formal pronoun **usted** in return from those of lower status. I never heard working-class informants **tutear,** even to intimates, although most reported that they used **tú** on occasion. It is certainly possible that my presence, assumed to represent middle class values, inhibited use of the pronoun. Both middle- and working-class informants gave a similar explanation for their nonuse of **tú:** they claimed they didn't know how to use it appropriately, i.e., they were unsure of the verb conjugations required to address someone correctly as **tú.** From this view, **tutear** is a grammatical practice that is learned largely in school, and a person who has not learned to **tutear** correctly runs a serious risk of embarrassing him/herself and displaying humiliating ignorance. A popular television comedy of the 1980s included a character who embodied this risk. The protagonist was a working-class male, Don Chinche, who frequently mixed pronouns and verb forms, such as ***"Doctor, ¿Usted sabes cuál es el remedio para esto?"*** (Doctor, do you [**usted**] know [**tú**] what the remedy for this is?) Though such errors do in fact occur among educated speakers, this character's sanguine mauling of the language drew roars of laughter from members of all social classes. Informants commented that they never used **tú** "because I would sound just like Don Chinche." The specific embarrassment associated with use of **tú** among lower- and middle-class speakers related to the perception that **tutear** was the province of highly educated, high-status people. Beyond the risk of making mistakes was the potential attribution of being **arribista** (i.e., a "pretender" or social climber, speech event #21): A social status would be claimed by use of **tú** that was not an accurate representation of the speaker's place in the class system. A connection to the upper classes would be claimed that did not actually exist.

Romance and friendship between people of different social status were prominent fodder in soap operas and gossip (the latter being widely known for the role it plays in social control; see, e.g., Goodman & Ben Ze'ev, 1994, and Bergmann, 1993). Such relationships generated widespread disapproval, ranging from backstage snickers to severance of family relationships. Such connections were described as unstable by nature because of the different life experiences, points of view, and customs of people born into different social classes. Friends and family members of the principals expected to encounter social awkwardness in situations where they were required to interact with such partners and sometimes refused to do so in anticipation of such difficulties. These kinds of relationships were seen as intensely problematic, both for the people involved and for others connected to them. That discomfort had effects both on the discourse and on the personal relationships of the middle-class people who were the primary respondents for this study.

First, characterizations of both people and settings by occupation were common in discourse, as in these two excerpts from field notes:

In a group of students discussing where to go dancing:

LEONOR: Let's go to *X* [name of bar].

JAVIER: Nooo, I went there a few weeks ago. ***Mucho obrero*** (lots of [blue-collar] workers).

(Nods of agreement and "oh, OK" from other members of the group; the talk then turns to other bars.)

PEDRO, age 24, catching up on news of mutual friends: Last time I heard from Yolanda she was dating this ***jardi-NERo*** (GARdener) from Yerbabuena.

Berta and Patricia (both giggle, trading wide-eyed looks with each other).

PEDRO: ***Quién sabe qué tendrá el jardinero. Será buen catre.*** (Who knows what the gardener has going for him. Maybe he's good in bed.)

In both of these instances, association with working-class people is invoked as relevant to action. In the first, the presence of "lots of workers" is grounds for avoiding a particular place. For these middle-class speakers, if there are lots of workers there, it is not where *they* belong. In the second, the fact that a middle-class female is dating a gardener is reported as noteworthy and greeted with surprise. The speculation about what attracts her to this man carries an implicit evaluation: given his occupation (which is either all the speaker knows about him, or all that is considered salient to this account), it is difficult to imagine what charm he might possess. Sexual prowess is at least plausible, defining the connection as one of physical attraction rather than a relationship expected to endure.

Given such reactions as these, the formation of a close relationship with someone from a vastly different social class was spoken of as an imposition on friends and family. College-educated middle class informants commented that, considering the sacrifices their parents made to help them attain the status of *profesionales,* it would be a significant disappointment if they did not marry other *profesionales.* The communal understandings of differences among members of different social classes are perhaps the clearest example of the types of constraints placed on potential friends and romantic partners by this community. Close personal relationships between people of different social classes were discursively constructed as unnatural, given the (presumed) lack of common experiences or a similar worldview, as uncomfortable and potentially disappointing to others in the partners' social worlds, and therefore as fragile and tenuous. Development of such relationships was thus not primarily a matter for individuals' decisions, volition, attraction, personality, and so forth, but a communally defined (and in this case, heavily constrained) event.

Two exceptions to this generalization serve to underscore it. First, employers and employees who worked closely together for extended periods of time sometimes developed extremely close, multifaceted relationships, as illustrated by the analysis of one such friendship in Chapter 5. Yet, those relationships were themselves significantly influenced by community constraints. They began in work contexts, which are virtually the only setting in which extensive daily contact among people of such different backgrounds is likely to happen. They developed over several years into intimate connections, yet the status differences between participants never entirely disappeared. Status differences remained embedded in task distinctions, discursive practices, and in the extent to which family and friendship networks actually mingled.

Second, illicit romances between people of different social status was at least represented in talk as extremely common (the actuality would be difficult to document, and may be less important than the widespread shared perception that such was the case). Middle-class boys' early sexual exploration with maids, and married men's "branch families" (i.e., long-term relationships with concubines, sometimes with children from that union) supported along with a communally legitimated spouse and children, attest to the power of the social world to bestow approval on certain partners and tolerate (or ignore) others.[4] Individuals may

4. Naturally, there are a number of complexities to the picture I have sketched all too briefly here. First, teenaged boys' liaisons with maids are less accurately viewed as "romance" than as dominance and misuse of their position. Nonetheless, such encounters are tolerated (though hardly condoned) as a kind of personal contact across social class differences that place them in the category being described. Second, concubines are not necessarily of lower social status than their married partners *when they enter the relationship*. When the community's reaction is disapproval, however, as is generally the case in Colombia, the concubine's status rapidly falls regardless of her occupational and educational level relative to the partner. Third, although clearly not all illicit romances involve a higher-status male and a lower-status female, that seems to be the predominant pattern, and for that reason I have used it as a prototypical case here. Finally, there is much to suggest that, by defining these relationships as illicit (and then pursuing or tolerating them), the middle class extends exploitation into the realm of sexuality and love relationships. Because in this area more than most I am presenting the view of middle-class Bogotanos, however (it was a delicate matter to pursue among working-class informants), I have very little information, about how working-class urban Colombians perceive these relationships, on which to base such a conclusion.

pursue relationships forbidden by the community, but to remain a member of the community they must develop those relationships in ways that do not fundamentally challenge or disrupt the basic social structure.

This belief that certain social facts were central to identity as well as behavior, and were powerful enough to override individual differences and uniqueness, may be stated as a cultural premise: crucial social identities are endowed at birth, largely indelibly by sex and social class, and to a lesser extent by region. Connections of this kind are enduring and pervasive bases for personal relationships. Persons who share those identities are to some degree connected to one another by virtue of the influence those circumstances of birth exert on experience, worldview, and behavior. Although that connection may be very slight, it is strong enough to facilitate certain relationships and pose significant barriers to others.

Certainly there were numerous evaluations of communication behavior, personal address and otherwise, that were linked to individual preferences, characteristics, and experiences, rather than presumed consequences of bonds to others. Yet, personal address both revealed one's roots and was taken as the basis for one's outlook on life. In a symbolically pervasive sense, social identity was constructed and displayed as a function of the connections of persons to fundamental circumstances of birth, and to other persons who shared those circumstances.

The understanding of status hierarchy as a fundamental aspect of identity and as an important influence on personal relationships, most obviously in social class separation (and to a significant degree in constraints on cross-sex friendship), was enacted more broadly in a cluster of speech events centered around the concept of ***respeto*** (respect). ***Respeto*** was enacted as deference to an achieved or ascribed status,[5] specifically through personal address that either:

5. This definition is consistent with Philipsen's (1992) description of a code of honor.

1. invoked the basis of the hearer's status (e.g., through use of a title);
2. invoked interpersonal distance, to show that the speaker did not presume intimacy (e.g., use of the first name rather than a nickname);
3. adhered to a code of conduct described as **culto** (well-mannered) and/or **formal** (e.g., use of a title plus the first name when the first name alone might be an option); or
4. made salient an important connection such as a kinship (or quasi-kinship) tie (e.g., use of **madrina** or **comadre**—terms denoting a godparent relationship—when the first name was an option).

The code of behavior embodied in the symbolic term **culto,** and the hierarchical overtones of this notion of **respeto,** will be described in more detail in Chapter 6. For now, it is useful to note that certain forms of address and reference were valued because they were associated with being **culto,** and that this understanding of well-mannered behavior included both knowledge of whom to respect and an expectation that important connections would be signaled through use of address terms that called attention to the symbolic aspects of the relationship (such as the implicit contract involved in godparenting).

A second premise underlying interpersonal connections in this speech community rests on a cluster of symbolic terms related to desirable and appropriate behavior between persons, primarily as configured by the nature of their connection. Personal address indexes a central dimension of personal relationships along a continuum pervasively signaled through uses of the symbolic categories **confianza** and **distancia.**

Further mirroring its centrality in the personal address system of this community, **tutear** is an indicator of relationship as well as social identity. **Tú** is the basic term of **confianza,** although only in a very qualified way. Among these Colombians, it was interpersonally meaningful action

to switch from **usted** to **tú** in order to change the configuration of a relationship:

> Alejandra, 30, in casual conversation: When I became a
> teenager I decided it was time to have a closer relationship
> with my father, so I started to **tutear** him. That helped me
> to feel closer to him.

It was also frequently the case that relationships marked
by a great deal of **confianza** were constructed within a
family or friendship framework marked by region, social
class or gender such that **tú** was never used:

> Fernando, 24, in individual interview: **En Bucaramanga
> es muy común que los hijos les hablan a sus padres
> de tú y a sus hermanos de usted. Así eramos en mi
> familia—si mi hermana llegara algún día tuteándome
> me incomodaría bastante.... Quizás sería algo de los
> celos entre hermanos, que el tú es reservado para los
> papás, entonces lo de usar el tú con los hermanos es
> como robar algo de la intimidad entre los papás y los
> hijos.** (In Bucaramanga it's very common for children to
> speak to their parents as **tú** and their siblings as **usted.**
> That's how we were in my family—if my sister showed up
> one day using **tú** I would be really uncomfortable.... It
> may be something to do with jealousy between siblings,
> that **tú** among siblings is like stealing some of the intimacy
> between parents and children.)

> Gabriel, 27, in a class discussion said that he and a female
> neighbor of the same age had been good friends for years,
> and that they always spoke to one another as **usted.** He
> commented that one time he did make a mistake; he turned
> around and asked her, **"¿Sabes a qué horas empieza la
> película?"** (Do you [**tú**] know what time the movie starts?)
> and said they both burst into embarrassed laughter. He
> thought their use of **usted** might have something to do with
> the proximity of their two families: Both of them generally

speak to their family members with *usted* and, because they live next door to one another, are frequent visitors in each other's homes.

Confianza may also be invited or extended through other address term means, such as use of a first name or diminutive, a metaphorical kin term (particularly *mijo/a* [my son/daughter] or *'mano* [brother]), or endearments such as *negro/a, mi amor,* and so forth. When informal address terms are used inappropriately, suggesting a closeness that does not exist in the perception of at least one of the parties, the action is evaluated as *ponerse confianzudo/a* (to get too chummy). Salespeople were perceived to engage in such facile ingratiation with annoying frequency and assertiveness, sprinkling their talk with transparently unfounded terms of endearment.

Distancia is an oppositional term to *confianza,* signifying both horizontal and vertical interpersonal distance. Maintaining distance was accomplished by way of insistent use of formal address terms and occasional correction of lower-status others:

> Walking into Miriam's apartment building one day, the doorman said *"buenos días"* to us both and directed a question at her. I didn't hear the question, but noted her tone seemed frigid when she answered. As we walked away she asked if I heard how the doorman addressed her: *"Me parece que me tuteó."* (It seems he used *tú* to me.) I said I didn't hear him. She said she'd listen more carefully next time *"y si le oigo tutear le digo 'tú, no. Usted.'"* (and if I hear him *tutear* me I'll say, *"tú, no. Usted."*)

The implicit danger of allowing informal address terms from subordinates to pass without comment was that the lower-status person would *ponerse confianzudo,* a highly undesirable state of affairs.

To the degree that two people have *confianza,* there is less need to be "careful" about address term use; a wider range of choices, such as *tú, usted,* first name, kin term (perhaps metaphorical), and nickname is potentially appropriate, according to settings and topics. To the degree that little or no *confianza* exists, a narrower range of choices is available and greater care must be exercised not to seem *confianzudo* (too chummy) or disrespectful.

> Juan, 30, went to a medium-priced clothing store to buy a suit. As he discussed various possibilities with the clerk (female, around 17), she addressed him as *tú* several times. As he left the store, Juan remarked in a disgusted tone that the clerk's use of *tú* irritated him: *"Yo creo que les estan enseñando hacer eso para crear más confianza con los clientes."* (I think they are teaching [salespeople] to [*tutear*] to create more *confianza* with the customers.) The next day when he went to pick up the suit after alterations, the clerk spoke to him as *usted.*

This extract illuminates two speech events associated with personal address. The first, *tutear* (to address someone with the informal pronoun *tú*) is a linguistic vehicle for relational change. The customer's disgust that a salesperson would try to *crear confianza* (create a relationship based on trust, affection, and connection to another person) through use of the informal pronoun was likely related to the artifice associated with salespeoples' easy intimacies. The salesperson's switch to a more formal, distant pronoun once the sale was complete reinforces the notion that the *confianza* suggested by use of *tú* was fleeting and instrumental.

The symbolic loads of *confianza* and *distancia* will be discussed further in Chapter 6. For now, it is sufficient to note that the opposition *confianza/distancia* forms the basis of a constellation of interpersonal meaning that is richly displayed in personal address terms, their uses, and the evaluative categories that offer a system of distinctions relevant to their deployment as communicative resources.

A third dimension of personal address reflected in the speech acts with names was that of sincerity or lack thereof. There were a number of personal address acts that were described as included within one category rather than another based on the degree of sincere feeling—either *confianza* or respect—that was perceived to motivate it. A third premise about personal relationships in this speech community is thus suggested by the recurrent distinction between sincere and/or appropriate behavior and that which was interpreted either as insincere or as resting on inappropriate claims to a desirable social status. Desirable relationships are those in which a level of respect is shown that corresponds to the earned or ascribed status of the other person and/or to the level of *confianza* that exists in the relationship. The respect displayed in talk and other behavior should (ideally) be sincere deference to status or should accurately reflect the *confianza* that exists. Whether or not the respect is sincere, however, a social duty exists to behave appropriately: to act in accordance with standards of *culto* behavior and to act in ways that accurately reflect one's position in the social hierarchy. These premises were most obvious in the speech events named to reflect violations of them.

Ser arribista (to be a social climber) and *echar cepillo* (to curry favor) are ways of laying claim to high social status that depend on establishing, or making visible, connections with powerful others rather than emphasizing aspects of oneself as the basis for such status. Because use of *tú* was associated with the upper classes, a risk incurred when working class people chose to *tutear* was a perception that they were trying to move up in the social order by adopting the linguistic habits of their target group. Likewise, family members were sometimes perceived as trying to claim for themselves some of the honor accruing when a relative achieved some important accomplishment.

> Pablo, 28, in conversation about family members: I was about 11 when my uncle became a priest. I had always called him Tomás, but now my mother and grandmother

insisted I call him ***Padre Tomás***. . . . I didn't agree with
that at all—he was still the same person to me, and I don't
think the title was all that important to *him*. For his mother
and his siblings, though, his being a priest was a big honor
to *them,* and *they* were the ones who needed everyone to
recognize what an important fellow he was now.

To this informant, the family members' insistence on
addressing a relative by his title was being ***arribista,*** in
continually calling attention to his high occupational status.
He perceived their motivation as less a matter of showing
respect for the priesthood (though presumably they would
label their use of the title as exactly, and only, that) than
heightening their own importance through an implicit connection with someone of high status.

Patricia, 35, told the story of a sudden change in her
neighbor's behavior shortly after the neighbor graduated from
college: ***Siempre nos hemos llamado por el nombre, y
un día apareció hablándome de Doctora—"ay, doctora
Patricia, ¿cómo me le va?" Claro que quería que
nosotros le hablabamos también de doctora, tan
arribista que es! Y yo me puse NEGRA de la risa!*** (We
had always called each other by name, and one day she
showed up calling me ***doctora***—"ay, ***doctora*** Patricia, how
are you doing?" Of course she wanted us to call her ***doctora,***
what an ***arribista*** [social climber] she is! I was BLACK with
laughing! [i.e., "I laughed myself black in the face"].

In this instance, the action of addressing a neighbor
with a title plus first name, rather than first name alone, was
interpreted by the person telling the story as a ploy for reciprocal use of a title designating high social and/or academic status. The social status designated by use of ***doctora***
is, as suggested earlier, an especially salient one in this
speech community. To have a college degree is to be a
profesional (professional) and thus indisputably a member of the middle class. Patricia's derisive reaction suggests
that the claim to identity as a ***profesional*** was inappropri-

ate in some way: either inconsistent with other aspects of the neighbor's identity or out of place in the relational context of interactions with neighbors.

By addressing her neighbor as ***doctora*** instead of the expected first name, the woman in this example signaled (in the hearer's perception, at least) a desire to be addressed in the same fashion. By describing the speaker as ***arribista,*** the hearer suggests that the claim to high status is an illegitimate one. Neither the action nor the identity desired by the speaker is, in other words, granted as appropriate.

A tentative conclusion based on this analysis is that Colombians oriented to interpersonal connectedness to a greater degree than to individual characteristics in their personal address behavior. In this speech community, status is pervasively important and thus encoded very frequently in address term use. It is a world in which relationships differ from one another in terms of a balance between trust, intimacy, and similarity on one hand; and an expectation that distance must be maintained from those of different status and/or where little trust, intimacy, or similarity has been established. This system of personal address revolves fundamentally around bonds between human beings. These bonds to family, region, social class, and sex establish the identity of the individual to a far greater degree than individual characteristics, abilities, or desires, and all are signaled through personal address. Titles reflect not only the status and importance of the individual to whom they are addressed; they index the status of the family to which that individual belongs. Use of ***tú*** marks a speaker as a native of a particular region (***costeño*** or Bogotá), a member of (or a pretender to) a high socioeconomic class, or a potentially inadequately masculine male.

In summary, status, respect, ***confianza,*** and masculinity are disputed territory in this speech community. All are negotiated through personal address, among other communicative forms. To insist on use of a title is either maintaining an (appropriate) distance, and seeking an (appropriate) measure of respect, or ***dándoselas de importante*** (putting on airs). To address someone with a first name or informal kin term rather than a title that they might legitimately claim is either being ***confianzudo*** (too chummy) or ***mostrando cariño*** (showing affection). Because address terms have no single, fixed meaning, they are malleable resources through which members of the community may lay claim to valued identities (e.g., middle-class status), relationships (e.g., ***de mucha confianza,*** or an appropriate distance), and valued modes of behavior (***culto***). Because communal understandings exist regarding the local hierarchy and one's place within it, conditions qualifying the extent to which ***confianza*** may develop, and numerous other aspects of personhood and relationships, those claims may be challenged, countered, and evaluated as insincere or inappropriate. Speech events with names reveal the dimensions of identity and the relationships that serve as the basis for these negotiations, and for defining connections to others.

In a universal sense, personal address both displays the nature of relationships between individuals and serves as a communicative vehicle for transforming those relationships. In this speech community of urban Colombians, certain personal characteristics and relationships were highlighted as significant (color of skin, hair, and eyes; regional origin; sex differences) that suggest that connections to others—of the same color, the same sex, region, social class—most fundamentally define personal identity. The implication of this conceptualization of personhood is that personal relationships are potentially more central to identity than individual, unique characteristics. Personal connections are facilitated (or favored) among those with whom a communal connection is perceived already to exist. This is distinctive from similarity/attraction dynamics as they are generally understood, because the impetus to form a connection comes not from within the individuals but from the expectations and beliefs of the community.

Although personal address terms have been at the center of this analysis, plainly such terms are not inserted into

interaction as isolated items. They occur during interactional
sequences, and to look at those sequences is to take a step
further into the stream of relational processes. Thus, the next
focus in the ethnographic study of this speech community
was on a speech act, to expand the analysis of interpersonal
communication to an interactive plane. In the next chapter, directive sequences are examined as a fundamental unit
of interaction through which these Colombians coordinated
their actions with each other.

CHAPTER THREE

DIRECTIVES

Requests and Commands

Like personal address, directives—that is, requests and commands—are a valuable source of insight into shared understandings of personhood and communication within a speech community. Directives exist in every known language and are a communication resource through which people coordinate their actions with others. In many cases, such coordination involves compelling others to act (or not act) in particular ways at particular times. Like personal address, directives have been studied ethnographically in a number of diverse speech communities. Those studies document tremendous variations across communities in the uses and functions of directives (see, e.g., Ahern, 1979; Blum-Kulka, 1990; Hollos & Beeman, 1974; Rosaldo, 1982; Rushforth, 1981; Weigel & Weigel, 1985). This body of work also suggests that distinctive systems of cultural beliefs about persons, relationships, and communication underlie directive performance in different communities. Because compelling the actions of another person implies some basic need or right of the person who makes the request (or issues the command, or slips the hint), directives also reveal understandings and enactments of power.

Beyond the empirical basis in previous literature that suggested directives would be a productive phenomenon for exploring culture, it is fair to say that directive performance was also the most profound culture shock I experienced in Colombia. I observed (and experienced) adults telling others what to do in Colombia with a frequency and firmness that I thought would be reserved for small children. For example:

> Mariela to Josefina: ***Ven acá y ayúdame hacer una cosa.*** (Come here and help me do something.)

> Imelda, to 40-year-old son: ***Venga, ¡sálgase de allí y váyase pa' su casa, que le necesitan por allá!*** (Come on, come out of there and go home—they need you there!)

> Man, starting to push a stalled car out of traffic, to a male bystander: ***¡A empujá mano!*** (To push, brother!—i.e., "Get over here and help me!")

Despite this abundance of stern-sounding directives, I noticed that people very often did not do what they were asked or told to do, even when serious repercussions seemed possible. Once I went to a bank during a labor strike and saw antimanagement graffiti spray painted on the mirrored and marbled walls *inside* the bank: ***¡Fuera con Jaime Diaz, rata represiva! ¡Viva la huelga!*** (Out with Jaime Diaz [the chief executive officer], repressive rat! Long live the strike!) I asked a companion how the graffiti could still be on the walls despite its being well past midday, and despite the fact that janitors were there in the building. He shrugged and said that the cleaning staff had probably been told to clean it up "and they probably said *'si, señor, right away,'* but then mysteriously have been *so busy* they just couldn't get around to it. The cleaning people, after all, are either members of the union or sympathetic to the strike."

Further, I observed and was told about people intervening in the lives of others in ways that astonished me: mending and ending relationships, choosing schools and

majors and living arrangements for college students, verbally (often vociferously) correcting the behavior of adults.
I heard people direct others to perform tasks that they could
as easily (or more easily) have done themselves. It was
obvious that Colombians generally were not offended by
these blunt, ever present directives, which suggested that
they attached quite different meanings to them than I was
used to. I realized that I came from a system in which people
mostly directed the actions of others in much more indirect, even timid, ways: orders were disguised as suggestions,
advice was couched in disclaimers, or people were careful
to give reasons and explanations to justify requests. Blunt
directives are reserved, in my speech community, for intimates, children, and emergencies, and may be avoided even
then. Colombians were indirect, and offered disclaimers,
much less often and seemed to order around everyone from
service people to their peers to strangers in the street. Behind the obvious differences in directive performance there
had to be a different kind of reasoning about the connections between directives and behavior, between people who
issued directives and those who received them, and between
the act of directing behavior and the identities and relationships signaled by such acts.

These Colombians plainly constituted a speech community that was rich in directives, and following up themes
and symbolic terms such as **confianza, distancia,** and
respeto by exploring directive performance was a logical
step. Nonetheless, it quickly became apparent that using
"directives" as a category of speech action was problemati-
cally broad in some ways. Unlike terms of address, a candidate utterance cannot always be easily classified as a directive rather than, for example, an informational statement.
To say to a parent, "Your child just walked into the street"
presumably counts as a recommendation for the parent to
take some action. Many other utterances with similar linguistic structures (e.g., "Your child is in bed asleep") generally do not. The pragmatic issues involved in indirect use
of language have been explored at length, with consider-

able attention to directives (see, e.g., Clark & Lucy, 1975; Labov & Fanshel, 1977; Levinson, 1983; Searle, 1979). Although most of that discussion is not relevant here, it is worth noting that the linguistic, pragmatic and cultural meanings of directives often diverge from one another in their natural habitat of everyday conversation. The distinctions between those levels of meaning affected data collection and analysis for this part of the study in the sense that selecting instances from the stream of talk to categorize as directives was a complex issue. Discovering the meaning of utterances that were linguistically constructed as directives meant going beyond linguistic form to explore the pragmatic force and cultural meaning of such utterances. Juxtapositions of this kind meant that part of the belief system I wanted to discover was the code rules about what kinds of utterances, in what kinds of contexts, counted as directives.

An illustration of this point can be made by considering the structure and function of offers among these urban Colombians. On any number of occasions, offers of assistance, food, drink, and so forth involved imperative constructions and an imperative tone:

> Mariela to Josefina: ***Toma ese jugo. Tómalo tú.*** (Drink this juice. You drink it.)

> Mariela, mother-in-law, to Kristine, daughter-in-law: ***Ve, trae la chequera y veamos cómo estás de plata.*** (Go get your checkbook and we'll see how you're doing with money.)

> Sister to brother #1: ***¿Quieres café o chocolate?*** (Do you want coffee or hot chocolate?)

> Brother #2: ***Dále café.*** (Give him coffee.)

Offers of this kind were almost never turned down, in my observation and in the reports of Colombian research assistants. A comment from a focus group interview suggested that under some circumstances refusing certain offers was such a violation of interpersonal expectations that the offer constituted a command:

Monica, 24: I used to go with my mother to visit friends of hers and they always offered us coffee. I don't drink coffee—I don't like it at all, so I just said "no thanks," and the friends looked at me like, is she crazy? Finally my mom said, "Listen, when people offer you something you *have* to take it. You can't just refuse—it's very rude, as if whatever they have isn't good enough for you."

This woman's reflection both suggests that some offers amount to imperatives and implies a cultural premise involved in such offers: *an interpersonal bond is formed by sincere offers of food, drink, and assistance.* An imperative grammatical construction reinforces the sincerity of the offer, and to refuse the offer is to deny or refuse the bond.

Naturally, not all offers were put forth with such sincere intentions that they be accepted, and not all offers counted as directives. Because so many offers were uttered as imperatives, however, and because relational imperatives underlay some offers, the possibility that offers might constitute directives at times had to be considered during data collection and analysis.

Methodological issues aside, the question of greatest interest in regard to directives was closely parallel to that pursued in examining personal address, namely, what premises about personhood, relationships, communication, and power are brought to bear on directive performance among these urban Colombians? As was true with terms of personal address, several speech events with names were used in connection with directive performance that constituted categories of interpretation and evaluation of such acts. Those speech events evoked symbolic terms that suggested a system of four rules for directive performance in this speech community. Those rules encoded the interpersonal objectives, balanced against constraints of relationships and power, that were the framework for compelling actions through communication in this speech community. The overall sense of directives as a part of the interpersonal ideology created by this configuration of symbolic resources was that directives, beyond compelling actions, create and sustain connections among persons by creating and calling attention to interdependence. As such, they are not construed primarily as the imposition of one individual will over another, or as a limitation of personal autonomy. Rather, they count primarily as signs of interconnectedness, the force without which human life itself would dissolve into chaos. Having given a brief synopsis of the symbolic system, I will describe the components—speech events, symbolic terms, rules, and the connectedness ideology they implicate—in detail.

DIRECTIVE SPEECH EVENTS

It is useful to open this discussion by noting that directives, like other speech acts, come in different degrees of illocutionary force (Austin, 1962; Ervin-Tripp, 1976; Searle, 1969). A hint, a request, and a command all attempt to direct the behavior of the hearer, but they differ in the strength of the attempt.

A distinction should also be made between linguistic labels that distinguish categories of directives on the basis of abstract assessments of illocutionary force, such as *dar una órden* (to give an order), *hacer una sugerencia* (to make a suggestion), and so forth, and cultural terms for talk that capture interpretations and evaluations applied to specific act sequences. Linguistic distinctions proceed *to some degree* from the structure of utterances, such that "Get your feet off the chair!" will generally count as an order because of its formulation as an imperative. Certainly there is no one-to-one correspondence between linguistic form and illocutionary force: "Why don't you get out of the car, sir," is not a suggestion despite its formulation.[1] Cultural interpretations of utterances incorporate an assessment of linguistic form and pragmatic force (whether an utterance counts as an order or a suggestion may depend on the relative ranks of the speaker and the hearer, for example) but also draw upon

---

1. I am indebted to Steve Duck for this example.

culture-specific understandings of personhood, relationships, power, and so forth (a point discussed more fully in Fitch & Sanders, 1994). Thus, the speech events described in this section are those invoked by Colombians when commenting on directive acts, both spontaneously and in interviews.

Ofrecer (to offer) was described earlier as a speech event that included some directives. A common courteous phrase illustrates the interpersonal climate in which offers bind people into relationships: *"De pronto se le ofrece algo"* (Maybe you can be offered something—i.e., anything you need, just ask). Apocryphal though it might be, the statement is in effect an invitation to issue directives. A related phrase reinforces the notion of a blanket offer in which directives would be welcome: *"Aquí estamos a la órden"* (Here we are, at your service).

Generally speaking, the more **confianza** that existed between interlocutors, the greater the magnitude of offers that were made and the greater the obligation to accept them. Sincerity was a separate issue: a level of **confianza** high enough to entail expectations that goods and services would routinely be offered did not make those offers automatically more sincere. When offers were recognized as potentially insincere, the obligation to accept them disappeared, as in the following exchange. Libia has been chatting about her son Ivan's options for a place to live while he finishes college with several family members.

LIBIA: *Puede vivir con Oscar, puede vivir con el primo Diego que vive allá en Chapinero* . . . (He can live with Oscar, he can live with his cousin Diego who lives there in Chapinero . . .)

DORA, a distant relative by marriage: *Allí está la casa a la órden Libia.* ([My] house is at your orders, Libia.)

LIBIA (*smiling*): *Ah bueno, gracias.* (Oh, good, thank you.)

DORA: *Claro, allí está el cuarto, él tiene allá la casa a su disposición.* (Really, the [guest] room is right there— he has the house at his disposition.)

LIBIA: *Muy amable.* (That's very nice of you.)

I showed this transcript to Leonor, who knows Dora slightly, to ask if she thought the offer was sincere. She asked how well Libia and Dora knew each other and I explained that Dora's husband is very close to Libia's husband; Dora and Libia have contact frequently but no particular affection for each other. Leonor inferred that the offer was not at all sincere, more a gesture that recognized the bond between the husbands; she doubted Dora would make such an offer to Ivan himself, for fear he'd take her seriously.

Pedir un favor (to ask a favor) is a counterpart to offers, generally involving requests for the same kinds of goods and services, and was a common label for directive acts in this community. Friends, for example, were distinguished as "people you could ask favors of," and the greater the degree of *confianza,* the greater the magnitude of favors that could be requested. Many instances of asking favors involved hints:

TEACHER, at a faculty meeting: *Qué rico un tintico caliente.* (Oooh, wouldn't a little hot coffee taste good?)

COLLEAGUE: *Voy a traer tinto. ¿Todos quieren?* (I'm going to bring coffee. Everybody want some?)

TEACHER, to a high school class: *Está haciendo mucho sol.* (It's really sunny out.)

STUDENT: *Mejor cerramos la puerta.* (We'd better shut the door.) (He gets up to shut it.)

A specific kind of favor that was both frequently requested and offered related explicitly to interpersonal connectedness. *Acompañarle a alguien* (to keep someone company) was used in reference to physical presence:

LUZ CARMEN: *Quiero hacer una llamada. ¿Me acompañas a la oficina?* (I want to make a phone call. Come with me to the office?)

ANDRES: *Como quieras.* (Whatever you want—i.e., "sure.")

And to moral support:

> A client discussing marital problems with a therapist commented that he really felt he should leave his wife but hated the thought of not seeing his son.

THERAPIST: ***Quiero que usted decida lo que siente. Si usted opta por la separación, le acompaño en la separación.*** (I want you to decide how you feel. If you decide on the separation, I'll accompany you in the separation, i.e., "I'll be there for you.")

In both the physical and the emotional sense, "to keep someone company" was specifically to provide the favor of human connection, to free someone from the less desirable condition of performing a task or undergoing a stressful situation alone. The frequency with which "keeping company" was both offered and requested as a favor, and the gratitude with which such actions were received, suggest that enacting interpersonal connectedness by physical or emotional companionship was highly valued in this community.

Directives issued to subordinates and service people frequently incorporated ***"me hace el favor de . . ."*** ("do me the favor of . . .") in their structure. Requests made to service people who controlled crucial resources (notably taxi drivers, clerks in public offices, and members of organizations who were in charge of audiovisual equipment, library materials, and other supplies) were often performed with elaborate care. This is from a focus group interview:

CAROLINA: ***Sería muy brusco decir "déme un formulario," digamos en una oficina pública.*** (It would be very rude to say "give me a form," let's say, in a public office.)

MARCELA: ***De pronto se ofenden y ni te lo dan*** (*laughter*). (They might get offended and not even give it to you.)

CAROLINA: ***Tienes que decirles "¿me hace el favor y me regala un formulario?"*** (You have to say to them, "Do me the favor and present me with a form?")

LIGIA: *De otro te miran feo y te dicen "ufff, no hay."*
(Otherwise they look at you mean and say "uffff, there
aren't any.")

MARCELA: *Y también uno tiene que tener cuidado con
los taxistas—todos saben que si les da rabia ¡te
bajan! Les dices por ejemplo "¿No le parece que
nos va mejor si bajamos por aquí?" Que si le dices
"Baje por aquí" no más, te dicen "Huy! Si quiere
manejar que compre carro!" y van por otro lado.*
(You also have to be careful with taxi drivers—everybody knows if you make them mad they'll kick you
out! You have to say, for example, "Doesn't it seem to
you we'd do better if we go down this way?" If you
just say, "Go down this way," they'll tell you, "Huy! If
you want to drive, buy a car!" and they go some other
way.)

Although control over scarce resources is part of the
configuration that makes these directives "favors" rather than
"commands," there are also broader issues of institution and
social class that make these requests delicate operations.
Shortages of resources—such as crucial forms—are so frequent in government offices that *"no hay"* is always a plausible response to clients' requests. It may thus be applied
whimsically, such that a low-status office worker can exercise gratifying control over the fortunes of those who come
to do business there, even those of much higher social status. Similarly, taxi drivers own their vehicles and answer to
no one, and the demand for transportation almost always
exceeds the supply, giving drivers considerable freedom to
"discipline" inappropriately directive clients. In both cases,
the client is much more dependent on the service provider
than the reverse and therefore treats the service as a favor
that may be refused.

Pedir limosna (to ask for charity, usually used to
describe the actions of beggars in the street) is a speech
event that is somewhat similar to *pedir un favor* in that
the hearer is free to refuse, and even ignore, such directives. Still, there are obvious differences between the two

speech events. Begging involves a very clear power imbalance and a lower expectation of compliance because of the lack of a preestablished connection between the beggar and the target of the request. It is worth considering as a directive speech event, however, in the sense that being the target of beggars' requests was a universal experience among these Colombians, and a certain admiration for the skill and spirit of some beggars was expressed. The formulation of requests by beggars was also noteworthy. Given the power imbalance and the lack of obligation on the part of the hearer, some interestingly nondeferential directive forms were commonplace:

BEGGAR, female in her late 40s, (*leaning close to the window as a car is stopped at a stoplight*): **Mi Dios me la atravesó en la vía, déme una monedita.** (My God brought you into my path—give me a little money.)

FEMALE DRIVER, 60 (*faint smile, no eye contact*): **No tengo.** (I don't have any.)

BEGGAR: **Ayyyyy déme una monediiiita, cinco pesos, 10 pesos, cuálquier cosita.** (Ayyyyyy, give me a little moooney—five pesos, 10 pesos, whatever little thing.)

DRIVER (*still smiling*): **Pero es que no tengo.** (But I don't have any.)

A strategy utilized by some beggars, particularly young ones, was to attempt to establish a short-lived service relationship with the target, in order to preemptively offer some service for which they could then be paid. Youngsters routinely walked out into lines of cars stopped at traffic lights, squirted water on windshields and rubbed with a rag, then stepped up to the driver's window with their hands extended for payment, often without a word to the occupants of the car. Similarly, children were often posted outside restaurants and stores. When cars parked outside, the child offered to "watch" the car while the passengers did business within, a service for which they were paid. One informant remarked that in some cases the child's offer to safeguard the parked car amounted to extortion: Either the driver paid or else returned to find the child gone and the car damaged or missing a hubcap, antenna, or rearview mirror. Nonetheless, these Colombians voiced sympathy for the plight of beggars generally, and respect for the efforts of some of them to perform some kind of work in exchange for pay, far more often than they expressed disdain or disgust (by far the more common response among U.S. tourists) at the nuisance they presented.

Pedir limosna was thus a speech event in which, like some instances of *pedir favores,* the actual relative power of the requester and the target was ambiguous—or even the reverse of what might conventionally be predicted. Beggars exercised a degree of control over their targets because of a general climate of sympathetic response and a measure of fear at the damage they might inflict. Dependence on the services provided by some lower-status people, such as taxi drivers and government clerks, gave them the power to refuse requests from clients, such that directives issued to those persons were considered, and formulated, as requests rather than commands.

Although subordinates occasionally had the power to refuse requests, and although even beggars were not without influence in the social system, directives given to these Colombians were overwhelmingly formulated as imperatives. One aspect of interpersonal connection that was signaled by imperatives was hierarchy, and status differences were far more often reinforced than they were negated by way of directives, despite the examples described above. Two speech events are particularly relevant to both the display and the maintenance of status hierarchy through directives: *hacerse respetar* (to make oneself respected) and *mantener órden* (to keep order).

Hacerse respetar incorporates the idea of respect, as discussed in the preceding chapter, in the sense of deference to a positively perceived personal quality such as hierarchical rank or educational status. The construction of this linguistic label for a class of directives suggests that at least part of the responsibility for appropriately respectful behavior lies with those persons who have that status. Respect is not automatic; those who desire respect must do something to bring about its enactment.[2]

Several of the Colombians who participated in this phase of the study, whether as members of the research team or as informants, were teachers, students, and/or parents. Perhaps for that reason, *hacerse respetar* was raised numerous times as a way of accounting for the structure and function of particular directive utterances, suggesting that issuing forceful directives was a primary way to make oneself respected. The need to maintain control over subordinates was described as the logical extension of respect: Without respect, there could be no control. Without control, a superior was no longer in the hierarchical position to which s/he had laid claim, a loss of tremendous consequence in this system. To lose hierarchical status was to lose a critically important aspect of personal identity and to make ambiguous a relational definition that was crucially relevant to a vast array of interpersonal dealings.

Furthermore, it was obvious that "respect" in this system often meant a degree of fear on the part of the subordinate. Coercive power, although remarked upon as distasteful, was a ubiquitous experience in directive discourse for these Colombians, as senders as well as recipients. A teacher who had taught at both high school and college level remarked in a focus group interview that

> *La gente tiene la idea de que el buen profesor es él que llega en punto, es él que grita, es él que es superestricto—que mantiene una barrera con sus alumnos. A mí no me gusta esa idea, se supone que uno debería hacerse respetar con lo que sabe y no con ser él que*

---

2. Notably, in this system that "something" goes beyond earning a degree or a position. It involves enforcement of ritual signs of respect, such as correcting an inappropriate term of address, or, more generally, imposing one's will on subordinates in overt (and often forceful) ways.

más duro grita, pero me ha tocado controlar con gritos muchas veces. (People have the idea that a good teacher is one who gets there right on time, he's the one who screams, the one that's superstrict—that keeps a barrier [between himself and] the students. I don't like that idea; you'd suppose that one should *hacerse respetar* with what you know, not by being the one that yells loudest, but I've had to control with yelling lots of times.)

The Colombians who participated in this study spoke of exposure to despotic authority as an experience with which they were all wholly familiar. Accounts of flagrant abuses of power, and of controlling subordinates through fear, were commonplace:

Tomasa, 48, in an individual interview: *Hay jefes que son todos mandones y todo, le gritan a uno y me trataban mál, me parece tan feo eso que le peguen un grito que "¡eso no estuvo bién!" y uno no es de palo ni nada, uno se siente muy mál con eso.* (There are bosses that are so [rough, pushy, bossy] and everything, they scream at you, and they treated me badly, that seems too ugly to me that they scream at you, that "that wasn't done right!" and one isn't made of wood or anything, one feels very badly with that [sort of treatment]).

Tatiana, 27: *Conozco el caso de una amiga que trabajó en una empresa farmacéutica. . . . Tenía una sicóloga de jefe, y era una mujer muy directa, muy brusca. . . . Cuando ella planteaba sus propios projectos y era más autónoma . . . la otra le callaba inmediatemente delante de todo el mundo.* (I know the case of a friend who worked in a pharmaceutical company. . . . She had a psychologist for a boss, who was a very direct woman, very rude. . . . When she [the friend] put forth her own projects and was more autonomous . . . the [boss] shut her up right away, there in front of everyone).

Nonetheless, there were comments on the importance of maintaining clear distinctions of hierarchical status:

Hugo, 45: ***No hay falla más grande en este mundo que decir que el papá es un buen amigo, no, el papá debe ser papá, si se pone en el de buen amigo está bajando.*** (There's nothing worse in this world than to say that the dad is a good friend; no, the dad should be a dad; if he gets into being a good friend, he's lowering himself.)

Mauricio, 31: ***En una buena relación laboral, cada quien tiene que hacer lo que le corresponde, osea yo no puedo ser patrón y subalterno a la vez. Si yo soy el jefe ejerzo mi papel, y si soy subalterno ejerzo mi papel tambien. . . . Ahi nace el respeto.*** (In a good working relationship, everyone has to do their part—that is, I can't be a boss and a subordinate at the same time. If I'm the boss I play my part, and if I'm the subordinate I play my part too. . . . That's where respect is born.)

The specific situation avoided by maintaining such separation and firm control was expressed as ***evitar que te la monten*** (to avoid their getting the upper hand). In this case, "they" are subordinates, and "getting the upper hand" means a loss of respect for the authority of the higher-status person. As noted in Chapter 1, other ideals for working relationships and parent/child relationships exist that center around mutual respect. Yet there was considerable sentiment that any breakdown in authoritarian control would lead to chaos.

Colombia's history suggests ample precedent for this perception. The Spanish conquerors were despots, enslaving the indigenous population as well as importing slaves from Africa. Even during the period of national unity in which Spanish rule was overthrown and the nation was founded, sharp distinctions among social classes sustained a status hierarchy that was virtually one of lords and peasants. During the time when political power seesawed between the two major parties, control over many of the relevant aspects of Colombians' daily lives switched hands with every election, creating social conditions that very often bordered on chaos. Even more recently, drug lords showed themselves able to thumb their noses at the Colombian legal system, and some guerrilla groups demonstrated their ability to terrorize and destroy, despite increased military and police efforts to control them. These developments further destabilized any sense Colombians might have had that people will, left to their own devices, follow rules set down by society. Rather, the violence reinforced the notion that only through continuous, visible signs of authority could even a tenuous grasp on social order be maintained.

Just as laws exert little real influence over the behavior of drug lords and criminals, however, the authoritarian demeanor of many parents, bosses, and teachers is noticeably ineffective in controlling the behavior of their subordinate counterparts. As striking as the number of blunt imperatives was to me, the frequency with which forceful, sometimes repeated directives were ignored was even more astonishing. Children nonchalantly disregarded the commands of their parents and teachers. Maids and secretaries murmured assent to the orders of their employers, and silently withstood scalding reproaches over tasks left undone—and then proceeded in whatever activity they were engaged, directives seemingly forgotten.

This tendency to voice intentions to comply with directives and then to disregard them extended to more equal-status relationships, as well. The Colombians I knew were generally very quick to agree to requests and favors that I asked of them, and to offer more assistance and company than I ever dreamed of asking for; yet the vast number of occasions when nothing materialized from those requests and offers was profoundly frustrating.[3] Naturally, there were individual differences in this regard. Some Colombians could be counted on absolutely to do what they agreed to do,

3. Unfortunately, it was not until much later that I read Kuiper's (1996) excellent analysis of formulaic speech as cultural performance, and learned to recognize both offers and agreement with requests within this speech community as formulae that were not necessarily meant to be taken literally.

while others were widely known as undependable. The pattern of giving a positive response to a directive and then doing something else was so commonplace, however, that the spontaneous comments of Colombians reflected a perception that it was a cultural characteristic.

Esperanza, 30, customer service representative at a credit card company: ***Hay gente que llegan a arreglar algún problema y ¡ya han pasado dos meses! Eso sí diría que nosotros los colombianos somos muy incumplidos, siempre decimos "¡ahh! eso voy mañana," esperamos y esperamos y ya es muy tarde.*** (There are people who come in here to fix some problem and two months have passed! I would have to say that we Colombians are very undependable—we always say "oh, I'll do it tomorrow," and we wait and wait and [suddenly] it's too late.

Dr. Gómez, director of a graduate program, to students: ***La gente que se inscribió para estas conferencias para quedarse bien conmigo, que no es de menos tampoco ... a la hora nona no aparecen. Y me he dado cuenta que somos nosotros los colombianos quienes nos damos ese lujo, porque los extranjeros ... no se han perdido ninguno.*** (The people who signed up for these [guest lectures] to get in good with me, which is not a minor consideration either—at the moment of truth they don't show up. And I've noticed it's we Colombians who allow ourselves that luxury, because the foreigners ... haven't missed a single one.[4]

4. These uses of the categorization "we Colombians" and the implication that these behavior patterns characterize a nation are worth noting. Billig (1995) discusses the development of conceptualizations of national identity and nationalism with rigor and insight that cannot be done justice here. One of his observations, however, is directly relevant:

> No prior sense of peoplehood could explain why a United States of America developed to the north of Mexico, but not to its south. The 13 colonies, which under George Washington's leadership overthrew colonial rule, developed into a single nation, while the five colonies liberated from Spain by Simon Bolívar went their

Although the teacher's criticism suggests that the failure is one of not living up to promises made, it is worth noting that the teacher had exhorted them to sign up and attend. The reproach, then, was a response to a directive with which the students had first complied—by signing up for the lectures—and then not complied—by not attending them. In the case of the credit card company representative, an appropriate directive to customers would have been instructions to settle billing difficulties within 10 days.

This acknowledgment that failure to comply with directives was widespread in the speech community, and the fact that it drew the spontaneous notice of natives, led me to ask Colombian informants their interpretation of the pattern. Typical comments:

Alberto, 43, in an individual interview: *Hay un dicho muy viejo que es, "Se obedece pero no se cumple." Quiere decir que uno debería tener la apariencia de cumplir con los órdenes de los demás pero no hacerlo de verdad. Creo que eso puede haber venido de la tradición histórica de dónde vinieron las leyes—fueron inventados por un poder extranjero que significaba muy poco para el pueblo colombiano, aplicadas por unos pocos representantes del rey, que no pudieron hacer mayor cosa para controlar las multitudes. Nunca había la idea de que la gente del pueblo estaba de acuerdo con las leyes, y entonces ningún sentimiento de culpa si uno no quería obedecer a la autoridad. Claro que ha habido muchos cambios en la última*

---

own national ways. In both cases, the sense of nationhood was to be created after the various declarations of independence, whether it was the sense of "Americanness" (the "one nation under God"), or the separate senses of being Bolivian, Peruvian, Venezuelan, Ecuadorian and Colombian. (p. 26)

Seen in this light, for Colombians to perceive something as uniquely "Colombian" reinforces the notion of a shared sense of history and identity, although it does not reduce the likelihood of strong similarities with neighboring countries.

generación—los niños nunca hubieran podido desobedecer a los padres como hacen hoy en día. La resistencia a la autoridad es parte de una transición de una sociedad autoritaria a algo distinto. (There's a very old saying that goes, "One obeys but does not comply," and it means to have the appearance of complying but not really do what you're told. I think that may come from the historical tradition of where laws came from—they were inventions of a faraway power that had little meaning for the local population, enforced by a very small number of the king's representatives that could only do so much in the way of controlling the multitudes. There was never a sense that the laws came from the consent of the governed, and thus no sense of guilt if you didn't want to obey authority. Of course there have been a lot of changes in the last generation—children in past generations could never have disobeyed their parents the way present-day children do. The resistance to orders is part of the transition from the authoritarian society to something else.)

Maria Fernanda, 25, in a focus group interview: *Eso de decir "sí, yo lo hago" y después hago otra cosa es algo muy nuestra—se llama malicia indígena. Yo no sé hasta qué punto sea resultado de toda una herencia de opresión que se enseñó a mentir. . . . Uno aprende a—a sacarle mejor partido a las situaciones.* (This business of saying "yes, I'll do it" and then I do something else is something very much ours [i.e., typical of us]—it's called natives' malice. I don't know to what extent it's a result of a whole heritage of oppression that taught one to lie. . . . One learns to—to get the best you can out of any situation.)

The speech events just described all contributed in some way to hierarchical authority, either underscoring it or undermining it. A separate cluster of directive speech events contributed to creating and maintaining **confianza,** the degree of trust, affection, and connection that characterizes personal relationships described in Chapter 2. The most basic of these speech events, in the sense that all other terms in this cluster were manifested in terms of it, was ***ayudar*** (to help). Many kinds of directives were described as motivated by a desire to help the recipient in some way, and in most cases that desire was described as based on the degree of ***confianza*** that characterized the relationship. The essence of an interpersonal bond of ***confianza*** might thus be described as a symbolic premise of help: both helping and allowing oneself to be helped.

Helping, of course, took many forms, from literal and material forms of assistance to offering goods, services, or company, as described earlier. Alternatively, help might be offered by the act of issuing directives, either to the hearer him/herself or to a third party whom the person being helped wished to influence. Each of these acts was encoded in a speech event enacted through directives.

A very frequent occurrence among these Colombians was intermediated directives, that is, directives issued by someone other than the person who originally desired to compel the actions of a hearer. These directives were described as falling within the speech event of ***ayudar*** in the sense that compelling the actions of others was something that frequently required assistance. Because telling someone to do something was no assurance that the task would be done, intervention by a third party to issue or reinforce the directive was common practice, as in the following examples:

> Dr. Enriquez, high school principal, to a group of students' parents: ***Estamos en un problema gravísimo de limpieza en este colegio.... Son sus niños para los cuales nos estamos esforzando a tener un medioambiente agradable y sano para aprender y son sus niños los que no saben cuidar a la propiedad pública. Esto no puede seguir, ustedes tienen que enseñarles que no se pinten las paredes de grafiti, que no hagan que los baños queden tan feos que no entraría ni un animal....*** (We have a very grave problem with cleanliness in this school. . . .
> It is *your* children for whom we are working hard to have a

safe, pleasant atmosphere in which to learn, and it is *your* children who don't know how to take care of public property. This cannot continue; you [parents] must teach them not to put graffiti on the walls, not to mess up the bathroom so badly that not even an animal would go in there. . . .)

In this case, parents were asked to intervene on behalf of the school to reinforce the school's rules about cleanliness. The basis for requesting this intervention seems to be that the parents are assumed to have greater authority over their children than the school has been able to exercise.

Gabriel, 23, to Patricia, 27, about a mutual friend: ***Oye Pati, Nancy quería preguntarte si le prestaras tu cámara mañana para sacar fotos de su niña. Ella lo cuidará muy bien y claro que comprará el rollo y todo.*** (Listen, Pati, Nancy wanted to ask you if you'd loan her your camera tomorrow to take pictures of her daughter. She'll take good care of it, and of course she'll buy the film and everything.)

Having overheard this request (Patricia readily agreed to loan the camera), I asked Gabriel why he had done the asking, if Nancy was the one who wanted to borrow the camera, given that Nancy and Patricia do know one another. He replied that Nancy had asked him to ask Patricia because ***"Patricia y yo tenemos más confianza de lo que tienen Nancy y Patricia"*** (Patricia and I have more ***confianza*** than Nancy and Patricia have).

In this instance, Gabriel is asked to issue the directive on the basis of having greater ***confianza*** rather than greater authority. In the first example, the directive was a command; in the second, a request. Both were attempted by way of intermediaries between the person issuing the directive and the target of the directive, and both instances involved "helping" someone to compel the actions of another by way of intervention of the third party. In Hymes's (1972) terms, this pattern of intermediated directives involved participants in directive sequences beyond the issuer and the receiver. The premise in operation here seemed to be that if *A* wanted *B* to do *X*, the chances that *B* would do *X* could be increased by participation from *C*.

A specific case of intermediated directives was described as ***recomendarle a alguien,*** to recommend someone. A "recommendation" in the service of obtaining a job or entry to an educational institution sometimes had approximately the same form and meaning as in the United States: a written or spoken substantiation of an applicant's qualifications that supported the application. Other times, ***recomendarle a alguien*** constituted a directive (a point discussed further in Fitch, 1994), amounting to a request or command issued to someone charged with the decision to hire or allow access to the institution on behalf of someone seeking entry. Such "recommendations" came either from peers or, more frequently, from superiors of the decision maker. Because it could count as either a request or a command, depending upon the relationship of the recommender and the decision maker, ***recomendar*** was usefully ambiguous in its illocutionary force. Hearers could make their own assessments of the consequences of compliance and noncompliance (some informants reported they could lose their jobs if they refused entry to a ***recomendado***) without the speaker needing to make explicit whether s/he was asking for a favor or obedience. An elaboration of this interpersonal pattern, mentioned here as it relates specifically to directive performance, will be described in more detail in the next chapter in relation to the widespread practice of obtaining objectives through personal connections.

A final directive speech event associated with helping was that of ***aconsejar,*** to give advice. In this belief system, ***aconsejar*** constituted helping in the sense that Colombians demonstrated a personal commitment to the success and happiness of the target by directing them, often quite directly and forcefully, to the course of action that the advice giver perceived to be most advantageous. Among these Colombians, advice was given frequently, with overtones that suggested that the speaker had no doubt that such directives were appropriate and would be welcomed:

Teresa, 14, commenting about a classmate during a class session in which all were invited to discuss everyone's strengths and weaknesses: *... **Lo que tengo que decir sobre Adriana es que siempre ha sido mi mejor amiga, y quiero aprovechar esta oportunidad de agradecerle toda la ayuda y todo el afecto que me ha brindado. ... Lo único que le aconsejo es que ponga más atención a las matemáticas, que le falta un poco de esfuerzo en ese campo y no quiero que le toque habilitar esa materia.*** (What I have to say about Adriana is that she's always been my best friend, and I want to take this opportunity to thank her for all of her help and all her support. .... The only thing I would advise her is that she pay more attention to mathematics—she's lacking effort in that subject and I don't want her to have to repeat the course.)

Clemencia, 62, speaking on the telephone to a nephew, 27, who has recently graduated from law school: ***Y usted que va a* buscar puesto, *siendo soltero, sin obligación de mantener a nadie, que Alfredo le ha ofrecido prestar la firma* gratis *para que* ejerce *su profesión! ... Bueno. No más. Ya no más, hemos hecho lo que pudimos por usted pero usted no sabe seguir los consejos. Hasta aquí llegó la relación familiar.* Adios** (slams down phone). (And you're going to *look for a job,* being single, with no obligation to support anyone [financially], when Alfredo has offered to lend you his signature for *free* [i.e., his uncle, who is also a lawyer, has offered to co-sign legal actions for his nephew, essentially enable him to engage in private practice before he gets his license—an employment path that is often better paid and more stable than working for a corporation] so you can *practice* your profession! ... Fine. No more. No more now, we have done what we can for you, but you don't know how to follow advice. Here ends the family relationship. *Goodbye* [slams down phone]).

Although the aunt's dark proclamation that the nephew was no longer a part of the family turned out to be an empty threat, her linking of advice to interpersonal relationship is revealing. In both of the examples above, ***confianza*** was the basis for giving advice. In one case a best friend, and in the other a close relative, issued directives to a hearer with whom they had a relationship of ***confianza,*** premised on assumptions that the speaker had the hearer's best interest in mind and was as knowledgeable (or more so) than the hearer about the course of action the hearer should take. To ignore the advice, as the nephew in the second example was apparently inclined to do, was to deny one or both of those assumptions: either the advice giver was not suggesting the correct line of action, and/or the giver did not truly have the receiver's best interests in mind. To openly reject advice, perhaps questioning the giver's rights to give it, would be even more negative in that it would question whether sufficient ***confianza*** existed to issue the directive at all.

FOUR RULES OF DIRECTIVE PERFORMANCE

Thus far, nine speech events have been described in this chapter that represented discursive links between directives and interpersonal relationships among these urban Colombians. The most noticeable of these links were the ways in which ***confianza*** and authority were enacted through directives. Although directives were not uniformly effective in compelling behavior regardless of the degree of ***confianza*** or authority that existed, the tension between them reflected a central challenge of interpersonal life, which was to maintain an adequate balance between these two forces.

A cultural premise evident in these patterns and symbolic components of directive performance is that, beyond compelling action, directives create and sustain human interdependence. ***Pedir un favor*** (to ask a favor) is to show that one values and depends on the goods and services of another, and to create or draw attention to a bond by sharing those valued assets. ***Ofrecer*** (to offer) goods and services is to allow or encourage participation of another in one's own life, again by sharing valued assets.

Creative and effective acts of ***pedir limosna*** (to ask for charity) created some relationship between the target and the person doing the begging, whether based on a service performed by the beggar, flattery, or a hint of coercion.

Ayudar (to help) is a ubiquitous measure of human connection. ***Aconsejar*** (to give advice) and ***recomendarle a alguien*** (to recommend someone) are kinds of directive events that underscore a desire to be helpful to another person, specifically by way of intervention in the other's tasks, decisions, and relationships.

Mantener órden (to maintain order) includes directives that serve to sustain hierarchical structure, a fundamental connection between persons of greater and lesser authority. Without directives forceful enough to ***mantener órden,*** the risk is created that subordinates ***te la monten*** (will get the upper hand), thereby destroying the hierarchical connection. Superiors must therefore ***hacerse respetar*** (make themselves respected), largely by way of directives.

The symbolic and pragmatic meanings of these linguistic resources (directives, named speech events, and dimensions of relationships indexed by directive performance, ***confianza,*** and authority) may be summarized in four rules of directive performance that encapsulate the shared understandings, in this speech community, of the force, the uses, and the limitations of directives within the broader scheme of interpersonal communication. The rules as they are presented here incorporate (in Hymes's [1972] terms) both norms for interaction and norms for interpretation.

1. To preserve a relationship, one should ignore directives rather than challenge or question them.
2. To increase the chances that a directive will receive compliance, one should:
   a. ask "nicely" when the hearer is of equal or higher status and/or no ***confianza*** exists;
   b. state it firmly when the hearer is of a lower status and/or ***confianza*** exists;

    c. get an intermediary of either more *confianza* or with more authority to issue or reinforce the directive; or

    d. remind and scrutinize—that is, police—the hearer until the action is completed.

3. To create or display **confianza,** one should issue directives that:

    a. emphasize concern for the welfare of the person directed; or

    b. presume the other's concern for one's own welfare (the issuer of the directive).[5]

4. To create or display hierarchical authority, one should:

    a. issue directives that make plain one's own (higher) status relative to hearer;

    b. be on guard against encroachments that could suggest **confianza,** unless it is **confianza** offered by the higher-status person; and

    c. be prepared to ignore some violations (i.e., unfulfilled directives).

This chapter has further developed the idea of a Colombian interpersonal ideology of connectedness by describing patterns and meanings of directive performance as a second discursive enactment of that ideology. Like terms of personal address, directives are enacted within a system of symbolic categories of intention, interpretation, and evaluation that is given voice in native terms for speech events related to uses of a particular linguistic resource. Like personal address, uses of a linguistic resource (in this instance, to compel the actions of others) reflect the positioning of

5. This rule invokes formulation "face wants and redress" (Brown & Levinson, 1987) particularly strongly, and thus might be taken as echoing a universal aspect of directive performance rather than constituting a culture-specific rule. It should be noted, however, that because **confianza** is presented here as a culture-specific dimension of personal relationships, enacting the rule will entail culture-specific performances. The rule is specified here as a part of the overall system of meaning of this speech community.

persons in relationships vis-à-vis two dimensions of interpersonal connection: **confianza** and, in the case of directives, authority.

A broader unit of interpersonal communication, the narrative, will be considered in the next chapter. The focus on a particularly common kind of narrative, **palanca** stories, corresponds to the category of *genre* in Hymes's (1972) analytic framework. The examination of **palanca** narratives that are told among these urban Colombians reveals the collective force of such stories as a cultural myth of interpersonal connectedness.

CHAPTER FOUR

PALANCA

A Narrative Genre

Like personal address and directives, narratives are a universal communicative phenomenon through which specific communities are constructed (Bochner, 1994; Fisher, 1984, 1985, 1987; Turner, 1980; White, 1980). Telling stories is a fundamentally human way to understand one's own experiences and the actions of other people. The conceptual link of narratives to shared understandings about the social world seems intuitively obvious: People interpret the social world to themselves and others by constructing plausible stories of actions and the meanings and motivations that underlie them. In doing so they draw upon, and thus make visible, the symbolic resources of their speech community. Those resources include ones that have been discussed in earlier chapters: the terms for talk that frame actions within sensible categories, the patterns of use through which meanings of communicative action emerge, and the premises that link actions to understandings of personhood and relationships.

Furthermore, the specific relevance of narratives to selfhood and personal relationships has been explored by Duck (1994; Duck, West, and Acitelli, 1997), McAdams (1993), and Harvey, Orbuch, and Weber (1990). This work makes the point that people draw on cultural resources such as metaphors to construct accounts and stories about their relationships, thereby coping with their personal circumstances in ways that are recognizable and sensible within particular cultural frameworks of experience and expectation.

It thus made sense to seek out narratives told by these Colombians that would relate specifically to personal relationships. *Palanca* was a term used frequently in everyday conversation that, it was soon apparent, indexed such a genre of narratives. Literally, *palanca* means a lever; symbolically, it is a connection, a personal contact who enables someone to obtain a desired objective. Because *palanca* in its symbolically pure form revolves around relationships (rather than money, a distinction that will be explored later in this chapter), *palanca* narratives invoke participants' experiences with power and helping as defining aspects of interpersonal relationships. Further, because *palancas* are used to pursue objectives that are often impeded by scarcity of resources and/or institutional rules and laws, *palanca* narratives evoke community understandings of connections between individuals and the institutions of their society, as well as the impact of scarce resources on everyday life. This chapter will first examine several naturally occurring *palanca* narratives and other uses of the term *palanca*. The nature of *palanca* is then described by way of several speech events associated with the actions of seeking and serving as such a connection. Finally, the status of *palanca* as a cultural myth, above and beyond the specific relationships it encompasses, is explored.

PALANCA NARRATIVES FROM EVERYDAY TALK

Palanca narratives were, for the most part, told in a key of easy familiarity, even pride. The Colombians I worked with in this study spoke of the people who provided and benefited from *palancas* in ways that suggested general acceptance of the system in which personal connections were required to achieve particular goals in life. There was some disgust, of course, when participants believed that *palancas* had operated on someone else's behalf and thus deprived them of something that was rightfully theirs. When the *palanca* worked in their favor, however, it was a morally approvable event. These were people who spoke with satisfaction of being able to serve as a *palanca* to obtain something for a friend or family member, or of knowing someone who could serve as a *palanca.* Although there were perversions of the system, which will be discussed later, the following examples should be heard in that tone:

> Mariela wanted a manicure on Mother's Day, although it was a major holiday and everything was closed. She called Luz Marina, a woman in her early twenties who occasionally worked at her mother's beauty shop, and asked her to come to her house to do her nails. Luz Marina complied, and I asked Mariela why Luz Marina was willing to drop everything and come on Mother's Day. Mariela replied that they had a long history: "I used to go to her mother's shop even though it was out of my way, because she always did a very good job. After a while Luz Marina started to learn the business, and her mother would send her to my house telling her to always be careful to do my nails correctly and be on time and everything. At the time, Luz Marina was working in a day care center, but she wanted to go to school to study psychology, so Alfredo (Mariela's husband, a professor) told her to apply to his university and he would take care of everything. And there she is today, studying psychology." (In other words, Alfredo served as a *palanca* for Luz Marina to be admitted to the university where he taught.)

> Ricardo, 25, a student, told the story of his earlier years: I went to a high school that was all teachers' children—you had to have that *palanca* or you had no chance at all. Then (*abashed grin*) I failed my junior year. Supposedly if you failed a year, you were out, they would never let you repeat. But my mother [a teacher, the one who got him ad-

mitted in the first place] had certain connections there, so I was able to repeat the year, and she even arranged for me to have different teachers so I didn't have to suffer through the same horrible experience I'd had before. The next year I really worked hard, and of course I did fine.

A female law student called the coordinator of an internship program at home one afternoon to discuss her site assignment for participation in the program, which was required for graduation. He explained to her that assignments were made by lottery; nonetheless, the person in charge of the lottery was *"muy amiga mía y si quiere le presto la carátula"* (a very good friend of mine, and if you want I'll loan you my cover, i.e., I'll speak to her on your behalf). When he hung up, I asked him who it was, and he said she was a very good former student of his, a mother with small children. "The lottery could end up with her assigned to work out in Tunjuelito or somewhere, and she called me to try to prevent that. She knows the assignments are by lottery but (*laughing*) we Colombians don't believe in lotteries any more." He emphasized that she was an excellent student, and he was happy to do what he could to help her out. Sure enough, she was assigned to work somewhere close to home.

The election of César Gaviria as President of Colombia in 1990 after an eventful campaign was described this way by Arturo, a businessman in his late 40s: Well, first of course there was Luis Carlo Galán—no, it goes back further than that. Misael Pastrana was President [1970–1974] and wanted Galán to be Minister of Education—only Galán hadn't yet finished his degree at the university. So Pastrana arranged for Galán's graduation . . . a little ahead of schedule (*wry smile*) so he could be Minister of Education. Then Galán did various things politically, and [in 1989] ran for President. He was assassinated during the campaign, and at the funeral, attended by thousands of people, of course, Galán's son called for Gaviria to pick up the torch, so to speak. Gaviria went from being campaign manager to being the candidate in a matter of a few days, and to no one's surprise he won the election—and in my opinion was one of the best leaders Colombia has produced in recent years. [In sum, Galán was able to graduate early because of *palanca* with the President, Pastrana; and Gaviria's transformation from campaign manager to candidate came about not because of his power within the party per se, but through his connection to the assassinated man's family.]

My own reaction to being the beneficiary of *palanca* may be an illuminating contrast to these events. I arrived in Bogotá from the United States quite late one night, and ended up at the very back of the line of passengers waiting to clear customs. I had several large pieces of luggage and an exhausted infant with me, and steeled myself for a lengthy wait. Within a minute or so, however, a woman in a business suit approached me and called me by name. I confirmed that I was who she thought, and she said, "Come with me—here, let me carry something for you." I started to demur, to protest that really I could deal with the wait, that I had prescriptions in hand to justify every medication in my possession, that my visa was in order. In short, I had nothing to fear in customs and was capable of managing both baby and luggage for however long it took. The woman silenced me with a firm look and a "Come *on!*" toss of her head. We walked past the line of passengers, paused briefly at the immigration checkpoint for the guard to stamp my passport, and then—after a nod was exchanged between the woman who was leading me and an official at the door—wheeled past the customs agents without so much as slowing down. I was aghast, thinking that surely those other people in line were just as tired as I was, and that it was unfair to them for me to walk out ahead of them. Even worse, I worried that the customs agents would think I was bypassing them quickly because I had something illegal in my luggage! And who was this well-dressed woman, anyway?

Outside the airport, she introduced herself as a former student of my father-in-law and explained that she did some legal work in immigration. For that reason, she had contacts in customs who let her in and took her word for who I was (a harmless communication researcher? a tired mother of a small child? a family member of a respectable Colombian citizen? I never knew how she explained my identity to them). My in-laws were waiting for me, and we all thanked her profusely for her help. In the days that followed, the story of how quickly and easily I had gotten through customs was repeated numerous times, as testimony to the important connections possessed by my father-in-law.

Other uses of, and needs for, *palanca* were evident in conversational references to it:

> David, commenting on his brother's application to dental school: He's done very well on all the entrance exams, and beyond that my dad has a friend there [at the school], and that's what's needed. You can do just great on the exams but when it comes to the interview and all, *se mueven palancas por aquí por allá y quién sabe.* (*palancas* move here and there and who knows)

> A news program outlining a government proposal for streamlining the Colombian bureaucracy included a comment from an official from the Chamber of Commerce: "It shouldn't be a matter of pride that people brag at cocktail parties, 'Hey, I have a *palanca* that does all my paperwork at that office— saves me a whole day every year.'" He illustrated this point with figures about the total amount of time lost by the average Colombian worker in the course of a year while standing in lines to do errands required by the government, such as renewing automobile registration. He added that the effect of the system was a lack of confidence in government institutions and progressive demoralization of the democracy that Colombia was still trying to establish.

> MOTHER (*to son, discussing how to schedule elective surgery at the hospital where the son is employed in the business office*): So when the surgeon comes back from vacation next week, is he all booked up for the rest of the week?

SON (*tone of outrage*): Are you *kidding?* His schedule is set in planning—*we're* the ones who schedule him for surgery. ***Es no más yo saco la palanca y estuvo.*** (I just whip out the ***palanca*** and it's done.)

The last excerpt, from my field notes, makes clear the identity stakes involved in being, or having, a ***palanca.*** The son's indignant reaction suggests that something about his mother's question maligns (or at least underestimates) him. Because he had worked in the hospital for a few years at this point, he implies it should be assumed that he would have developed sufficient contacts within the system to exert some control over a doctor's operating schedule. For his mother to imply that the patient (her husband) was at the mercy of some disconnected, disembodied scheduling system ignored the son's power as a ***palanca,*** drawn from his connections to the interpersonal system at the hospital.

The meanings of ***palanca*** may be summarized as follows: First, because it is a matter of pride to have acted effectively as a ***palanca,*** stories in this genre are told to honor the people who carried it off. Credit is due to the provider for being sufficiently powerful and clever (and perhaps well-connected him/herself) to have secured the objective. Credit is also due the beneficiary, who had a sufficiently strong connection with the provider to have asked for (or deserved) the effort and consideration required to enact the ***palanca.*** There is for the most part no dishonor to the recipient, and no inference that s/he had to resort to ***palanca*** because of lack of qualifications (although such interpretations are sometimes suggested by unsuccessful aspirants). Rather, there is recognition that the system could work against any candidate without ***palanca,*** however well-qualified s/he might be.

Second, ***palanca*** revolves around ***confianza,*** like personal relationships more generally. A ***palanca*** has to trust that the recipient will perform reasonably well or not get caught outside the rules, which would cause the ***palanca*** him/herself trouble. To seek a ***palanca,*** some degree of personal connection is required, even if that connection is several steps removed (a brother's boss's wife might be a *palanca* for some things, for example—the personal connection is not necessarily a direct one from provider to beneficiary).

Finally, it should be obvious from the varied uses of the term that a *palanca* is both a person (someone who can intervene on behalf of someone else), and the use of a personal connection for an instrumental purpose. A friendship or a service relationship, with a doorman for example, might go on for many years with no hint that *palanca* will ever be sought or offered. When the friend's father needs elective surgery or the tenant needs to hire a driver (for whom a trusted doorman is a good source of candidates), *palanca* may come into play. The friend becomes a *palanca,* intervening into scheduling procedures. The doorman provides a connection to someone of *confianza,* thus extending the services depended on by the tenant into the arena of employment relationships.

SPEECH EVENTS ASSOCIATED WITH PALANCA

The types of objectives that required *palanca* are suggested in the examples already given. Admission to educational institutions, employment, exceptions to rules (e.g., that a student who failed a year would not be allowed to repeat the year in that school, or that students must complete certain requirements before graduating), rapid access to services ranging from medical care to telephone installation, bypassing official channels that required long waits, and favorable outcomes of "lottery" assignments were all achievable by way of connections with appropriately positioned others.[1] In cases where the objective was to obtain some kind of service (such as a plumber or manicurist willing to

---

1. There were, however, some institutions regarded as *palanca*-proof, such as the Universidad Nacional. Admission to that, one of Colombia's finest universities, was based strictly on test scores that were published in the newspaper.

work on holidays), the *palanca* might be of lower social status than the recipient, yet uniquely able because of their class position to make contact with that service provider and/ or prevail upon them to provide the service as desired.

In each case of *palanca* described here, the beneficiary was ultimately worthy, on some grounds, of the preferential treatment. Luis Carlos Galán graduated "a little ahead of schedule" because of his connection to the President, who wanted him to take a Cabinet post, but proved his qualifications by performing competently enough in that role to move on, and up, in political life. The student who originally failed his junior year buckled down when given another chance, passed on the second try, and went on to do well in college. The student whose internship assignment was not left entirely to chance was given extra consideration on the basis of being "a really good student" and a mother with small children. Even my quick passage through airport customs might be justified, I reasoned, on the basis of sympathy for the baby. Although having, and serving as a *palanca* is generally a matter of pride and admiration, scorn is reserved for beneficiaries who prove to be unqualified. It is one thing to use *palanca* to get a job, or admission into a university, and then perform well enough to show that you deserve to be there. It is quite another to obtain access and then ultimately fail to perform, thus abusing the *palanca* and possibly making the person who provided it look foolish.

The interpersonal dynamics of *palanca* are also evident in several speech events associated with uses of the term:

1. ***Hablar con un amigo que conozca*** (to talk with a friend who knows something, e.g., whom to talk to, or how to arrange an exception to a rule). This is a common way to seek out a *palanca* and is also offered as a suggestion that the best chance to achieve an objective may be through *palanca* rather than directly.

2. ***Recomendarle personalmente a alguien*** (to personally recommend someone). To give or ask for a "recom-

mendation" had two meanings among these Colombians. One was equivalent to the traditional understanding of recommendations in the United States: the recommender wrote a letter commenting on an applicant's qualifications for a position. Such a recommendation might or might not be followed by the decision makers faced with several qualified applicants. A more powerful form of "recommendation" was a *palanca* that was a well-positioned connection willing to give a personal endorsement to an applicant. If the connection was particularly influential or trusted, the endorsement virtually guaranteed success for the applicant. In some cases, employers looked for employees by way of "personal recommendations" from people in similar positions. A teacher leaving a job might be asked to recommend a replacement; a doorman might be asked if he knew of someone trustworthy to be a chauffeur. In other cases, a personal recommendation might overcome substantial barriers to entry:

> Anastasia, a housewife, late 40s, catching relatives up on the events of a younger nephew's life: You know how Luis was never much of a student. Well, he dropped out of high school when he was 16, thinking he would find a job. He couldn't, of course, so after a while he ran away from home and joined the *guerrillas.* His parents were frantic, and they called Julio [Anastasia's brother, a colonel in the Army] and asked him if he could do something to get Luis away from the *guerrillas.* It was agreed that the Army would be a good place for Luis, teach him some discipline, give him a way to earn a living for a while—but there was the problem that he hadn't finished high school. With Julio's recommendation, though, it was all arranged.

In this case, neither the fact of choosing to be a member of the *guerrillas* (whose activities include, among other things, attacks against the Army) nor the lack of a high school diploma outweighed the "recommendation" of a highly placed official. It might also be noted that, in this instance, to call the colonel's intercession a "recommendation" is

euphemistic: as a military official, he could issue commands
to admit his nephew that subordinates were not really in
any position to refuse. Nonetheless, the fact that Anastasia
refers to his action as a "recommendation" evokes an image of persuasion rather than coercion, that *palanca* is
extended on the basis of interpersonal connection rather
than raw power to force others to accept the circumstances.

3. ***Ser un allegado, e.g., a la casa*** (to be someone
who is close to, e.g., the family) is an expression of a kind
of relationship in which serving as a *palanca* is expected.
If one family member has a close connection with an influential person, that connection might be extended to other
members of the family (or asked for on behalf of other family
members). The possibilities of being able to ***mover/sacar
palancas*** (to move or shake out *palancas*) thus increased
not only through one's own relationships but by way of the
relationships formed by other family members and friends.
Similarly, the more contacts one had with influential people,
the wider the network of potential *palancas,* adding to the
stakes involved in sending children to the schools and universities attended by the social and political groups to which
one aspired to membership.

4. ***Pedirle el favor de . . .*** (to ask someone the favor
of . . .) referred to asking someone to exercise their influence on another's behalf. Significantly, *palanca* (in its symbolic form, at least) is viewed *as a favor,* not as a service
provided for money. Providing *palanca* was, to be sure,
an expectation of close relationships strong enough to be
considered an obligation in some cases. The impetus for
providing *palanca* in such cases was twofold: the interpersonal connection that was strengthened by providing this
kind of help, and creation or reinforcement of one's own
identity as influential or trustworthy.

It should also be noted that the existence of ***confianza***
carries obligations to ***hacer favores,*** including to act as a
palanca when possible. To the degree that a personal
connection exists to someone, it can be awkward to explain
why one is unwilling to serve as a *palanca* if one is in a
position to do so. Naturally, there are grounds that are cultur-

ally recognized as valid when one declines to be a *palanca*—
e.g., this position requires very different skills than you have,
I'm not really in a position to influence that decision, and
so forth.

5. *Estar pendiente (de ayudar; de alguien)* (to be
attentive [in order to help; to someone's needs]). This speech
event captures the protective, mentor-like connotation of
palanca as a kind of assistance that might be offered or
provided without any request from the beneficiary. Extending reassurance that one will "be attentive" to another suggests a willingness to intercede on her or his behalf when
necessary, along with other forms of helping. A friend commented to me once that he knew someone in the *Oficina
de Relaciones Exteriores* (Foreign Affairs Office) and that
if I ever had any trouble with a visa or documents of any
kind I should let him know—*"de pronto se te ofrece algo"*
("perhaps you can be offered something," as in Chapter 3).
In this case, the offer was plainly to serve as a *palanca* if
needed. It sounded like a sincere gesture of friendship, an
effort by this man to show attentiveness to needs that I, as
a foreigner, might have. Whether this person, a university
student, could actually have helped out by way of his contact in the government agency is unclear. Because offers of
palanca involve claims to connections with higher-status
people, they can also be ways to *hacerse el importante*
(make oneself seem important).

6. *Ser interesado/cepillero* (to curry favor). This
speech event was described in Chapter 2 as it related to
strategic use of address terms. One way to curry favor with
an influential other was to make reference to their exalted
status through use of respectful address terms. The difference between being a *cepillero* (an apple-polisher) and
showing genuine respect was, in that instance, the perception that motivations were more instrumental than sincere.

In a similar way, relationships might be sought with
people in the hope that they could one day serve as *palanca,*
rather than on the basis of genuine similarity or liking. The
relationship sought was one of sufficient *confianza* to
warrant the amount of influence provided. Seeking a *palanca*

or serving as one implies that a degree of *confianza* exists between provider and intermediary or recipient relevant to the magnitude of the favor requested. When the service required is easily provided, the position sought is unimportant, or the scarce goods are not risky or difficult to secure, *confianza* may be minimal. When stakes are higher—when the service desired is difficult even for the *palanca* to obtain, the position is one that will directly affect the future and/or reputation of the *palanca,* or the goods are carefully controlled—a significantly higher degree of *confianza* must exist for the favor to be appropriately requested or safely granted. A *cepillero* with a slight relationship to someone influential might thus attempt to create more *confianza* in preparation for seeking that person's help. The suspicion that someone of lower status might attempt to increase *confianza* in order to have some basis to ask for *palanca* constitutes, in this system, a significant constraint on the development of such relationships.

To complete the definition of what *palanca* is, it is useful to discuss what it is *not.* Long-term mentorship relationships include providing favors that are generally perceived to be within the scope of *palanca,* such as moral support, financial backing, and access to jobs or institutions. Neither party would describe this as *palanca,* however, because the recipient is viewed as someone who is exceptionally deserving. The Colombian term for mentorship in a professional sense is *apadrinar,* to "godfather" someone, and is viewed as a particularly noble kind of connection that exceeds the usual time frame and objectives sought by *palanca.*

Three other types of transaction that transcend regulations or scarcity are, by contrast, perceived as clear perversions of the *palanca* system. First, service relationships may be established with *tramitadores,* persons who make their living by performing bureaucratic duties for a fee. *Tramitadores* bypass official regulations in providing the service, and it is helpful to establish a working relationship with a particular individual if the task will need to be performed on a regular basis. They are not, however, ***palancas,*** because their motivation for providing their services is not an interpersonal bond but an immediate economic benefit.

A similar instance of bypassing regulations by way of financial exchange is bribery. When stopped by traffic police, for example, some Colombians may offer money to the officer to avoid a ticket. Evaluation of bribery is more negative than for either ***palancas*** or the services of ***tramitadores.*** The motivation behind the favor is purely material rather than interpersonal, and the desired end is clearly not one the recipient legitimately deserves.

A third way in which institutional laws may be bypassed is by individual initiative to ***hacer trampa*** (to play tricks, or beat the system by illegal means). Falsifying documents, lying about qualifications or eligibility, and subverting procedures by way of personal dishonesty all fall into this category. Evaluation of this means of achieving desired ends is strictly negative, partly because of the suspicion that people will fabricate, lie, and subvert regulations at every turn. That suspicion clearly permeates Colombian bureaucracies, both public and private, and is the apparent motivation for ever more elaborate and cumbersome verification procedures. Those procedures make simple tasks, such as opening a checking account, more difficult for everyone. Ironically, they seem to have little effect in deterring such behavior.

The ***palanca*** system, although part of the Colombian interpersonal ideology of connectedness, is acknowledged to have drawbacks. Informants pointed out that ***palancas*** are unfair "when they work against you" that is, when another person's having ***palanca*** enables him/her to reach a goal that is therefore denied to oneself. One informant, the son of a wealthy family, said that ***palancas*** undermine democracy and that acceptance of ***palancas*** in the legal system decreased the chance that Colombia would ever reduce the crime rate with which it chronically struggles. Others mentioned instances when ***palancas*** had been used in what they considered to be morally indefensible ways and was a symptom of "everything that's wrong with the country these days." That is, Colombians do *not* necessarily believe that ***palanca*** narratives embody the most morally desirable course of human action. They do view the ubiquity of ***palanca*** as consistent with human nature and as being the most effective strategy available to pursue many objectives. Further, the obligation to do favors, including providing ***palanca,*** as a marker of personal connection itself carries significant moral weight.[2]

The belief that people are essentially sets of bonds to others is central to Colombians' distinctions between ***palanca*** and the less acceptable ways of bypassing laws just described. "Playing tricks" to beat the system by dishonesty means breaking the law on one's own. It is perceived as morally corrupt because it results from individual action and benefits only the individual. ***Palanca*** sometimes involves evading the law, but the beneficiary has at least done so via an interpersonal bond, thus acknowledging the fundamental truth that humans viewed as individuals are incomplete entities. Using a ***palanca*** also creates an expectation of reciprocal favors, so that the recipient may not in the long run be the only one to benefit from the situation.

Still, ***palancas*** are connections that generally reinforce power inequities. The benign, even approving tone of ***palanca*** narratives among these largely middle-class informants would probably have been far more bitter among the working classes who are routinely denied certain opportunities because they lack access to those kinds of "connections." The ubiquitous existence and general effectiveness of ***palanca*** thus deepens and maintain class divisions. It excludes deserving people from admission to educational institutions and professional positions, lets well-connected people get out of various kinds of trouble they get themselves into, and sometimes puts unqualified people into

2. I would argue that there is an obligation to let others *do* favors for you that is nearly as strong. See the excerpt in Chapter 3 (p. 91) in which a nephew's declining to let his uncle help him professionally caused a rupture in family relationships, at least temporarily.

positions where they perform inadequately but are protected by the same connections that got them there.

Nonetheless, it is a relational system that is consistent with understandings of human beings that exalt connections to others over individual abilities and performance. It is a system that, however unfair it may be, rests on cooperation rather than competition (with attendant advantages in human relations, as well as drawbacks to efficiency). The importance of *palanca* narratives to this study is that they reveal shared understandings of the nature of persons and the importance of relationships. In this ideology, people need to be connected to others in order to survive in a world where important services and access to opportunities are most often controlled by connections to other people. Helping friends and family members to get those services, and to have that access, is a positive contribution to those relationships and increases the provider's status in the eyes of the community. Asking for such help acknowledges the fundamental interdependence of humans, rather than suggesting that the asker is inadequate in some way. Such requests also pay homage to the identity of the person whose help is sought as someone who is sufficiently influential and/or trusted to provide a highly valued kind of assistance. Finally, belief in *palanca* as an effective and necessary means to obtain certain objectives embodies the conviction that the social world is arranged hierarchically, such that people naturally differ in their abilities to influence life's events. For that reason, laws and rules cannot be expected to apply equally to all people or to all situations. Connections to powerful people are often more relevant to pursuing certain objectives than the laws and rules that may exist in some official sense.

A final question about *palanca* narratives remains to be addressed, as they pertain to the general questions of culture and personal relationships pursued in this book. Although personal address and directive formulations are obviously resources available to the speech community in that they are built into the structure of the language, it is less apparent how *palanca* stories—as individual narratives—converge in force and meaning to become part of the resources of culture. For stories of personal triumph to be communally meaningful, there need to be common threads to link them to broader contexts of social life. The question that remains then is how *palanca* stories, like other stories told by members of this speech community, contribute to and draw significance from a shared system of premises about personhood and relationships centered around connectedness.

PALANCA AS A CULTURAL MYTH

It is possible to be far more precise in describing the process through which individual narratives converge in force and meaning to construct cultural myths. Fisher (1987) points out that humans are storytellers by nature. As people tell their stories, they are interpreted, responded to, and retold by hearers. As a group of people tells stories of similar events and experiences, collective beliefs are expressed as to efficacious courses of action to pursue or central truths about the nature of persons and the world. Narratives offer implicit advice for peoples' lives, suggesting good reasons for pursuing a particular course of action or accepting a particular interpretation of events. Stories like the ones reported earlier in this chapter make *palanca* a compelling force in present-day Colombia because they are perceived to be more true to the way people and the world are, in fact if not in value, than are contrasting stories wherein desired objectives were pursued by adhering to institutionally established rules, laws, and procedures.[3]

Concepts that encode something symbolic about the nature of persons, relationships, and the world perform what Philipsen (1987) has described as the cultural function of

3. This is consonant with this community's views of laws as imposed from *outside* (see Chapter 3) and the consequent emphasis on how to evade their impact.

communication. Individuals come to understand the social world around them through the talk of other members of the community. Narratives that are interpreted as revealing some significant truth about the world are construed as providing good reasons for choices between alternative courses of action. In pursuing a desired objective, Colombians face choices between "going it on their own" and trusting to skills, abilities, and rational systems of decision making within which those who are most deserving are most likely to be treated well; or seeking out personal connections to help. They make those decisions within a framework of stories of *palanca,* which suggest many good reasons not to trust in one's individual abilities or in the fairness of a system of rules.

As aggregates of shared experience and meaning, *palanca* narratives become cultural myths, which suggest "a supersensible world of meaning and value from which the least member of a tribe can borrow something to dignify and give coherence to his life" (Philipsen, 1987, p. 252). Cultural myths are the symbolic expression of individual narratives. In expressing collective beliefs about persons and relationships, they "hold together the imagination of a people and [provide] bases [for] harmonious thought and action" (Philipsen, 1987, p. 251).[4]

The cultural myth of *palanca* is built up of countless personal stories that tell of goals achieved by way of connections to others. This myth, in its most idealistic form, claims that no earthly end is unachievable given interpersonal bonds with adequately powerful others. One's individual prospects for achievement are enhanced by way of contacts with other persons. There is a limit to what any individual may do; there is virtually no limit to what may be accomplished by *palancas.* Thus, the moral judgment of seeking and exercising *palanca* rests not on transcend-

---

4. It should be noted that "myth" is not used in any sense of an imaginary or untrue story, but as a collective story of mythic proportions, that is, that stretches beyond the circumstances of individuals to symbolize a truth about the life of a community

ing a law or obtaining goods that others desire. Rather, evaluation of *palanca* rests on the worth of persons, measured in terms of where and how they are connected to other persons of influence and their willingness and ability to do "favors" for deserving others. As stories of success through *palancas* are told, they express good reasons for cultivating interpersonal relationships and for pursuing goals by way of influential intermediaries. Thus, the myth of *palanca* both reflects, and contributes to, an interpersonal ideology of connectedness among Colombians.

A more detailed examination of how cultural premises come into play in the construction and interpretation of narratives can be pursued through a contrasting case. Below is a story told in the context of a focus group interview, in response to the question of what matters may be pursued through *palanca.* Thus, the story is an elicited, rather than a naturally occurring, narrative. Nevertheless, it is a useful instance through which to observe the incorporation of cultural premises into a narrative in that it involves retelling events that occurred in one culture within the interpretive framework of another culture.

A: Yesterday in that program about Castro Caycedo . . . some guys rotting away there in a jail in the U.S.

B: And two Colombians free.

A: The ones in jail didn't commit the crime—worse than that, [the police] caught the one who *did* commit the crime.

C: Nonetheless they haven't let [the other ones] go.

B: Because they're Colombians and they don't have a lawyer.

C: They're Colombians and they didn't want to, they never wanted to become citizens, and they've been there some 20-odd years, living in the States until now and everything. But they didn't want to become citizens. . . . And they were still Colombians, and [the police] say well, there they are, and there they are in jail, all because they're Colombians.

B: They're ruining them [the prisoners' lives are ruined].

C: And one sees for example the ***palancas*** that they had, that the other guys [who went free] had, right? The ones who confessed to the crime, even though they confessed and everything, they turned in the other guy and they told them that the deal was, if they confessed they'd let them go, right? So he—that's a big ***palanca*** too.

This story is told in the way stories often are in conversation: it is messy, repetitive in some places, and sparsely detailed in others. Some aspects of the actual events (such as who exactly is in prison, and why, and who has been released, and under what circumstances) are not distinguishable in the narrative as told. Yet a brief gloss of the narrative is possible. Two Colombians are presently in jail in the United States, accused of crimes that they did not commit. They remain in jail even though the real criminals (an indeterminate number, also Colombians) were captured and have confessed. The innocent men, who have no access to an attorney, are still in jail for two reasons. First, they are Colombians who have lived in the United States for 20 years without seeking to become citizens. Two, they did not have ***palancas*** (connections), which the real criminals did have and which they used to get out of jail. There are unspoken assumptions in the story, for example, that ***palancas*** work in the United States in similar ways, and in similar circumstances, to those in Colombia.

Ten middle-class Americans[5] were presented with this story and the gloss just given, and were then asked what

5. The intention of asking these opinions was to have some evidence, however inconclusive, that my own middle-class Anglo-American interpretation was not idiosyncratic. The discussion of these responses was intended to provide at least an informal basis for the comparisons made here. All of the respondents to this informal check were people I knew: I asked six in person, in Boulder, Colorado, and four others by electronic mail in various parts of the United States. All were graduate students, faculty, or staff in communication departments at research universities.

they believed actually occurred. The question put to them was, How did the real criminals manage to get out of jail? Seven of the ten said that the story suggested a plea bargain had been made, that is, the guilty parties had traded information about other persons or crimes for a reduced sentence. One of these respondents remarked that, although such deals were occasionally regrettable, in that some criminals got off lightly, they were completely legal. They were also "fair," because the rules that govern plea bargains presumably applied equally to everyone.

Two respondents said the story made no sense to them at all. They remarked that the speakers must be confused about the nature of the U.S. legal system, leading them to construct an essentially meaningless story. This was evident, one said, in the suggestion that people might be kept in jail because they had never renounced their original citizenship. This seemed highly improbable, because it is legal in the United States for noncitizens to stay in the country as long as they have secured the necessary documentation. Therefore, either the prisoners in question did not have that documentation (in which case they would be deported, not incarcerated), or some other crime must have been committed. This respondent also noted that, in any case, a lawyer would have been appointed by the court to represent the accused.

The final respondent said she believed the account presented by the speakers. The people who got out of jail must have had some contacts within the police department or the prison system, who arranged for them to go free. This interpretation was the explanation given by 15 of 18 Colombians who gave their opinions about what happened[6] The other three said there was too little information for them to

6. In this case, the most practical way to get Colombian responses was COLEXT, described in the Introduction. I posted the transcript and question to the list in the same format I used to poll North American respondents, explaining that my interest was in interpretations by Colombians of the story. I asked subscribers to respond with their interpretations, and received 18 answers.

know what had really happened. Is it the case that this one American, and the 15 Colombians, are somehow "mistaken" about the nature of the U.S. justice system? Is it the case that the seven Americans who agreed on a "plea bargain" as the most logical explanation are naive about the actual operations of their courts and prisons?[7]

The narrative paradigm as formulated by Fisher would call "plea bargain" and *palanca* competing narratives in this instance. The two narratives should be evaluated, Fisher suggests, on the basis of narrative probability and fidelity.[8] For the two informants who thought the story made no sense as constructed, the text itself suggests a lack of narrative probability. From the perspective of those individuals, the elements of a coherent story are not present.[9]

The suggestion that, between "plea bargain" and *palanca,* one story will be more coherent—that is, will ring more true to the stories that people know to be true in their

7. Such is almost certain to be the interpretation of many Colombians, who argued to me that *palancas* must be operating on occasions when I couldn't imagine that was the case. "At least here we *know* that's what's happening," one pointed out. "[North Americans] are kidding themselves if they think this couldn't happen in their system."

8. Presumably this evaluation would occur within the context of the cultural assumptions of the tellers, though Fisher is largely silent on this point.

9. There is an obvious parallel here to the differing reactions in the United States to the verdict in the O. J. Simpson criminal trial in 1995. One narrative coherent to many African Americans (and others) involved Simpson being framed by the police, inconclusive evidence, and a verdict that was thus logical and justified. Another, competing narrative, coherent to many Anglos (and others) was of a mountain of evidence pointing toward Simpson, a jury very likely swayed by rhetorical shenanigans, and an illogical verdict. Assumptions about what police officers can and would do lay at the heart of these competing narratives, and it seems likely that those premises are culturally based, despite the obvious difficulty in defining the boundaries and membership of the cultures that are relevant. Race alone is not sufficient basis, since neither Anglos nor African Americans were completely unified in their responses to the verdict.

own lives—brings up the problem explored by Rowland (1989). He points out that, as Fisher has defined narrative fidelity, the question of narrative coherence thus becomes: coherent to whom? The story may be incoherent to U.S. Americans because it revolves around a premise they find culturally incoherent (that *palancas* can get someone out of any kind of trouble, and that without *palanca* innocence may be beside the point), but it is widely coherent to Colombians precisely because of that premise. Fisher's account of narrativity gives little sense of how culture-based differences of this kind might be reconciled. In fairness, I have no elegant theoretical response to the question either. I would note that cultural analysis of narratives at least offers a framework both for locating the communal beliefs that give shared narratives their power and for highlighting the premises that make narratives coherent in one speech community and not another.

Colombian Beliefs about Laws and Rules

A Colombian perception of institutional rules of Colombia's legal system is captured in a well-known saying: *"Las leyes son para los que se visten de ruana"* ("Laws are for those who wear *ruanas*" [similar to Mexican ponchos]—i.e., the poor, uneducated, and powerless). Like the English motto that "rules are made to be broken," this saying is usually a tongue-in-cheek rationalization for doing something illegal. Yet, the phrase expresses a rueful truth about Colombians' dealings with their government and other official institutions. A legal opinion offered by the Consejo de Estado stated that influence peddling—including *palancas*—was not, and could not, be prohibited. Such action could neither be controlled nor punished because it was unprovable, being carried out verbally rather than in writing. The report concluded that influence peddling was a national institution that could only be controlled by the moral standards of the individual (*El Tiempo*, December 15, 1987).

U.S. Beliefs about Laws and Rules

This view of laws and rules contrasts sharply with the perceptions of those in the United States. Based on a cultural study of kinship in the United States, Scheider proposes that, for Americans,

> the order of law is the outcome of the action of human reason on nature. The good (from nature) is selected, discovered, chosen; rules and regulations (the order of law) are established to maintain and perpetuate the good. . . . Government is regarded in American culture as the formulator of laws and rules in the light of reason. (1980, p. 109)

To break or evade laws is thus regarded as morally deficient and even, to some extent, nonrational, because of the close connection between reason and law. Breaking laws that reflect the "good" in nature implies selecting or perpetuating some course of action that is "bad" or unnatural.

Colombians, on the other hand, spoke of laws and rules as invented by human elements that are defined by their linkages to other human elements. Rules and procedures exist to provide at least some appearance of systematic process and orderly conduct, but they are not necessarily reflective of reason.

> Veronica, 27, student: [Institutional rules] are necessary to show people that such things exist in the organization, to maintain the good image of the institution. Even though everyone knows that getting a job there or getting admitted is not a question of following the procedures but in having some *palanca.*

Laws are thus viewed, in this community, as reflecting the lawmakers' responsibilities to those with whom they have some important connection. Deserving people who are *not* connected to lawmakers and law enforcers may thus not reach their desired ends if they rely entirely on the formal system prescribed for doing so. Establishing a personal contact by which one may transcend institutional rules is a demonstration of interpersonal competence. In order to establish a bond of *palanca,* one must show oneself to be deserving to some degree, that is, at least minimally competent or eligible.

Although Schneider does not make this extension explicit, it seems plain that law in the United States reflects a belief that persons should be regarded and rewarded on the basis of their individual actions and abilities. This belief has resulted in a legal system that decrees that people be treated impartially, as atomistic units. By contrast, the Colombian system of *palanca* gives some persons advantages over others by virtue of interpersonal bonds. Americans perceive the law as consistent with nature because it is based on the good in nature, as determined by human reason. Colombians perceive *palancas* to be consistent with nature because they are based on human relationships. Where there is no bond, there is no *palanca* and, at *that* point, an impartial, objectively defined procedure exists to ensure orderly conduct.

The story constructed from the sequence presented earlier by most of the Americans I asked is that one man confessed and was able to reduce his prison time by way of a plea bargain. "Plea bargain" is a term that middle-class Americans understand and accept; it is consistent with their views of their legal system. *Palanca* is not consistent with what Americans believe about how the law operates in this country, nor is it consistent with their understandings about people and their motivations. Consequently, the *palanca* narrative lacks coherence for middle class Americans. *Palanca* is sensible only within a framework of belief that constructs persons as being, most importantly, sets of connections between human elements. "Plea bargaining" is sensible within a framework in which persons are individuals first, and may thus be expected to protect their individual interests, sometimes at the risk of affecting others' interests negatively.

CONCLUSION

In Chapters 2–4 of this book I have presented the details of some communication practices in a speech community of urban, largely middle-class, Colombians. Three categories of communicative resources were described, and analysis centered on identifying the patterns of use and the meanings of those resources. Meanings were uncovered largely through named speech events in which the intentions and interpretations of personal address, directives, and *palanca* narratives are encoded. Cultural premises embedded in these patterns of talk, and terms for making sense of those patterns, were described in specific reference to the particular categories under discussion. Chapter 5 presents a detailed case study of a long-term personal relationship to explore the uses of these resources within a lived relational context and to illustrate some ways in which cultural premises about relationships are adapted and applied by relational partners to their unique circumstances, history, and personal characteristics.

CHAPTER FIVE

FRIENDS, FAMILY, AND WORKMATES

A Situated Enactment of a Personal Relationship

Relationships and the social world are intertwined systems of meaning, and neither can ever break free of the other. Relational partners can never start from scratch to define their relationship in truly unique ways (not even those partners marooned on the proverbial desert island, for if they have acquired a language, they have acquired with it a system of expectations and interpretations for communicative behavior). Nor can a social structure remain intact and unchanged in the face of renegotiated relational contracts among its members.

What follows is an extended look into a specific relationship, both on the microscopic level of everyday talk between relational partners and in the broader context of their relational history. The social context that shaped that history, and finds its expression in their discourse, is also discussed.

FRIENDS, FAMILY, AND WORKMATES:
MARIELA AND JOSEFINA

The relationship I examine here was one I had unique access to. As mentioned in the Introduction, I lived with my in-laws while doing the fieldwork that formed the basis for this book. Along with family members and friends who made frequent appearances, there was another person who was a constant fixture through the years, both when I was present and when I was not. On the first morning of my first visit, this person was introduced by my (then future) mother-in-law, Mariela: "This is Josefina," she proclaimed. "We have worked together for 20 years, and one of us will bury the other." The description is significant in that Josefina occupied (and continues to occupy) a role in the life of my in-laws that has a conventional term of reference. She is the person who comes to their apartment several times a week to clean, cook, do laundry, and during some periods of time, provide child care for grandchildren. That role is ordinarily designated with the term *la muchacha* (the girl) in Colombian dialect, although in recognition of Josefina's age (mid-50s at our first meeting, roughly the same as her employers' age) she would more often be described as *la señora que ayuda en la casa* (the woman who helps in the house, as distinguished from *la señora de la casa,* the lady *of* the house).

Mariela's identifying comment that she and Josefina had "worked together for 20 years" was later elaborated. The two women met when both were working at the national telecommunications company. Mariela was first a supervisor in accounting and then a lawyer, Josefina was the *señora de los tintos,* a person who serves coffee to employees at their desks and does custodial work. "Josefina knew I liked a particular kind of tea, and she always brought it to me," Mariela explained, and thus a bond formed between them on the basis of Josefina's special consideration for Mariela's needs. That bond deepened when Josefina retired from the company. She needed to continue working for financial reasons,[1] but at age 50 wanted a flexible schedule. Coming to work for Mariela was a way to accomplish that: given that there was already some ***confianza*** between them, she knew Mariela would be willing to give her time off as she needed it.

By the time I met them, the talk between these two women reflected thoroughly blurred relational boundaries. They teased and argued like sisters, confided as to a close friend, and gave and received orders as employer and employee. Each spoke often of the other, at times in disgust and frustration and at other times with the highest regard, affection, and respect. Their connection reverberated through the personal networks of each of them: a relative of Mariela's rented a room in Josefina's house for a time; Mariela and her husband were godparents for one of Josefina's grandchildren. Each attended, with the special attention and consideration accorded an honored guest, many of the important events in the other's life: anniversary celebrations, funerals, weddings, christenings of grandchildren. Because the blending of relational types so evident between them seemed to contradict the idea of rigid social class distinctions emerging from other data,[2] I asked their permission to leave a tape recorder on top of the refrigerator in the kitchen, where many of their extended conversations took place. I proposed that I would turn it on and off at odd moments, but that they could always turn it off or take it away altogether any time they wanted. They agreed, saying they preferred not to know when it was on or off. Thus, either I or my husband recorded conversations in 1986, 1987, 1989, and 1992, for a total of approximately 10 hours of tape. Of that corpus, perhaps 30 minutes are transcribed.

1. Obligatory retirement at age 50 is not uncommon in Colombia, largely as a cost-saving measure for businesses that may be required to give substantial cost-of-living raises each year.

2. That was not quite the way I explained my interest to them. I said I wanted to tape their conversations because they had such a long and interesting relational history—which seemed, under the circumstances, an adequate level of disclosure.

The fragments below were originally selected because of the relative clarity of the recording and because of address term use (the original focus of the ethnographic case study) that seemed particularly interesting. In all of the tapes, the two women are together in the kitchen, sometimes briefly joined by other family members. Josefina was generally involved in food preparation or cleaning; Mariela often came in on various errands and stayed to chat, direct operations, or perform some task of her own. (For an explanation of transcription symbols relevant to this chapter, see Table 5.1.)

Transcript 1: J. (Josefina), S. (Mariela's son), and M. (Mariela), January 1986.

1 J. Municipal? Buses. Buses.	Municipal? Buses. Buses.
2 No troleys sino BUSES. Orita ni	Not trolleys but BUSES. Right now
3 YO ya no. Eso no me aFECta.	not even I, not now. That doesn't afFECt me.
4 (door slams) HUY—ay::!	(door slams) HUY! oops,
5 Llegó la mamá=	the mother has arrived=
6 S. =LleGO ja jefa (.) lleGO la	=The boss has arRIVEd (.) the
7 patrona y::: aca estamo	boss has arrived an::d here we are
[ ]	[ ]
8 M. VIEJA CULICAGADA	THIS OLD DOO-DOO HEAD
9 PASEADORA E¡SA!	WALKABOUT!

10 HUH! puh-puh-puh
     [   ]
	HUH! puh-puh-puh
	     [ ]

11 J. Si me regaña me	If you scold me I'm
12 VOY=	LEAving=
13 S. =hehhehhehhehuh	=hehhehhehhehuh
14 M. Pues VAYase YENdo	Well GET GOing then

TABLE 5.1. Transcription Symbols (developed by Jefferson and described in Sacks, Schegloff, & Jefferson, 1974)

Symbol	Meaning	Example
[ ]	Speakers' turns overlap	HUH! puh-puh-puh [ ] If you scold me I'm LEAving=
Capitals	Increased volume	THIS OLD DOO-DOO HEAD WALKABOUT
Equals sign	Latched turns: there is no interval between the end of the prior turn and the start of the next	If you scold me I'm LEAving= =hehhehhehhehuh
Punctuation	Intonation: period (.) indicates falling contour, question mark indicates a rising contour	In the PLA?za MO?ther he could
Colons	Lengthening: the sound immediately preceding has been noticeably lengthened	WHA::T
Parentheses	Comments: material that is not part of the talk being transcribed, for example, to describe a noise or non-speech sound or to elaborate on a translation to make it idiomatically sensible	(whistle—admiration)
Series of h's	Outbreath	hh—it's up to you
Phonetic representation	Laughter: intended to represent length, volume	hheehheehahaha
Numbers in parentheses	Silences in seconds and tenths of seconds, according to rhythm of speech (see Hopper, 1992)	Should we put them in toGETH?er? (.5)

126

15 S. hheehheehahaha	hheehheehahaha
16 M. AY::: JoseFITA enconTRAS?te=	AY::: JoseFITA you FOUND? it?=
17 J. =Mire 'quí	=LOOk here
18 S. QUE, qué encontró?=	WHAT, what did she find?=
19 M. =(whistle—admiration)	=(whistle—admiration)
20 J. En la PLA?za MA?dre	In the PLA?za MO?ther
21 lo pudo sazonar y todo pa'que	he could season it and everything so
22 le quede tan rico como	it would be just as delicious as
23 aquel día ES?te sin sal=	that day it DOESn't have any salt (on it)=
24 S. =QUE::: [ ]	=WHA:::T [ ]
25 M. Está sin sal?	It doesn't have salt?
26 J. El pescao	The fish

As the fragment begins, Josefina is chatting with Mariela's son as she prepares lunch for the family. Her commentary on buses and trolleys is formulated in a style that is idiosyncratically hers, in which sentences begin in the middle of previous, unfinished sentences, overlapping in rapid layers of words:

1 J. Municipal? Buses. Buses.	Municipal? Buses. Buses.
2 No troleys sino Buses. Orita ni	Not trolleys but BUSES. Right now
3 YO ya no. Eso no me aFECta.	not even I, not now. That doesn't afFECt me.

This relaxed moment is interrupted by the arrival of Mariela. Her identity is remarked on by both the son and Josefina, each referring to Mariela in terms of the connection between her and the other person:

4 J. (*door slams*) HUY—ay::!	(*door slams*) HUY! oops,
5 Llegó la mamá=	the mother has arrived =
6 S. =LleGO la jefa (.) lleGO la	=The boss has arRIVEd (.) the
7 patrona y::: aca estamo	boss has arrived an::d here we are
[ ]	[ ]

The son's comment might have continued as "here we are talking instead of working to get lunch ready"—an illusory inclusion, since he holds no responsibility for food preparation at his mother's house. As Mariela walks briskly from the front door to the kitchen, her voice gets louder and louder on the tape. Her "greeting" to Josefina is, at least in a literal sense, a stream of insults, and Josefina responds by "threatening" to leave:

8 M. VIEJA CULICAGADA	THIS OLD DOO-DOO HEAD
9 PASEADORA E!SA!	WALKABOUT!
10 HUH! puh-puh-puh	HUH! puh-puh-puh
[ ]	[ ]
11 J. Si me regaña me	If you scold me I'm
12 VOY=	LEAving=

The son's laughter across the next two turns makes it plain that the two are teasing rather than seriously insulting and threatening each other. Mariela's use of "walkabout doo-doo head" further reinforces the playful nature of her invective, although the phrase is uttered in a deadpan screech. *Culicagada* is a term of address and reference ordinarily reserved for children, sometimes used with real disgust but more often with some degree of affection. Speaking to a woman in her 50s in this way signals a high level of *confianza* between the two; it is an instantiation of Ricardo's comment (in Chapter 1) that "a good friendship is when you can make rude jokes with each other and everyone

understands it's not really an insult." Reflecting the employer–
employee aspect of their relationship, however (and perhaps the social class differences between them as well),
Josefina's address term choices are more circumscribed. She
addresses Mariela, obviously metaphorically, as **madre** a
few lines further down, a term that Mariela never uses with
Josefina. The only other term I heard Josefina use, or that
appeared on tape, was **Doctora,** a reference to Mariela's
status as a **profesional,** someone with a college degree
(or of the middle classes more generally, as described in
Chapter 2). Both terms refer to Mariela's identity as a person of higher status than Josefina herself.

The theme of the joking exchange suggests reference
to interdependence between the two women:

11 J.	Si me regaña me	If you scold me I'm LEAving=
12	VOY=	
13 S.	=hehhehhehhehuh	hehhehhehhehuh
14 M.	Pues VAY ase YENdo	Well GET GOing then

The truth of their situation is that if Josefina left and
never came back, Mariela would have an extremely difficult time managing her household on her own. She does
not cook and has various health problems that limit her
ability to do housework, yet enjoys frequent visits from family members who may stay for several days or weeks at a
time. She would have to hire a new **muchacha,** a difficult
and risky proposition given the shortage of trained household help and the frequency with which such employees
compensate for their inadequate wages by stealing from their
employers. Josefina is similarly connected through needs
of her own: she depends on the steady income she gets
from working for Mariela, a relatively easy and secure position, to supplement a very meager pension. It would be
very difficult for a woman her age to find a new job, and it
would almost certainly pay less and require longer hours
than her present position. The interdependence between
them is routinely enacted in Josefina's leave-taking ritual:
She always announces "I'm leaving," to which Mariela re

sponds, ***"Dios te pague, Josefina"*** (God repay you, Josefina, i.e., thanks for everything), and Josefina often responds, giggling, ***"El placer no ha sido cualquier lagaña de mico"*** (roughly: The pleasure has been no small thing, i.e., the pleasure was mine).

Mariela's tone quickly changes to one of appreciation and admiration when she gets far enough into the kitchen to see what Josefina is preparing for lunch. Fish is scarce and often of poor quality high in the Andes, yet is a particular favorite of Mariela's. Josefina has gone to a great deal of trouble to secure the fish, going all the way to the plaza to shop instead of making do with what the corner store had to offer. The trip downtown took up most of the morning, accounting for Josefina's absence, to which Mariela has called attention by referring to her as "walkabout." The seller has seasoned the fish in a special way that Mariela enjoyed on a previous occasion, yet left it unsalted in consideration for Mariela's dietary needs. This has almost certainly required careful recollection and extended direction of his efforts on Josefina's part, reminiscent of the special teas she brought to Mariela when they both worked at the telecommunications company. Josefina's extra efforts may have been in honor of the presence of a nephew who arrived a bit later for lunch, rather than entirely on Mariela's behalf. Nonetheless, Mariela is the official hostess of the event regardless of her part in bringing it off, such that a special meal will count as attentiveness to her family. Josefina has gone beyond the duties expected of a paid employee to help Mariela carry out a crucial relational duty—in the sense that she has helped as much as might be expected from close friends and family members. She will be thanked by everyone present, who will recognize her exertion and her talents in preparing an unusual and highly valued dish, and she will very much share in the glory Mariela will enjoy as hostess.

Transcript 2: J. (Josefina) and M. (Mariela), June 1989.

1 J. Suena el teléfono y se despierta	The phone rang and (he) woke up, so

2 entonces por esto lo acuesto yo?	for that reason I should put him to bed?
3 (water running) A mí no me hace	(water running) To me that doesn't make
4 —eso's cierto—no más me	—that's for sure—I no more
5 despego porque pa qué (se pone	get loose because for what (why would I
6 a buscar capules—a destacar	look to make myself more
7 más) (1.5) Yo le digo a la niña	central) (1.5) I said to the (little) girl
8 que esa estufa pa quién era y dijo	that stove who was it for and she said
9 pa TODOS Mamá, aquí pa la casa	for EVERYONE Mama, for Everyone here at
10 para TOdos. Y ayer le dió en las	the house. And yesterday she punched her in the
11 narices HEE	nose. HEE
12 heeheeheeheh	heeheeheeheh
13 M. Quién	Who
14 J. Pues la NI?ña=	Well the (little) GIR?l=
15 M. =Le dió en las narices	=She punched her in the nose
16 J. MaRIna.	MaRIna.
17 M. La castigó?	She punished her?
18 J. Pues era que ella estaba, yo no sé,	Well it's that she was, I don't know,
19 YO NO sé de dónde (le dijo) dizque	I DON'T know where (she told her) she says
20 raTERa que yo no sé qué le dije	THIef I don't know what I said to her
21 QUIEN, dijo uSTE, le dije sí? y esa	WHO? she said YOU, I said yeah? and that
22 china se fue detrás de la mamá	kid went right behind her mother
23 pa'rriba, diciendo se paró en las	upstairs, saying, she stopped

24 escaleras que raTEros, y le dije por / on the stairs "THIEves" (she said), and I said

25 qué cerraron, por qué cierran / why did you close—why are you closing (locking your door)

26 arriba? Para que no se'ntren los / upstairs? "So the

27 raTERos, y le dije cuáles rateros, / THIEves don't get in," and I said which thieves,

28 entonces la chinita ( ) me / so the little kid ( ) she

29 dijo que uSTE, le dije Sí? GRAcias / said to me "You," I said Yeah? THANk you

30 mijita por la recohhmen-daciON hh / sweetie for the recohhmenDAtion hh

31 se devolvió la mamá y hh TENGale / Her mother came back and hh "TAKE that kid." (.5)

32 mijo. (.5) hheheehee QUE es lo / hhehheehee "WHAT's that

33 que 'stá ste' diciendo? que no je / you're saying?" and I don't

34 qué. Y ella es que de todo es que / know what all. It's that everything is . . .

35 (le lleve / (she talks back

36 la contraria). / to everything).

37 (1.0) / (1.0)

38 M. (*swallows*) Es que ese sí es un lío / (*swallows*) That's a bad habit

39 que tiene uste? Josefina. Por qué / you have? Josefina. Why

40 le gusta llevarle la con-traria a las / do you like to talk back to

41 personas si eso no es NAda bueno. / people if this is NOT good.

42 [   ] / [   ]

43 J. y y enTONces= / and and THEREfore=

44 M. =Así enseña a las personas ah ser / =That's how you teach people to uh

45 peleadoras y eso no debe ser=	be disagreeable and that shouldn't be=
46 J. =Las echamoh JUN?tas? (.5)	=Should we put them in toGETH?er? (.5)
47 M. hh—Uste verá	hh—it's up to you
48 J. Pero entonces al doctor no le	But in that case we won't
49 damos mm carne	give the doctor mm meat
50 M. Que se echa juntas QUE Josefina.	If you put WHAT in together Josefina.
51 [ ]	[ ]
52 J. Pechugas.	(Chicken) breasts.
53 M. Pues uste verá lo que va'cer hh	Well it's up to you what you're going to do hh
54 yo hh qué voy a saber que's lo	I hh how would I know what you're
55 que va'cer? [ ]	going to do? [ ]
56 J. (pues) la pasta con pollo	(well) the pasta with chicken
57 M. BUE?no (.5) hh - Hágalo (.5) heh hh	FI?ne (.5) hh DO it that way (.5) heh hh
58 J. No::: le pregun?to=	No::: I'm ask?ing=
59 M. =Todos los días le tengo que	=Every day I have to
60 d-decir la misma cantaleta y	t-tell you the same dumb thing and
61 VUELVE la JoseFIta, no?	BACK comes JoseFIta, no?

This fragment begins near the end of an extended narrative, once again made somewhat difficult to follow because of Josefina's habit of running sentences together, changing topics, protagonists, and time frames in rapid, unmarked order. Despite decades of experience following Josefina's train of thought, Mariela apparently has some of the same confusion, which she tries to clarify in midstory (lines 13–16).

In the narrative(s) presented in Josefina's two long turns, however, some glimpses of what life can be like in a family that lives out the ideal of **unidad** by living together in the same house are apparent. Josefina has six sons, the youngest of whom was in his late teens when this recording was made. She lives in a large house in a quiet working-class neighborhood about 20 minutes' drive by car, or 30–50 minutes' ride by bus, from Mariela. Some of her sons (as few as two and as many as five) have lived with her at times during the past 10 years, along with their wives and children. The house has some self-contained bedroom/bathroom combinations, almost like small apartments, clustered around a central living area. When those units have been vacated by sons who moved out on their own, they were offered to renters (always people Josefina knew well, such as Mariela's relative). Together, the family runs a small grocery store next door to the house, sharing in the work and profits from that business as well as coordinating household tasks, child care, and so forth.

The arrangement plainly has its advantages: Although it is unclear who "the (little) girl" is in line 14 (the use of **Mamá** is plainly metaphorical, since Josefina has no daughters. The speaker may be a daughter-in-law or a granddaughter, of whom there are several living in the house at this time), the object under discussion is a new stove that some family member has purchased for everyone's use. There is another side as well: family conflicts are inevitably witnessed or overheard by several people, and family members may say brutally negative things to one another. The sequence involving the girl who was punched in the nose involves some rude comments from a child to Josefina, her grandmother, to the effect that her parents have taken to locking the door to their apartment upstairs so that thieves won't get in. When she explicitly names her grandmother as the "thief" she has in mind, her mother rebukes her physically. Whether Josefina was hurt by the child's accusation, or whether the child meant it as a joke that seemed too cheeky for her mother, who overheard it, to let pass without comment, is unclear. Plainly, it was a noteworthy moment in the life of the family, and is reported as such to Mariela.

Josefina's extended narrative about the event, including the potentially rude comment of the granddaughter and the mother's punch in response, is a commonplace kind of conversation for her to have with Mariela. Mariela has heard so many of the scenes of Josefina's home life over the years that Josefina assumes she is well acquainted with the characters:

13	M. Quién	Who
14	J. Pues la NI?ña=	Well the (little) GIR?l=

Josefina's intonation suggests surprise—"The little GIR?l, of course. Who else would I be referring to?"

To the extent that a child insulting her grandmother, or a mother punching a child in the nose, are considered sensitive issues that cannot be revealed very far outside the family circle, Josefina has offered significant disclosures about her home life in this conversation. Mariela's response is neither sympathy nor reciprocation, but a rebuke:

34	J. Y ella es que de todo es que	It's that everything is . . .
35	(le lleve	(she talks back
36	la contraria).	to everything).
37	(1.0)	(1.0)
38	M. (*swallows*) Es que ese sí es un lío	(*swallows*) That's a bad habit
39	que tiene uste? Joscfina. Por qué	you have? Josefina. Why
40	le gusta llcvarlc la contraria a las	do you like to talk back to
41	personas si eso no es NAda bueno.	people if this is NOT good.
42	[ ]	[ ]
43	J. y y enTONces=	and and THEREfore=
44	M. =Así enseña a las personas ah	=That's how you teach people to uh
45	ser peleadoras y eso no	be disagreeable and that shouldn't be=

Although the rebuke focuses on Josefina's behavior with her family, it is also a theme in the relationship between her and Mariela, who frequently accuses Josefina of disagreeing with her about anything and everything. Josefina lets the critique pass without comment:

43 J. y y enTONces=	and and THEREfore=
44 M. =Así enseña a las personas ah	=That's how you teach people to uh
45 ser peleadoras y eso no debe ser=	be disagreeable and that shouldn't be=
46 J. =Las echamoh JUN?tas? (.5)	=Should we put them in toGETH?er? (.5)

This conversation is typical of a pattern of talk between them: Josefina often recounts family matters in what might, to some people, be excruciating detail. Her sons' successes, failures, and idiosyncrasies in both work and personal life, as well as the comings and goings of their respective romantic partners and spouses, are well known to Mariela and other members of her family. Mariela does not respond with stories or confidences about her own family members, although Josefina's daily presence in the household means that there are few secrets about what goes on there. Mariela does frequently give Josefina advice, on the somewhat abstract level seen above (i.e., "you shouldn't talk back to people all the time, that's how they learn to be disagreeable").

A final exchange of interest here is the discussion of the lunch about to be served. Josefina interrupts Mariela's comment on her "talking back" with a question about arranging the food, inviting her to exercise some influence:

46 J. =Las echamoh JUN?tas? (.5)	=Should we put them in toGETH?er? (.5)
47 M. hh—Uste verá	hh—It's up to you

Mariela passes, making plain she does not consider herself involved in this decision. Her half-chuckle suggests ridicule: "What a question to be asking ME!"

Josefina's next attempt to involve Mariela includes an indirect warrant: "the doctor" is Mariela's husband, and she may be considered, as his spouse, to know better than Josefina whether he would prefer to have meat or not. Because Mariela frequently gives detailed directions to Josefina on what "the doctor" should or should not eat, based on Mariela's assessments of what is good for his health (particularly his waistline, about which she voices concern almost daily), Josefina's question is an invocation of that pattern. Instead of taking this opportunity to direct "the doctor's diet" as usual, however, Mariela expresses confusion over what Josefina is referring to.

48 J. Pero entonces al doctor no le	But in that case we won't
49 damos mm carne	give the doctor mm meat
50 M. Que se echa juntas QUE Josefina.	If you put WHAT in together Josefina.

Presented as a parallel to the "what girl?" confusion several lines earlier, Mariela reiterates her lack of involvement in, and responsibility for, the shape of lunch. She implies that whatever happens is "up to you" (Josefina), as though she has never considered directing her husband's diet. Again, her response is interspersed with chuckles, as though Josefina has asked an entirely novel, strange question to which Mariela cannot possibly be expected to respond.

52 J. Pechugas.	(Chicken) breasts.
53 M. Pues uste verá lo que va'cer hh	Well it's up to you what you're going to do hh
54 yo hh qué voy a saber que's lo	I hh how would I know what you're
55 que va'cer?	going to do?
[ ]	[ ]

When Josefina specifies her plan once more, Mariela voices agreement, in a tone of amusement, as if humoring a whimsical child. This time Josefina pursues the issue, insisting that she truly wants an opinion (and involvement?), rather than a differently phrased "do whatever you want."

56 J. (pues) la pasta con pollo	(well) the pasta with chicken
57 M. BUE?no (.5) hh - Hágalo (.5) heh hh	FI?ne (.5) hh DO it that way (.5) heh hh
58 J. No::: le pregun?to=	No::: I'm ask?ing=

Mariela's response is another rebuke: When Josefina isn't "talking back" and "making people disagreeable," she is forgetting simple instructions and asking unnecessary questions:

59 M. =Todos los días le tengo que	=Every day I have to
60 d-decir la misma cantaleta y	t-tell you the same dumb thing and
61 VUELVE la JoseFIta	BACK comes JoseFIta, no?

In this exchange about lunch, Mariela's refusal to get involved with decisions about cooking and serving may subtly emphasize her role as employer rather than coparticipant in food preparation. As mentioned earlier, she does not cook, and she might well defend her disavowal on the grounds that she really is ignorant of whether chicken should be cooked with noodles, or separately, or whatever. From Mariela's view, Josefina might be obstinately calling attention to Mariela's lack of cooking experience, or asking questions when she has already made up her mind how to prepare the food, thereby giving herself openings to disagree "as usual." Refusing to respond in that case could merely be deftly closing those openings.

On the other hand, it is easy to imagine that Josefina brought up the cooking task at hand just when she did as a way of changing the subject, shifting talk away from criticism of her into discussion of cooking, something about which she is an acknowledged expert. She does not dispute Mariela's claim about her tendency to "talk back," quite likely recognizing the remark as an indirect reference to her interactions with Mariela. Mariela's remark invokes an unequal footing between them, despite its cloak of warmth of a long-term relationship, a cozy chat in the kitchen. Although Mariela might well claim to be enacting involvement with Josefina, offering "helpful" analysis and advice on Josefina's situation as a mark of friendship and family relationships, it is not a conversational move that Josefina is at liberty to reciprocate. Mariela creates a superior position for herself through her criticism: Josefina is the one with family members who behave in shocking ways, and Josefina herself may be at fault because she tends to "talk back" to everyone, thereby making them disagreeable. She, Mariela, is in a position to "helpfully" point this out and "share" in Josefina's troubles by suggesting that a reason for her granddaughter's smart mouth may be Josefina's own behavior.

When Josefina tries to extend this spirit of involvement into a topic area and activity that entail positive aspects of her identity, however, Mariela denies there is any connection between her self and the task of cooking. Josefina is clearly the expert at cooking, and Mariela is willing to admit her ignorance and helplessness in that arena (and thus her dependence on Josefina for a basic necessity of daily life). Her amused tone can also be heard as arch: cooking is, after all, something she can pay someone else to do. She, as a middle-class *profesional*, can afford to be ignorant and helpless about something that Josefina earns a living doing for other people—like Mariela.

In the talk of these two women, then, there are echoes both of their unique personal relationship—people who have lived through many of life's most significant events in the context of some contact with each other—and of the class system that distinguishes between them and conditions their interpretations of, and responses to, each other's actions. Their close personal connection, extending across decades and encompassing some of the most meaningful events in the lives of each of them, is not separable from the social context in which it was formed and maintained.

There are a number of parallels between the relationship of Mariela and Josefina and those between Black domestic workers and their employers in the American South, as described by Tucker (1988), Harris (1982), and others. In Colombia as in the American South, legalized slavery gave way to an institutionalized relationship between social classes, in which women of the working classes left their own homes and children to provide household labor for the middle classes. Long-term relationships between domestics and their employers were often (and sometimes still are) characterized by mutual affection, loyalty, and interdependence. That closeness notwithstanding, the social arrangement was one that consistently exploited domestic workers and perpetuated a system in which the standard of living of whites (or members of the middle class) rested on the cheap labor of those workers (cf. Tucker, 1988).

From one view, these conversations between Mariela and Josefina are enactments of many of the relational ideals described in Chapter 1. Two women transcend the usual boundaries of class difference to create a close, quasi-familial relationship that clearly (and equitably) enriches the lives of both partners. They plainly count on each other for help in difficult times. Josefina spoke once, with tears in her eyes, of how Mariela's husband had provided legal assistance: "Oh, **Señora,** if it hadn't been for the doctor, I would have lost my house!" Mariela, in equally emotional tones, told of times when Josefina seemed her only support, more constant than many of her own family members in "keeping her company" through her illnesses. They refer to one another as to kindred souls, both **verracas** ("tough broads") who have overcome the barriers of circumstance to achieve worthy, difficult goals: Josefina, despite very little education, worked hard all her life to ensure that all of her sons finished high school. Mariela, despite vehement opposition from her siblings, attended night school and obtained a law degree while working full-time. The material and emotional bond between these women has obviously contributed a great deal to their respective successes.

Another view is that their relationship enacts and perpetuates the social inequities that permeate Colombian society. Mariela was able to attend night school because Josefina took charge of the housework and cooking, while Josefina was never allowed to take time off for the literacy courses she longed to take. Although the two of them worked for the same company for approximately the same length of time, Mariela's pension was substantial enough for her to stop working altogether when she retired, while Josefina was still working 15 years later. The power differences between them are also made plain in discourse: although Mariela's insulting address terms are meant as teasing, Josefina is not free to respond in kind. Although Josefina freely offers her confidences about her family matters, she cannot respond to criticism with a show of anger. Mariela controls movement between the ***confianza*** of their long, intimate association and the distance created by separation of roles and tasks.

This analysis has highlighted a number of factors that contribute to the rich, complicated relationship between Josefina and Mariela. Their similar personalities, their long and multifaceted shared history, and the social structure that has given form to (and inevitably been played out in) their interaction all play a role in the configuration of their relationship. In significant ways, what has emerged between them is a unique code of meaning. The unique aspects of their relationship, as conceptually linked to the idiosyncratic patterns and meanings that emerge in long-term close relationships generally, are a useful note on which to end this chapter.

RELATIONAL CODES

Personal relationships have long been conceptualized as unique entities, created by specific individuals within a specific historical context (Altman & Taylor, 1973). The notion that shared meanings and expectations for behavior arise within relationships that are specific to the dyad or group, and that those meanings and norms are unique, was explored conceptually by Wood (1982) and empirically, in subsequent studies of romantic couples and friendships (Baxter & Wilmot, 1985; Baxter, 1987; Bell, Buerkel-Rothfuss, & Gore, 1987; Hopper, Knapp, & Scott, 1981). "Relational culture" was the term coined to describe the unique symbols, meanings, and patterns of interaction that emerge within close relationships, often bearing little resemblance to public language rules. In its early formulations, there was heavy emphasis on relational culture as a dyad-specific, individual system of meaning. Wood (1982) proposed that relational culture was "created by individuals. . . . [It is] an extensive set of definitions, values, and rules which comprise a unique-to-the relationship world order" (p. 77). Montgomery (1988) concurred: "[R]elational standards are phenomenologically *unique* for each partnership. They are developed entirely within the confines of a particular relationship" (p. 354).

Even with this heavy emphasis on the uniqueness of relational codes,[3] the influence of a social world on relationships was also acknowledged. First, it was pointed out that the impact of relational codes on behavior extended beyond private interaction. Following Goffman (1971), researchers noted that using intimate idioms to coordinate action in public allowed couples to create a teamed identity, thereby underscoring the link between them and leading others to make attributions of intimacy (Bell et al., 1987; Wood, 1982). Second, social groups communicate expectations for relational partners that are incorporated into the relational standards developed by each couple or friendship, in the way of relational prototypes (Montgomery, 1992)

3. Rather than juxtapose "relational culture" with communal systems of meaning as culture, I will use relational "code" (in the Philipsen, 1987, sense of "culture as code" of meaning and for behavior) as a counterpart term to culture, defined as a *communal,* historically transmitted system of premises and symbolic meanings. The elaboration of relational codes offered here is, nonetheless, drawn from work that used the term relational culture to describe relationship-specific configurations of meaning.

and understandings of what constitutes "good" communication within relationships (Montgomery, 1988). It was obvious that people did not merely follow instructions for being friends, marital partners, siblings, and so forth, passed along whole cloth from their social world. In healthy relationships, at least, they adapted, adjusted, or substituted alternatives for social expectations in ways that were unique to their personalities and circumstances (Gottman, 1979; Montgomery, 1988).

The code constructed between Mariela and Josefina is in many ways an instantiation of certain relational ideals of friendship, family, and employer/employee relationships described earlier in this chapter. There is ***confianza,*** there is togetherness, there is a good measure of mutual respect. Still, their relationship also enacts—and thus perpetuates—class inequality. The relational code is most profoundly a basis for ongoing negotiation of meaning between these two people, rooted in their shared history and a commitment to a shared future. It seems highly likely that one of them will, in fact, bury the other.

A question that remains to be addressed is just how relational partners draw on cultural resources, and how personal relationships construct culture. Baxter and Montgomery (1996) propose that both processes occur through dialogic interchange between culture and personal relationships. Relational partners simultaneously react to and create the cultural context. At the levels of institutions (such as marriage ceremonies), media[4] (such as popular songs, TV shows, films), and social networks (friends, family, workmates), social collectives with distinctive interests in how personal relationships are conducted prescribe appropriate behavior for relational partners, both toward each other and in terms of the relationship's participation in the

4. Baxter and Montgomery describe mass-mediated influences as "cultural artifacts." Here I refer to them simply as media in order to distinguish this aspect of culture from the more abstract systems of symbolic understanding that I have presented in this book as a broader instantiation of interpersonal ideology.

life of the community. At the same time, partners' choices about their own relational configuration can influence the decisions of others in their network and lead to larger-scale cultural changes in definitions of appropriate and desirable forms of relationships.

To the extent that distance between relational ideals and the realities that never quite match is obvious in conversational transcripts such as those analyzed here, critical discourse analysis suggests an avenue toward analysis of social life with tremendous potential to effect change.[5] Presenting members of a culture with transcripts that capture the kinds of relationships they assign meaning to, and showing the perpetuation of oppression through discursive practices, might create a basis for renegotiation of relational contracts between partners and thus serve as the impetus for social change.

To attempt such "enlightenment" carries significant interpersonal risk. Confronting people with interpretations of their talk that are at odds with their own intentions and meanings is more likely to incur defense than conversion, particularly if it comes from a nonmember of the culture. To present either analysis of their conversation—the benign cultural one or the class-conscious one—to Mariela and Josefina would almost guarantee that future chats in the kitchen would be less cozy, less unguarded, and perhaps less frequent. Whether they could ultimately be more satisfying for either party is a separate question. In any case, the fact that these women have borrowed from the resources of their culture—however flawed those may be—to create a relationship that comforts and sustains them both as they grow old together, seems an accomplishment worth noting.

The last four chapters have sketched the outlines of an interpersonal ideology of connectedness. Within that

5. The liberationist turn of recent work in the coordinated management of meaning (Cronen, Chen, & Pearce, 1988) and critical discourse analysis (Fairclough, 1992; Hodge & Kress, 1993; van Dijk, 1993) each pursue precisely this type of project.

framework of premises and meaning, urban Colombians like Josefina and Mariela formulate relational configurations that are partly unique constructions arising from their own particular relational histories and partly are extensions of that system of enablements and constraints. Chapter 6 draws together the premises sketched in these chapters into a more coherent picture, characterized nonetheless not by uniformity and consistency but by dilemma and contradiction.

CHAPTER SIX

"A SET OF BONDS
TO OTHERS"

Elaborating an Ideology
of Connectedness

This book began with a glimpse of personal relationships in an urban Colombian speech community in terms of abstract ideals of relational types. The three chapters that followed elaborated communicative resources and ways of speaking through which members of the speech community both construct their social identities and display the nature of, and their orientation to, their personal involvement with others. Finally, Chapter 5 illustrated the utilization of these resources in conversation, and the influence of the speech community in shaping a specific long-term personal relationship that blended elements of the ideal types discussed in Chapter 1.

What these communicative resources display and construct is only recognizable to the extent that participants know certain cultural premises on which personal relationships are grounded. Those premises have so far been presented in a somewhat fragmented and disconnected way, to tie them as closely as possible to specific resources and patterns as they were discussed. A further descriptive move needed at this point is to synthesize and elaborate on those premises to show the system of meaning as a reasonably coherent whole. Despite the utility of such synthesis to show connections across contexts and communicative forms, any summary of this kind is likely to sound (and be) more monolithic and unitary than the more untidy performances that constitute social life. Thus, a brief discussion of some predominant strands of meaning will be followed by a longer description of some contradictions and dilemmas that emerge from those strands.

A member of the speech community studied here, an economist in his 40s, offered a succinct formulation of a central, perhaps overriding premise under which many others might be subsumed. He said that for Colombians in this group *"una persona es un conjunto de vínculos"* (a person is a set of bonds to others). In other words, the fundamental unit of human existence for Colombians is the *vínculo* : the bond between human pair-parts,[1] between a family and its home (*la casa*), and between a human and his or her homeland (*tierra*). This premise cuts across a very wide range of Colombian interpersonal experience. Many diverse aspects of contexts, situations, institutions, and interpretations of action are made sensible within this view of persons.

Other comments in focus group interviews supported this notion.

> Pilar, 34, librarian: We humans are incomplete . . . as persons, individually, because we need to share our experiences with others in order to develop, to grow. We need other people.

---

1. I use the term "pair-part" in the sense that has been incorporated into conversation analysis. A question is one pair-part in a sequence, one in which the pair-part required to complete the sequence is usually an answer. In the same way, an individual human is an incomplete pair-part, needing another human element to be a fully developed being

Fernando, 24, lawyer: It's like the saying, *dime con quien andas y te digo quien eres* (tell me who you walk with and I'll tell you who you are)—you are who you're connected to. Your family, your friends, your neighbors, the people you work with—they make up your life story. Well (*laughs*), not *all* of it, but a lot.

From this view, each human is born with a *forma de ser,* a unique way of being, and must develop a capacity to think and act independently. Life's tasks and events must primarily be experienced, however, in the context of connection with other humans to be meaningful. Being alone is being lonely, linguistically as well as culturally. A state presumed to be desirable at most times is to be *acompañado,* with company,[2] that is, in the physical presence of people one is connected to, neither physically alone nor surrounded by strangers. In Colombian Spanish, the same word is used for alone and lonely: *sólo.* It can describe an empty physical space (a street, a house, a building, or a room with no one in it is said to be *sólo,* not *vacío,* empty) as well as a person who is alone. In a country that has struggled with a staggering crime rate for the past few decades, to be alone is often physically dangerous. Little wonder, then, that being alone generally has such negative connotations.

As mentioned in descriptions of an ideal family, individualism as a habitual attitude or mode of action poses a significant threat to *vínculos.* A relationship wherein the parties view themselves first as individuals and secondarily as part of a family, couple, or friendship is described as inherently unstable. There are times, of course, when personal needs must take precedence over the needs and well-being of the other pair-part, but sacrifice and/or "helping" (in all the forms "help" assumes) generally takes evaluative preference over individual assertiveness.

2. The Latin term *vinculum* originally designated a chain used to restrain prisoners. The more positive connotations of its Colombian Spanish form are derived from the metaphorical transition to denoting a tie that bonds, rather than binds. I am indebted to Steve Duck for this observation.

Interpersonal bonds come partly from nature, and partly must be nurtured. Ties of kinship, regional origin, and sex are formed at birth. They are based on "natural" elements: blood, for kinship; telluric forces (geographic features, e.g., mountains, the sea, the wind), for regional origin; male nature (strong and violent) and female nature (nurturant), for sex. One response in a focus group interview to the proposition that "Each person is indelibly marked by home-land, gender, and social class. . . . people do not change their fundamental way of being" was:

> Ana María, 27, biologist: It's like the old saying, "The mon-key that dresses in silk is still a monkey." Whatever has formed the person, their social class, their sex, their home-land—they will always be fundamentally *that*, even if they move to another region or go up or down in their economic status or whatever. Maybe superficial things about the way they act will change, but the fundamental kind of person they are is rooted in those early experiences.

Other bonds may be formed through shared experiences that shape one's worldview, an ***acercamiento de conciencia*** (closeness of consciousness) derived from one's social class, political affiliation, and/or exposure to religion.[3]

Still other bonds form by experience and choice. The particular experiences and choices that serve as the bases

---

3. Nonetheless, political affiliation and religion seem to have much less influence on Colombians' behavior than they used to. That may be more true of their actions than of their worldview and self-presentation. People are liberal, or conservative, or sometimes socialist or Christian Demo-crat, but no one is "none of the above." Declaring oneself to be politi-cally neutral has no meaning in the system. In terms of religion, the Colombians I worked with and observed were either in favor of the church or against it, but religious imagery was inevitably part of their discursive world. That imagery was derived from mysticism, Catholicism, or often a combination of these. Speaking of events, including many relevant to personal relationships, in terms of attributions to specific mystical and/ or religious forces was an experience shared by all of these Colombians, whatever their inner views may have been.

for *vínculos* are different for each individual, but how they function to form interpersonal bonds is part of the cultural meaning of *vínculo*. If persons share pleasantly memorable experiences, a *vínculo* forms or is strengthened. If they share a common vocation or interest or circle of associates (e.g., schoolmates), rituals and activities are often constructed with the express intention of strengthening those *vínculos*.[4]

In sum, some *vínculos* exist from birth; some arise naturally from commonalities of worldview; some are chosen or encouraged; others (notably those characterized by differences in background such as social class and education) are actively discouraged and constrained. People in the environment with whom a *vínculo* has not been established cannot be depended on to cooperate or assist in accomplishing life's large and small tasks. In the absence of a *vínculo*, people often must compete for scarce resources, which members of the culture perceive to be numerous (a perception perhaps partly due to living in an overcrowded, fast-paced capital city). Because important tasks in life cannot be accomplished by individuals acting singly, *vínculos* are also formed around the necessity of performing particular tasks.[5]

4. One such activity is a *fiesta de integración*, an "integration party" held early in the school year. Students at all levels of education go through several years of schooling with essentially the same group of people. Establishing a feeling of unity within the group is spoken of as crucial for a satisfactory learning environment, while voluntary extracurricular activities unconnected to one's classmates, such as sports, music, or other clubs (typical in North American schools), are not, and are rarely made available. Activities are planned with the express intention of creating class unity, especially during the first year of the group's existence. This parallels the structure and function of "gibush days," designed to promote coherence among groups of Israeli students (Katriel, 1992).

5. Parallel to the notion of *palanca* discussed in Chapter 4, service *encounters*, where one interacts with a business establishment only briefly and thus is merely a face in a crowd, are therefore dispreferred to service *relationships*, in which the client attempts to establish a bond with the service provider in order to efficiently complete the task.

Formation and strengthening of ***vínculos*** is the most important task to be accomplished in many situations. There is a shared understanding that engaging in activities that will strengthen ***vínculos,*** for example, ***charlando*** (chatting), ***estar con alguien*** (be with someone), ***estar pendiente de alguien*** (be aware of someone's needs, desires, and general well-being), ***acompañar a alguien*** (keep someone company, i.e., accompany them to run errands or perform a task), and so forth, may take precedence over paid employment, being on time, and (for the culturally ideal person) personal achievement. Ability to comply with this cultural preference for behavior may be dependent on occupation and position in an organizational hierarchy: a mark of one's importance is the freedom to lay aside work tasks in order to service personal relationships.

Vínculos are defined and regulated by two forces: ***confianza*** and respect. Every ***vínculo*** carries some level of ***confianza,*** even if that is intentionally minimal. To the extent that ***confianza*** exists, expectations and obligations are created between the pair-parts that are a natural outgrowth of the connectedness—the trust, commonality of worldview, and shared effects—between them. Maintaining distance avoids those expectations and responsibilities. ***Confianza*** and ***distancia,*** on one hand a continuum of relational quality, on the other hand present an oppositional force of costs and benefits. Survival and, indeed, personal existence depend on the establishment of ***confianza*** with other pair-parts. Social order depends on maintaining distance from them.

Respect stems from the natural occurrence of differences between pair-parts. Persons must be respected both as human elements and as status incumbents within hierarchies of authority and importance. The interpersonal world is organized along several parallel hierarchies, and persons occupy particular positions within them. Fundamental con-

---

Service relationships are especially important in cases where the client anticipates that the task will recur frequently, for example, buying groceries, having a car repaired, or making travel arrangements.

nections exist between a person and his or her place in each hierarchy, and *vínculos* between pair-parts are shaped by being of the same or unequal status positions with relation to each other. Specifically, persons of higher status have the authority to influence the actions of lower-status persons. Showing respect for the person implies showing respect to the hierarchy, in that the grounding for the *vínculo* is placement within the hierarchy.

This synthesis of an interpersonal ideology of connectedness, however coherent it would sound to Colombians (and testing and refining these claims were, in fact, the central activity of the focus group interviews), is rather too neat and tidy to be an accurate reflection of the pulls and tugs characteristic of all social life. To paraphrase Rosaldo (1989), the conversation of communal life is more a lively argument than a cozy chat. It would be profoundly unsatisfying, and certainly misleading, to leave description of the ideology at this level of abstraction, where sense and consensus seem to predominate and the conduct of personal relationships seems a relatively straightforward matter. Thus, the remainder of this chapter focuses on four dilemmas of social life that arise from this ideology of connectedness as those are relevant to personal relationships. The value of seeing these dilemmas as cultural instantiations of dialectics of personal relationships theorized to be universal is then discussed.

DILEMMA #1:
SINCERITY VERSUS APPROPRIATENESS

There is significant evidence to suggest that in this system it is open to question whether people will, or should, act in accordance with their actual feelings and predispositions. First, the frequency with which sincerity was mentioned as a characteristic of ideal friendship suggests that it is not taken for granted that genuine liking and appreciation will motivate efforts to be friends. Because social status is so central to personal identity, and because identity is defined so pervasively as a question of the status of those to whom one is connected, suspicion that people will seek to establish relationships for instrumental rather than personal reasons is frequently voiced in evaluations and interpretations of friendly overtures.

Second, the existence of a code of appropriate or ***culto*** behavior specifies certain actions as proper and others as inadequately so. That code is referred to in descriptions of conduct and persons as ***formal*** (*"formal"*). Roughly speaking, the code reflects the experiences and mores of the middle and upper classes; its basis was described by one informant as "a moral formation found among persons of a certain level of culture." There are inevitably members of society who fall below that level of "culture," such that they may not be expected to understand or to be able to put into practice the behaviors that constitute "formality." By the same token, even persons who were ***bien educados*** (brought up well), so that they know and are able to enact the code, may choose not to do so on occasion or habitually. Both those who cannot, and those who do not, act in accordance with "cultivated" conduct, in situations when that code is required, are evaluated negatively.

Specifically, ***formal*** applies to attitudes and behavior that are orderly, dignified, and restrained. ***Un niño formal*** is a well-behaved (and clean, tidily dressed) child; ***una señorita formal*** is a socially poised (and well-dressed) young woman. Both are ideals that parents encourage their children to attain, often quite forcefully.[6]

---

6. There may be no better way to see the cultural premises built into childrearing practices than to see one's own children endure the norms of a different culture. During one period of fieldwork when they were preschoolers, my son and daughter were suddenly expected to wear shoes at all times, keep their clothes clean even during playtime, show expertise with eating utensils, and keep toys and books meticulously in their places except when actually in use. I realized I had been conditioned to see all of these habits as outside the capacities of 3- and 5-year-olds, and to see freedom, choices, and informality as the most natural and healthy environment for children of that age. When

Some events are required to be relatively ***formal*** in order to count as appropriately celebratory of persons and their accomplishments, such as birthdays, graduations, and welcome and going-away parties. Relationships may also be celebrated, on anniversaries, Mother's Day, and Father's Day. The family unit is generally an explicit cohonoree in both kinds of events. That is, a graduation is not merely the achievement of an individual but a goal reached by the family, a positive reflection on the hard work and persistence of the family unit as much as the person graduating. In order for such events to be marked as significant, clothing must be elegant, food should be elaborate and, whenever possible, prepared by someone other than the principals, and drink should be ***aguardiente*** ("firewater," a distilled sugar cane liquor), imported whiskey, and/or wine rather than beer, to the extent the family is able to afford such expenditures. Speeches are generally made on such occasions that extol the idealized characteristics of the person or relationship being celebrated, and they are typically formal (by North American standards) in tone and content. One marker of formality in such speeches is a suppression of any allusions to departures from cultural ideals: although not all marriages are happy and harmonious, all anniversary speeches must depict blissful mutual devotion and uninterruptedly tranquil relational histories.

Although ***formal*** implies restraint, the restraint is not expected to apply to displays of emotion. On many formal occasions, such as Mother's Day and going-away parties, attempting to suppress feelings in keeping with the event would be far worse than giving them free rein. Emotional displays are expected to show sincerity. Rather, what must be restrained are vulgar speech and action, and feelings contrary to the spirit of the occasion. Formal occasions are meant to ***darle importancia a la persona*** (to show a

---

I saw my four-year-old niece and her cousins do all of those things, apparently effortlessly and with few parental reminders, I could only shake my head in wonder.

person's, or relationship's, importance), and an informal, relaxed event would not accomplish that objective to nearly the same degree.

Certain settings are also marked for formality, such as classrooms, offices, churches,[7] and places reserved for cultural events such as theaters, museums, and libraries. Social events may take place in offices and schools, during which some expectations of formal conduct are suspended while others are maintained. Dancing and singing may be perceived as appropriate, for example,[8] while vulgar joking and use of informal nicknames remain taboo. During the time I did observations at a linguistics institute the students there

7. Colombian expectations for "formal" behavior in church contrast with those perceived as formal by North Americans, however. Some religious ceremonies such as weddings, baptisms, and Mass may in fact seem relatively casual by North American standards. People who are not part of the event in progress wander in and out, chit-chat is common, and there is little emphasis on carefully orchestrated and rehearsed progression of the ritual. What looks to an American like informality may more accurately be a reflection of the degree to which participation in religious activity is an everyday event for these Colombians. Because the population is overwhelmingly Catholic (at least by upbringing and name), participation in church events is a routine shared experience instead of an out-of-the-ordinary event. Nonetheless, these Colombians expect behavior in church to be *formal* in many of the ways that characterize *formal* conduct in other circumstances: vulgarity (but not necessarily emotion) should be restrained, order should be generally maintained, and for the principals involved in ceremonies elegant dress is required.

8. In his recent journalistic work mentioned earlier, Gabriel García Márquez concurs: "The night that Maruja and Beatriz were kidnapped, the Villamizar home was full to bursting. People from political life and the government arrived, along with the families of both the kidnapped women. Azeneth Velázquez, patroness of the arts and a dear friend of the Villamizars, who lived upstairs, had taken on the role of hostess, and only the music was lacking for it to be the same as any other Friday night. It is inevitable: In Colombia, any reunion of more than six people, of whatever type at whatever hour, is doomed to become a dance." (1996, p. 32; my translation).

organized a *tertulia,* which they described to me as a highly informal gathering to celebrate the end of the semester. The gathering was held in a classroom, with plentiful snacks, wine, and general merrymaking. Some of the faculty participated, though they were not asked (as someone reported when I queried) to contribute toward the refreshments. They were addressed as *usted* throughout the evening, though there seemed to be an increased use of first names and casual touching among students and faculty. Toward the end of the event, the two most senior administrators made an appearance and were asked by the student organizers to say a few words. Although they each said essentially, "Isn't this nice, let's do it more often," I was struck by the formal tone of their remarks. As one of the administrators ceded to the other, he said, *"Ahora quiero darle la palabra al estimado Dr. Bernal"*—"Now I want to give the floor to the esteemed Dr. Bernal." Dr. Bernal was this man's subordinate, and I had heard him both address him as *tú*—reflecting the upper-class background of both men—and refer to him as *Jaimito,* a first-name diminutive.

This seemed a puzzling juxtaposition of ceremonial tones in what had been a very relaxed (and increasingly tipsy) gathering, yet none of the other participants seemed to find it odd. I asked a few of them their interpretations later on, and one commented: "Well, the usual structure of things was suspended for the evening. At some point there had to be something to bring everyone back to business as usual." "A close parenthesis," chimed in another listener, and there were nods of agreement. My interpretation is that the administrators heightened the perceived importance of the event by attending, and that they were asked to speak in recognition of that importance. Their presence made the event more *formal* both in the change of tone they brought about and in the sense of adding an official blessing that the students deeply appreciated.

Third, a distinction between sincere actions and ones that are hypocritical, or which lay deceptive claim to high status, is encoded in several of the native terms for talk discussed in previous chapters. Notice the difference between **ayudar**—to help—and **echar cepillo**—to curry favor. Bringing someone coffee could be interpreted either way, depending on the relationship between the giver and the receiver. Similarly, to correct a subordinate's use of an informal address term (insisting that one be addressed as **Dr. López** rather than **profe,** "Teach," for example) might be interpreted as **hacerse respetar**—to make oneself respected, considered a crucial aspect of maintaining order and thus a legitimate action. The same action could be heard as **dándoselas de importante** (making oneself seem important) in relationships where status differences are assumed to be nonexistent or unimportant. Other examples of actions which suggest sincere motivations and accurate claim to high status are

pedir un favor	to ask a favor
mostrar confianza	to show **confianza**
mostrar cariño	to show affection
mostrar respeto	to show respect
dar importancia a la persona	to show someone's importance

Actions which violate the premise of sincerity pursue a desired object—either the appearance of high status or the pretense of a close relationship—in the absence of true interpersonal interest or a basis for claiming the high status. Such violations are encoded in such actions as

ponerse confianzudo	to get too chummy
echar cepillo	to curry favor
coquetear	to sweet-talk
ser arribista	to be a social climber
dárselas de importante	to act important
ponerse títulos	to put on titles
ser interesado	to be an opportunist

Sincerity and appropriateness are not mutually exclusive evaluations of behavior. Some formal ceremonies and speeches can be profoundly sincere. Even when they cannot be performed with the deep affection, admiration, and respect expected in such ceremonies, however, those sentiments must still be elaborately conveyed for the actions to be perceived as appropriate.

For Colombians, nonetheless, many agonizing dilemmas are grounded in conflicts between sincerity as a motivation of human interaction and appropriateness as a dimension of evaluation. The mandate to show respect to an institutional or familial superior sometimes cannot be carried out with any sincere sense of deference to higher status, and often directly conflicts with the emotional climate of the moment.

The tension between sincerity and expectations of *formal* behavior are writ large into personal relationships, particularly friendship and romantic relationships. Proscriptions against close relationships between people of different social classes were described in Chapter 2. A symbolic term that encodes communal standards for a relationship that is desirable and appropriate is ***una relación formal.*** The cognate formal/*formal* would be misleading in this context; an accurate translation is "a proper relationship," with "proper" understood as conforming to shared understandings of desirable and appropriate bonds between persons. The term ***una relación formal*** is one I heard numerous times in discourse about romantic relationships. In this speech community, heterosexual romantic partners do not "date around," nor do they move from a period of casual dating to a more serious commitment that adds an expectation of exclusivity to the relational mix. Generally, unless they are introduced by someone connected to each of them, single people get to know one another as members of a larger group. If they are introduced by a friend or relative, their early interactions are likely to be in a larger group. "Blind dates" are almost unheard of. After some contact in such a group, often including seeking information about one another and vocal encouragement from other members of the group, the couple pairs off (***se cuadran,*** literally, "they square off"). Importantly, exclusivity is assumed from that time forward if the pairing off is defined as the beginning of an actual romantic relationship rather than a one-nighter.

Ironically (to my North American ears), fidelity to these unspoken contracts of exclusivity is rarely maintained. I asked one man in his late 20s, who always seemed to be juggling two or three romantic partners at a time with promises to each of them of his undying (and exclusive) love, why he didn't just admit to all of them that he was playing the field. He answered that none of them would accept such an arrangement; each would insist on ***una relación formal*** or nothing at all. This view was confirmed by several women: it was one thing, they said, for a boyfriend to see other women behind their backs (men were like that, after all), but to openly admit he planned to date other people meant that he wasn't a boyfriend at all. Fidelity might be semiopenly acknowledged as a fictitious premise, but it is a defining premise nonetheless for a publicly admissible romantic relationship.

It seems reasonable to infer from this configuration of dating practices, alongside the frequency (in discourse, at least) of extramarital affairs described in Chapter 2, to infer an assumption in this community that the existence of a prior romantic commitment does not extinguish or diminish the attraction between men and women. The concept that someone may be "off limits" because they are married or significantly involved with someone exists only to the degree that the involved person insists on remaining loyal to that pre-established bond. Although such loyalty is clearly the most appropriate stance toward extramarital (or extrarelational) invitations to romance, it runs counter to peoples' basic desires and therefore cannot be depended upon to control their behavior.

A great deal of public social control is exerted on male/female relationships, largely through norms of socializing in groups rather than in pairs. This may be partly due to a sense that sexual attraction is too powerful a force for individual persons to consistently resist on their own. Additionally, choices of significant others and mates have substantive consequences for people other than the principals.

Because contact between romantic partners and family members, friends, and perhaps workmates is inevitable, persons with **confianza** feel they share a stake in selection of such partners. Private advice, open statements of approval or disapproval (usually under the guise of joking or indirect compliments or criticism), and active intervention to facilitate or constrain romantic connections are thus commonplace. The only way to avoid the participation of others in one's love life is to keep it a secret. Explicitly requesting connected others to desist would either not be taken seriously or would jeopardize the relationship with the person attempting to intervene.

DILEMMA #2: CONFLICT BETWEEN VÍNCULOS

In an interpersonal context where persons are fundamentally defined by and through their connections, people and their actions are not surprisingly, evaluated on the basis of how adequately they sustain and show the importance of the connections. Because connections must be numerous and varied (to friends, classmates, workmates, service providers, among others; and family—a widely extended net all its own), and because of parallel hierarchies within society, each of which is accorded great importance, there are inevitably moments when responsibilities to one relationship conflict with the rights of other relational partners. Obviously I do not mean to suggest that such conflicts are unique to Colombian society or collectivist societies more generally; a recent study by Baxter and colleagues (Baxter et al., in press) suggests that they are probably inherent in most, if not all, speech communities. It does seem reasonable to infer that the greater the emphasis on personal involvement (particularly when defined as physical copresence, given the impossibility of being two places at once) and the greater the symbolic weight placed on relational responsibilities as opposed to personal desires, the more frequent and significant such clashes will become. In addition, some instances of conflict between relational ties may be noted that seem particularly characteristic of the Colombian ideology sketched thus far.

One poignant example of such a conflict was the subject of a family counseling session I observed. The therapist told the family's story this way, as summarized in my field notes:

> This is the mother and the five children (adults, 24–37 years old). The father, who is not married to the mother, is not with the family because he has children with another woman, to whom he *is* married. They are his legitimate family. His illegitimate family is known as his branch family (**el sucursal**). His children in the legitimate family are all **profesionales,** but in the branch family the father has never helped out his children at all. He returned to live with his first wife and family when the kids in his second family were all very small. Their mother has had to work very hard to support them on her own. Sometimes she slept 2, 3 hours a night and worked the rest of the time, sewing. Now her children are—well, they're doing OK—they have a family business, and they all work in that. Some of them have studied at night, and they've made some progress. But the father always throws in their faces that his *other* children are **profesionales** and everything. The children see their father, but their mother doesn't. She has said she just wants to forget about him and starts to cry if anyone mentions his name. All of the children have a lot of anger over their father's abandonment.

The family's reason for seeking help from a counselor was a series of nervous breakdowns for which the youngest son had been hospitalized several times in the previous year. The therapy session centered around his problems and the part the family played in causing, and should play in solving, them. A central question deliberated during this session was whether he would be better off continuing to live at home or moving somewhere else. Three of the five children lived at home and all of them, including the other two who were married, had lunch at home with their mother every day of the week. The therapist and several observers of the session, all Colombians, found this an unhealthy extreme of family unity, even within relational ideals that prized frequent contact and extensive involvement with family members.

Of more interest than the family's therapeutic issues, however, are the culturally situated reasons for their collective situation. The father's relationships with his two sets of children are clearly shaped by an ideology that values "legitimate" relationships over "nonlegitimate" ones and **profesionales** over those who run their own business despite limited education. He has helped his legitimate children become **profesionales,** thus securing their position at a socioeconomic level close to his own. In abandoning them the father did not entirely destroy the **vínculo** with his branch family children. By refusing to pay for their education, however, he created a social class distance that they are unlikely ever to bridge based on their own efforts. The emotional cost is also obvious. Ironically (or maybe predictably) enough, this group of therapists concluded that anger at the father who had treated them all so shabbily was what held this family so close together.

Another conflict of **vínculos** that appeared frequently in the discourse of these urban Colombians was rooted in the expectations of the workplace (both the work itself and personal ties to coworkers) and the needs and wants of friends and family members.

> José, 35, in a casual conversation about plans for the upcoming weekend: Tonight (Thursday) I have to go to a going-away party for one of the guys here at the hospital. I don't want to go. I really need to meet my cycling friends at the gym and work out, but what can I do? My boss called me in and told me about this cocktail party, and if I don't go (*points at his eyes, looking pointedly around, with a resigned expression* —i.e., "my absence will be noticed and commented on unfavorably"), they'll say "what's with this guy that he didn't show up to say goodbye?" But if I don't work out, the guys at the gym will ask the same thing, think I'm not serious about this ride we have planned for Saturday.

Aside from noting that he didn't really want to go to the cocktail party, this man's elaboration of his dilemma is centered squarely on his responsibilities to two different sets of connections, to the friends who cycle and to the workmates who expect him to socialize as well as work. The logic by which he made his decision was framed (at least in his account of the dilemma) within those connections to others and their attendant responsibilities, rather than his own preferences.

A similar situation was described in a recent report on the ongoing connection between the women described in Chapter 5. Josefina, now nearly 70, continues to work for Mariela a few times a week, over increasing protests from her sons and their families who claim they need her much more at home and that, after all these years, she deserves to retire. It is obvious to those who know them that Josefina enjoys the social contact with Mariela and her friends and family a great deal, and that she would work at least as hard at home if she were there rather than getting paid for working at Mariela's. According to Mariela, however, that is never what is said. Although Josefina's own desires certainly come into play in decisions about her continuing to work, they are clothed in the more culturally sensible garb of loyalty to an employer who has treated her well for many years and still needs her help.

A final piece of evidence for the frequency (or at least intelligibility) of conflicts between work ties and personal connections is suggested by a sign I saw posted in the lobby of one of the largest commercial organizations in Colombia. On top of the receptionist's desk, near a sign-in sheet on which all visitors were expected to register their presence, was an engraved message that I have never seen in a U.S. workplace. It stated that if the visitor wanted to see a company employee for personal reasons, the employee would have to come downstairs to the lobby. Visitors were allowed to the upper floors only for business reasons. In this company (and I am certain they were not unique in this regard, given the casual reception I got on personal visits to a number of organizations of various sizes and kinds), it was assumed that personal visits would happen on com-

pany time. One type of control the company could reasonably expect to exercise over those visits (and there are bound
to be other, more tacit ones) is their physical setting. Making personal visits openly visible both acknowledges their
importance and allows for overt influence on their frequency
and duration. The premise that personal relationships will
carry with them responsibilities that are not necessarily
suspended in favor of employment responsibilities is embodied in this company policy and derived, I would argue,
from a social context that accords importance to both types
of demands much more nearly equivalent than the counterparts in many U.S. speech communities.

DILEMMA #3: CONFIANZA VERSUS AUTHORITY/RESPECT

As noted in Chapter 2, **confianza** is the degree of trust and
closeness that exists in a relationship. The greater the **confianza,** the greater the latitude in interaction for address
term use, joking, asking favors, seeking **palanca,** and so
forth. Yet the cultural premises that (a) **confianza** is basic
to human social existence and (b) authority is an organiz-
ing principle for orderly conduct present a contradictory pull
in a wide range of personal relationships. **Confianza** carries the risk of abuses, and authority carries the opposing
risks of distance and subversion.

Families in particular are a system of personal relationships that incorporates **confianza** and authority in their
most complex configuration. On one hand, the people with
whom one's worldview and life experiences most closely
overlap, and with whom one's future is most securely intertwined, are members of the family. On the other, because
of the primordial significance of the family of origin in interpersonal life, status as a "family member" is a characteristic that must be accorded the greatest possible respect.
Parents spoke of the need to exercise authority over their
children in order to guide their development, yet insisted
they would never wish to maintain distance from the per-

sons they are most directly connected to by blood and affection. Because authority ordinarily requires some distance (as described in Chapter 3), a dilemma is created. Some of the latitude Colombian children seemed to have to ignore their parents' and teachers' directives may derive from a slow erosion of rigid family hierarchy, in favor of an ideal that emphasizes unity (and thus **confianza**) instead.

Among the Colombians I knew and worked with, of all social classes, offspring lived at home until they married (and sometimes even after they married, particularly among the working classes, where living independently was not always an option). In this community it was unusual for young people to seek out a job or educational opportunities somewhere besides where their families lived. If they did need to move elsewhere to pursue some opportunity, they generally lived with extended family members or at least with family friends. The idea of renting a room or an apartment from a stranger was regarded with horror because of the enormous risk (and assumed isolation) perceived in living someplace where the only connection was a financial one. Thus, adult children often well into their 30s, perhaps well established in their careers, very commonly lived with their parents. The degree to which parents would continue to exercise authority over those offspring often (though certainly not always) created significant tension in those situations.

Within the general postulate that hierarchy is a logical, even necessary, condition of human social life, there are a number of parallel hierarchical structures in Colombia that are meaningful sources of power and authority. Table 6.1 details some of those structures, their bases of power, and other dimensions of contrast among them.

Parallel hierarchies can present many instances of conflicting **vínculos** in public and private life. Teachers who work in upper-class private schools, for example, are generally from middle-class, sometimes working-class backgrounds. In this speech community, where class is pervasively attended to as a relevant attribute of social identity, this disparity frequently creates problems in keeping order

TABLE 6.1. Component Analysis: Dimensions of Authority in Urban Colombia

Basis of authority	Positive (+), negative (−), neutral (0) affect	Participation by choice?	Basis of power[a]	How acquired	Effects of/on social class	Bond linking members to hierarchy
Family	+	No	Legitimate; reward	Social agreement that family exists	Individual position linked to family's	Blood; social sanction
Occupational status (e.g., client/service provider)	0[b]	Somewhat	Reward	Social class, educational level, family membership, *palanca*	Experience being servant/served	Service-oriented economy dependent on human labor
Education	+	No[c]	Referent	Social class, "godparents," personal talent, *palanca*	Social class largely determines access and quality	Belief in education as scarce resource; connection of education to social status
Organizations (schools, corporations, etc.)	0	Yes	Legitimate, expert, reward	Education, experience, *palanca*	Type of school (public/private), rank in organization	Membership in organization (sometimes) inspires loyalty

Military status	–	Yes[d]	Coercive	Enlistment or draft	Rank depends on educational level[e]	High in-group cohesion; fear and distaste among population
The church	+/–	Yes	Legitimate; referent, to some	Decision of individual, or family for offspring	Access to some services influenced by palanca[f]	Tradition makes this a pervasive metaphor, at least
Government/ the law	0[g]	No	Some reward, coercive	Participation in mainstream society	Degree to which people are subject to enforcement	Common experience of government as capricious and law as tenuous force

[a]French and Raven (1971) describe five bases of power: reward, referent (power of A derives from B's desire to emulate A), legitimate, expert (power is derived from expertise), and coercive (power to punish).

[b]I.e., "that's just the way the world works"—see Chapter 3 for elaboration.

[c]Educational opportunities are strongly tied to class position. Members of middle and upper classes are unlikely ever to consider not taking advantage of opportunities to pursue education; members of lower classes infrequently have such opportunities. One informant noted, "There's no such thing as a dropout in Colombia. Anyone who can go to school, does."

[d]Those with money, palanca, or a convincing excuse (such as medical conditions or family responsibilities) can avoid military service if they desire. Legally, it is obligatory for every male at age 18.

[e]Lowest ranks are therefore always from lower socioeconomic classes. Belonging to the military is the first position of power many of them have ever had, one reason why they are widely feared: this is their chance to resist the system in which they have always been powerless.

[f]E.g., palanca can enable Mass to be conducted in one's home. Other services such as baptisms and weddings may be out of reach of poor people because of the festivities expected to accompany them. Marriages may be annulled only through complex, lengthy processes usually requiring both money and palanca, putting that completely out of reach of working classes.

[g]Laws are perceived as so ineffective that little affect is attached to their existence. Enforcement is seen as a remote possibility, but enough of one to create some fear of punishment (or, at minimum, police brutality) on capture.

among the students, who may be openly disdainful of teachers' authority. Foreign teachers and Colombians who have
studied abroad are eagerly sought in some schools of this
type because the cachet of internationalism outweighs one's
actual economic status.

DILEMMA #4: BEING *VERRACA* IN A *MACHISTA* SOCIETY

In Chapter 5, the fact that both Mariela and Josefina were
verracas (tough broads) was mentioned as one basis for
the close relationship between them. The term and its symbolic implications for identity, as well as personal relationships, are at the center of a fourth dilemma embedded in
the ideology of connectedness among these Colombians.

The term ***verraca*** is derived from the male form ***verraco***—literally, an uncastrated pig. In both female and male
forms, the word can be used as an adjective to describe
actions, people, and situations more generally. ***Una tarea
verraca*** is a difficult task; *¡qué verraco!* can either mean
"what a jerk!" or be a semiadmiring comment on a man's
daring and bravery.[9] The common threads of meaning that
link these diverse uses of the term are boldness, bravery,
and strength: a difficult task or situation requires strength,
a bold person may act in ways that are offensive and thus
be a jerk.

Given the communal understanding that Colombia is
a ***machista*** society (a sentiment I heard voiced any number of times by both men and women, though notably only
middle-class ones), it is significant that many uses of the
term are compliments when used to describe women. A

9. Carlos Lleras Restrepo, President of Colombia in the late 1960's, is
an easily recognized typification of a **verraco.** On one occasion he
appeared on national television at 5 P.M. and declared a curfew in Bogotá
for 6 P.M. that same day, promising that violators would be jailed. At
6 P.M., the streets were empty. "Now *that* was a *leader,* " is the admir-
ing recollection of many Colombians these days, weary of continuous
violence and the government's inability to control it.

response to an inquiry about meanings of **verraca** (or **berraca,** as it is sometimes spelled) posted on the internet hotline described in the Introduction was the following:

> One says that a woman is a **verraca** *(es una verraca)* when no one can get the best of her, no one can dominate her or fool her, when she is capable of coming out ahead in the face of difficulties. One says that a woman IS **verraca** (**está verraca**) when she won't stand for contradiction, when you'd better stay out of her way.

Both men and women can also be **verracos,** that is, exceptionally accomplished, in a particular area (playing soccer or the violin, arguing politics, doing mathematics, etc.) Excellence and toughness are thus celebrated by the term as applied to women as well as men. These positive connotations might seem surprising from a stereotypical notion of **machista** ideals, if those ideals are assumed to revolve around female submissiveness or subordination. Yet there have always been arenas in which Colombian women legitimately took control in interaction and decision making, and in which they could establish and claim valued identities. Traditionally, of course, their primary arena of influence was in matters of home, family, children's education, and entertaining. In a society that values relationships so highly, particularly those with members of extended family, it would be inaccurate to assume that this sphere of control became less important when it was assigned to women. Tales also abound of brave women who played important roles during Colombia's years of political turmoil, such as the following:

> One, named Elvira, tied to an olive press, asks that [her captors] kill the newborn son in her arms if she is to die in the flames . . . . The lieutenant looking at the woman suffocating in the smoke of her own home asks her: "Are all you women like this?"
> "This is how they all should be!" responds Elvira . . .
> "Release her for her courage!" responds the official. (Franco Isaza, 1959; quoted in Gúzman, Fals, & Umaña, 1986, p. 145; my translation).

In the past two generations, women in Colombia have had more opportunities to develop their abilities and exercise their influence, although such chances are predictably confined largely to the middle and upper classes. Although education was (and still is) sometimes discouraged for, or denied to, female members of a family, for a daughter to become a *profesional* is widely perceived to enhance the family's stature. In the workplace and politics, Colombian women (particularly upper class ones, with upper-class connections) have oftentimes had greater access to powerful positions than their U.S. counterparts.

These positive connotations of being *verraca* nonetheless contrast with expectations that women be more tender and nurturant, and less vulgar and violent, than men are perceived to be. The dilemma presented by these contrasting virtues applies to social identity. Being *verraca* is good, being *mandona* (domineering) is bad, and demonstrating a strong will may be evaluated either way. It is certainly possible that women's actions are evaluated differently than men's are, in much the way that gender research in the United States has suggested, making the identity of *verraca* a finer line for females to construct than enacting forcefulness is for males. There is a linguistic difference here, however, that may suggest a cultural one: *verraco* and *verraca* are variants on the same word and both carry positive connotations (and male and female forms of domineering, *mandón/mandona,* are equally negative). In American English, the term "bitch" applied to women perceived to be too forceful has no male equivalent.

This dilemma extends to personal relationships as well. In some cases, the positive attributes associated with being a *verraca* can be the basis for attraction, in both friendship (as in that between Mariela and Josefina) and for heterosexual romantic relationships, as noted by some male members of the community.

E-mail respondent Mauricio: For many men, including me, we would be delighted to have a partner who was a *verraca,* in the sense of someone who is not fragile, who was very good at something, and who could be a partner in times of difficulty. . . . I know that if it weren't for my wife's **verraquera** (**verraca**ness) I wouldn't be where I am.

Germán, 39, engineer: The women I dated seriously were all **verracas**—strong, opinionated, ambitious to have careers, and that was always what I was looking for—and found—in a wife. I never wanted someone who would defer to me.

Certainly it is difficult to know how widespread this admiration for **verracas** is compared to the opposing, **machista** ideal that would still opt for a protected (and subordinate) role for women. I also observed many instances where women who were forceful and outspoken with their male partners in private adopted a much more soft-spoken, indirect manner with them in public, suggesting that under some circumstances it might not be acceptable to admit just how much influence the woman exerts in the relationship. Although I have only minimal data to bring to bear on this point, I suspect that being a **verraca** creates complexity within romantic relationships as well as attraction, particularly when the male partner is **machista.** Those difficulties are likely also to be evident in the public self-presentation of the couple to a social world from which the contradictory premises about desirable characteristics emerged in the first place.

The complementary dilemmas created by the value placed on being a **verraca** in a society that labels itself **machista** suggest the analytical utility of a theory of personal relationships framed around contradiction. Four dilemmas of social identity and personal relationships have been described as they are specifically implicated by an interpersonal ideology centered around connectedness. Alongside the culturally distinctive contours of these dilemmas, however, there have been obvious parallels to issues faced by friends, romantic partners, family members, and so forth in the United States, and probably many other cultures as well. Those parallels suggest that these contradictions and dilemmas may be culture specific instantiations of more universal dynamics of personal relationships. Thus, the final section of this chapter discusses integration of the Hymesian framework of cultural analysis that has been at the heart of the Colombian case study with a dialectical theory developed by Baxter and colleagues that enlightens the relational dynamics of the four dilemmas just described. That integration captures empirically, analytically, and conceptually the nature of interpersonal ideology as I have sought to develop it here.

CULTURAL DILEMMAS AS RELATIONAL DIALECTICS

According to Bakhtin (1929/1984, 1981), the contradiction between unity and separation—what he termed the dialogic condition—is central to sociality. Baxter and her colleagues (Baxter, 1992, 1993; Baxter & Montgomery, 1996) propose that personal relationships are a paradigm case of this central contradiction. Personal relationships are characterized by a fusion of multiple voices and constituted within contradictory forces; they are part of the social order as well as separated from the social order through participants' construction of a system of meaning specific to the relationship. From this view, the ongoing tension between unifying and differentiating forces is organized around three dialectics: integration–separation, stability–change, and expression–privacy (see Table 6.2). These dialectics are manifested, in turn, in six basic contradictions, three of which are internal (i.e., constituted within the relationship) and three of which are external (i.e., tensions between the relationship and the social system). These contradictions may be experienced both intrapersonally (though Baxter and Montgomery emphasize the social self, not a monadic, cognitive self, as traditionally construed in personal relationships literature) and interpersonally, and may be managed through communication strategies of selection, separation, and integration (Baxter, 1988, 1990; Baxter & Montgomery, 1996).

TABLE 6.2. Internal and External Contradictions in Personal Relationships (Baxter, 1993)

	Dialectic of integration–separation	Dialectic of stability–change	Dialectic of expression–privacy
Internal	Connection–autonomy	Predictability–novelty	Openness–closedness
External	Inclusion–seclusion	Conventionality–uniqueness	Revelation–concealment

It is worth noting that relational dialectics is a heuristic theory, intended to orient observation and discussion of personal relationships in particular directions rather than to predict behavior or provide the basis for testable hypotheses. In that sense it is similar to Hymes's (1972) model of language and social interaction, and the SPEAKING framework (see footnote 2 of Introduction), which served as the theoretical basis for description of urban Colombian culture presented here. These two heuristics emerged from distinct disciplines, of course, and were directed at quite different questions. Hymes's mnemonic and the conceptual scheme of speech communities, speech events, speech situations, and so forth provided a vocabulary for discovering patterned and meaningful ways of speaking within particular cultures, and making cross-cultural comparisons to advance understanding of the integral connection between language and social interaction. Baxter and Montgomery's dialectic theory provided a way of seeing and hearing contradictions, discerning opposing (centripetal and centrifugal) forces, and locating the particular issues around which those forces are enacted, in personal relationships.

It is precisely at the interstices of these two heuristics that I mean to locate interpersonal ideology. The SPEAKING framework captures the cultural specificity of speech activities; it is a perspective very closely tied to everyday

communication practices through which people form, maintain, and understand their personal relationships. Relational
dialectics, in turn, highlight the multivocal, dilemmatic tugs
and pulls of the interplay between relational partners (and
between them and the social collectivities that surround
them), discouraging any notion of a unidimensional or uniformly coherent system of meaning shared equally among
members of a social group.

Neither framework on its own adequately captures the
concept that I have approached in this book as interpersonal ideology. A cultural perspective intended to describe
all speech activities may be applied to interpersonal activities, such as describing those actions that work to increase
confianza or distance, thus negotiating the nature of a
relationship. Yet it gives only a vague sense of what happens within particular relationships, how close relationships
function differently from casual ones, how relational partners come to influence each other to the extent that they
do, and so on.

Relational dialectics, on the other hand, situates personal relationships very firmly within social contexts, and
in fact presumes the boundary between a relationship and
society to be blurred and permeable. The "communicative
interface between couples and culture" (Baxter & Montgomery, 1996, p. 162ff.) is itself assumed to be the site of
dialectical tensions and dilemmas. Social collectivities have
considerable interest in the shape and conduct of personal
relationships, and those interests are conveyed persua-
sively, even directively, to relational partners. Relational
partners, in poaching and adapting cultural resources, re-
create their social collectivities. Yet this perspective on
relationships, committed as it is to the interplay of culture
and relationships, offers no descriptive apparatus for discovering and describing the particular dialectics (and particular instantiations of dialectics) that characterize specific
speech communities.

In Chapter 7 I will elaborate on a concept of interpersonal ideology that incorporates the emphasis on cultural
distinctiveness characteristic of Hymes's approach to speech

activities with the emphasis on dilemmas and contradictions of personal relationships illuminated by relational dialectics. I will pay particular attention to the nexus of institutional power and social accountability through which interpersonal ideology exerts its force in social life. In the final section of this chapter, however, I elaborate on connections between some Colombian practices and premises of interpersonal life and the dialectics described by Baxter and Montgomery, to demonstrate congruencies and distinctions that suggest the conceptual richness of the integration I propose.

COLOMBIAN RELATIONAL DIALECTICS

There are some obvious points at which the Colombian data are easily subsumed within the exact dialectics described by Baxter and Montgomery (1996). Conflicts between *vínculos,* for example, such as decisions about spending time with friends or family members, or whether to include a romantic partner in a group of same-sex friends, are consistent with the inclusion–exclusion contradiction. There are certainly culture-specific tinges to the dynamics of that dilemma, specifically the value system that privileges connections among people of similar social status and severely constrains cross-sex friendship.

Further, the dilemma between authority and *confianza,* particularly embedded within ideals of showing respect through "formal" behavior, can be understood as a tension between the predictability of traditional hierarchy and the novelty allowed by relative freedom (granted in equal measure as *confianza*) from the restrictions entailed by that system. Similarly, limits on the extent to which a *verraca*'s strength and influence in a romantic relationship may be publicly displayed could reflect a tension between conventionality (appearing to adhere to traditional *machista* ideals of dominant males) and uniqueness (the couple's shared expectations of rights, responsibilities, and roles within the relationship).

Finally, the monologic conception of openness characteristic of much U.S. research and theory in personal
relationships was usefully reformulated by Baxter and
Montgomery (1996) as a dynamic contradiction between
openness and closedness. From the relational dialectics
perspective, all interaction revolves around the unsaid, as
well as the said. Outer speech (utterances) reflects inner
dialogues about how one's relational partner may respond,
how distant others might interpret one's actions, whether
one is behaving in an ethical and moral manner, and so forth.
With this dialogic conceptualization of openness–closedness,
Baxter and Montgomery facilitate analysis of relationships
on a culture's own terms about desirable models of communicative conduct and the kinds of communication that
constitute "good" relationships. This formulation breaks free
of the notion that relational partners necessarily grapple
with dilemmas of revealing or concealing an inner, private, unique self, a notion of personhood discussed by some
ethnographers as specific to U.S. middle-class culture (cf.
Carbaugh, 1988; Katriel & Philipsen, 1981; and others).

An interpersonal ideology such as the one described
in earlier chapters that revolves around connections between
persons and on appropriateness much of the time locates
the desires and preferences of the individual as subordinate
to appropriate public performances of roles. These premises
about personhood and relationships are reflected in what
may (must, should, can) be said as well as what may not
(must not, should not, cannot). In this system, **confianza**
increases license for sincerity, though it is very often not
equivalent to openness in any sense related to candor. Family members may, because of very high degrees of **confianza** with one another, be very sincere in expressing
preferences, dislikes, annoyance, and so forth. Yet any rev-
elation of feelings or experiences that violates the code of
appropriateness—notions of hierarchy, relational ideals of
harmony, and so forth—though it may accurately represent
the inner state of the speaker, threatens the bond between
that person and the hearer. Thus, feelings that constitute
such violations are rarely expressed openly. For Josefina to

say honestly to her employer, close friend, and godmother of one of her grandchildren, "It hurts my feelings when you call me a walkabout doo-doo head, when after all I went all the way to the market just to buy you a fish;" for an adult child to say to his or her parent "I think I'm grown up enough now to make my own decisions about who I go out with and when I come home, so why don't you mind your own business"; or for a child from a "branch family" to confess to her father that "I feel really disrespected when you throw it in my face that your other kids are professionals and we're not; after all, that's more your doing than ours, isn't it?"— none of these expressions of candor would be seen as sensible within the culture.

Nonetheless, it is simply not the case that openness is less highly valued in urban Colombian society than in the United States. Among people of even moderate *confianza*, questions may be asked ("So how much money will you make in this new job?" "Whom did you vote for?") and information may be offered ("My daughter-in-law punched her child in the nose last night") that would be heard as sensitive disclosures by U.S. middle-class standards. Plainly, however, the inner dialogues are framed much differently, and the outward expressions are differently constrained, congruent with the contours of the specific interpersonal ideology that underlies them. The license for sincerity in relationships of high *confianza* does not cover expression of inner states that would challenge certain basic definitional premises of personal relationships, but it does allow for other kinds of information exchange.

In some other aspects, Colombian dialectics of personal relationships seem to be shaped quite differently than those described by Baxter and Montgomery, who acknowledge that the dialectics they propose are based on a large body of primarily Euro-American research on personal relationships. The notion that connection versus autonomy is a dilemma central to personal relationships, for example, is almost certain to be perceived and experienced differently in a speech community that so highly values interdependence and connection than it would be in an individualistic culture, such as many middle-class U.S. American speech communities. It is an empirical question whether, and how, such a dilemma applies between relational partners who take seriously an interpersonal ideology that defines persons as sets of bonds to others. There may well be such a dilemma, and I hasten to emphasize that I have no data to support any claim that these urban Colombians do not experience autonomy–connection as a dialogic process in their personal relationships. It could well be, in fact, that such tensions were all around me and I missed them because of being struck by (and thus focusing primarily on) the connectional ideal of personhood elucidated and so frequently enacted. Nonetheless, it seems more useful to ask the question of *whether* autonomy–connection is a relational dilemma in this speech community, given its particular interpersonal ideology, than to ask (as most cross-cultural research does) *how* that dilemma, proposed and tested within an individualistic culture, is enacted.

A second implicit assumption of the relational dialectics that emerges in light of the Colombian case concerns the notion that the primordial configuration of relational partners is the "couple" (see particularly Baxter & Montgomery, 1996, ch. 7). When describing relational *partners,* Colombians seemed often to envision a larger cast of participants than North Americans do. Friendship seems to happen more commonly in groups than in dyads, for example, and references to "my family" almost certainly include extended family in most cases. Even romantic partnerships and marriage may be less intrinsically conceptualized as dyadic arrangements in Colombia. Rather than assuming that romantic pairs must have privacy in order to develop, for instance, the frequency and vigor of these Colombians' interventions in couples' relationships may mean that relationships require help and company more than they need space. Similarly, rather than viewing a child "in the middle of the parents' marriage" as a dysfunctional state of affairs for both child and marital pair, there was much to suggest that once a couple had a child they were no longer uniquely (or even primarily) a couple. I saw children integrally involved in adult activities in Colombia to a much greater degree than in the United States, and I found no way to explain to Colombians the practice of U.S. married couples seeking time for themselves (and their "relationship") away from their children. It could be that the dyadic emphasis of much personal relationships research in the United States is a further reverberation of individualistic bias noted by a number of theorists (Duck, West, & Acitelli, 1997; Lannaman, 1991; and others) that is embedded to a certain degree in relational dialectics as well.

In sum, there are several aspects of relational dialectics theory that usefully encompass the Colombian data, showing the configurations of personal relationships dilemmas to be culture-specific instantiations of more widespread, perhaps universal, dynamics of relationships within a social context. There are other particulars of the Colombian data to support the notion, foreseen by Baxter and Montgomery, that the particular relational dialectics in operation must be discovered for each culture.

Chapter 7 elaborates on the concept of interpersonal ideology as a subset of culture specifically relevant to personal relationships by unpacking the ontological status of premises as the central component, and by considering the nature of power inherent in this conception of ideology. Subsequently, the unique perspective offered by comparison of cultural case studies for building theory is elucidated.

CHAPTER SEVEN

PERSONAL RELATIONSHIPS IN COMPARATIVE PERSPECTIVE

The usual assumption in personal relationships research and theorizing has been, until recently, that what develops between people is entirely the result of their individual qualities and needs, and what they have communicated to each other about themselves. This book has taken an opposite approach, attributing much of what happens between people in relationships to what is possible within the framework of their culture's premises, beliefs, and values about personhood, relationships, and communication itself. Further, it has implicitly challenged the notion that the values and assumptions embedded in personal relationships research and theory constructed in Euro-American contexts are universal. The task that remains is to make explicit how research and theory in personal relationships can be enriched by the kind of detailed consideration of interpersonal ideology undertaken in Chapters 2–6. Two benefits of research of this kind may be briefly sketched:

1. The cultural approach illustrated here suggests new categories of communicative phenomena to attend to in studying relationships that tie them directly to the social context in which they exist (in this case, personal address, directive sequences, narrative genres that specifically encode cultural symbols, and everyday conversation). Talk practices through which relationships are developed and maintained are interrogated for their patterns and meanings on a social level, as well as within the relationship itself.

2. Case studies of speech communities allow for comparative research, which itself carries several implications. First, comparison across cultures offers a basis for examining (and expanding) scope conditions of communication theories beyond Euro-American late-twentieth-century society. By studying personal relationships in other speech communities we, as people who live in speech communities and have relationships, as well as studying, theorizing and teaching about them, come to know ourselves better. We can see more clearly (and thus be in a better position to show others) how specific cultural premises shape the construction of identities and relationships and the role of communication in those constructions. Finally, understanding other models of personhood and relating offers new alternatives for analyzing relationship processes, and being in relationships, that are not apparent from within a single system.

Each of these implications requires some expansion. First, the concept of interpersonal ideology suggested throughout the book will be elucidated further, with specific attention to the ontological status of cultural premises and to the nature and conceptual role of power. Second, the kinds of comparisons across community-specific case studies that may show the impact of cultural systems of symbolic meaning on configurations and processes of personal relationships will be illustrated.

INTERPERSONAL IDEOLOGY

Throughout this book, certain symbolic resources that cohere and warrant social interaction have been referred to as *interpersonal ideology*. Interpersonal ideology was proposed in Chapter 1 as *a set of premises about personhood, relationships and communication around which people formulate lines of action toward others, and interpret others' actions*. Interpersonal ideology, then, is a subset of cultural premises related most specifically to interpersonal relationships, as opposed to (for example), beliefs about wellness and illness, pedagogical concerns, economic and religious practice, and so forth.

To describe a system of symbolic premises as ideology is to incur a historical residue of meaning embedded in the term "ideology." Specifically, power becomes an issue. From the critical tradition of social theory, power has generally been understood in terms of conflict and contradiction between interested parties, implying struggle for domination between classes, races, sexes, or other social groups. Lannaman (1991, 1994) and others have shown the utility and reasonableness of connecting this notion of power to the localized actions of interlocutors. When social accountability is examined as a locus of power, the interactive constraints through which interlocutors position themselves and are positioned by others in conversation are interrogated as the means for joint action and construction of meaning.[1]

1. The power aspects of the interpersonal ideology of connectedness described in this book have been somewhat implicit, in favor of a Hymesian–Geertzian tradition of ethnography that privileges the natives' point of view. The analysis relied heavily on native terms for talk, above all, speech events with names, as the starting point for elucidating the premises of the ideology. Nonetheless, the power of ideology to enable and constrain action in both hegemonic and social accountability terms is central to the definition I have proposed here.

This vision of power is consistent with the notion, widely accepted within interpersonal conflict literature (e.g., Duck, 1994) that power is relationally constructed, not a static property of individuals. People in relationships exert influence with (and over) one another by way of symbolic resources poached (de Certeau, 1984) from a culture-specific framework of premises. Retrieving the relational dialectics perspective discussed in the last chapter, power may be further conceptualized as a dynamic, contradictory set of forces that constrain and enable the relational configurations that partners work out between themselves.

In the urban Colombian system described in this book, connections to others, hierarchy, and/or role enactment are in many circumstances more highly valued bases for action than are personal characteristics or preferences. That valuation, stemming from premises about the fundamentally incomplete nature of a human individual and the primal importance of interpersonal connectedness, carries direct consequences for formulating and interpreting lines of action. Framing personal objectives in terms of connectedness or in ways that acknowledge (though they may subvert as easily as uphold it) the hierarchy will more readily be heard as coherent, and often will be accorded more legitimacy in such a system, than invoking the rights of individuals to realize their unique desires.

Although frameworks of shared understanding are a natural outgrowth of (and a facilitative condition for) communal life, their existence does not enable or depend upon consensus. Membership in a community is accomplished through recognizing and participating in comprehensible, valued ways of speaking; yet membership, like relational partnership, is contested and negotiated dialogically. People deploy shared symbolic resources to pursue social ends that deny or resist the configurations of meaning most highly valued in a community, just as they seek legitimation within that same symbolic system. They may inwardly rage or outwardly protest the constraints placed on selves, relationships, and communication by particular systems of meaning. Nonetheless, living within a community requires shared symbolic resources that make ways of speaking patterned and meaningful, and thus enable coordinated social action. Ideology may be defied, and indeed, defiance is a strong form of recognition. It can rarely be ignored. Likewise, although ideology may be imposed (Chang, 1992, is a fascinating account of this), it will never survive in lived experience as a monolithic voice. There will always be some possibility for opposition, resistance, and contradictory forces and voices.

Throughout this book I have emphasized *shared* understandings as fundamental to interpersonal ideology. Such a focus on the communal aspects of interpersonal ideology does not negate the possibility—even probability—of asymmetries, in which some voices are heard too softly, or are illegitimately interrupted or ridiculed. Certainly there are instances in which participants in conversation have unequal access to resources (information, experience, credibility, valued identities) relevant to the task at hand, which show up in discourse as asymmetrical patterns of positioning and influence (e.g., Markova & Foppa, 1991). Clearly there are connections between hegemonic social structures and everyday interaction; some were readily hearable in the talk of these Colombians. An offhand remark that the GARdener must be good in bed (for a middle-class woman to date him); ridicule of, and discrimination against, **costeños** for their perceived lack of sophistication and manners; linking women and children together as persons who should be talked to "tenderly"; an employer whose address term alternatives allow for many more constructions of an employee's competence than vice versa—all of these are moments in which hegemony and social accountability arguably become one, and are enacted in the processes of personal relationships. There is no question that institutionalized asymmetries are constructed through and played out in (and may be challenged through) interaction, and that those asymmetries are performed through discourses of power that emerge from shared, perhaps conflicted, experiences of pursuing interpersonal objectives. Those discourses of power, in turn, are shaped by cultural premises that value certain patterns and interpretations of action and thus legitimate and reinforce them over other possible lines of action and interpretations (Montgomery, 1988, makes a similar point).

These questions of power are significant ones for researchers and theorists in personal relationships to consider in that they suggest a dimension of connection between partners in relationships and the social context of those relationships that has been suggested, yet inadequately explored. Although the primary focus of this book has been on social context as inseparably tied to processes of relating, the conceptualization of interpersonal ideology formulated here can readily be applied to some of the traditional concerns of personal relationships research (such as relational expectations and satisfaction; e.g., Zimmer, 1986; Fincham & Bradbury, 1990; Allan, 1993) by making explicit the communal basis of those aspects of relationships. By locating power within relationships as well as in communal understandings of relating, interpersonal ideology offers a lens through which to see variations in enactment as well as common themes.

A second issue of some importance in this notion of interpersonal ideology is to clarify the nature of premises. To say that interactants draw upon the premises of interpersonal ideology to construct meaning *through talk* implies that premises are retrievable *from talk*. It does not imply, as some have construed, that ideology is either a fixed and static set of "instructions" to apply to an ordered variety of circumstances, or that culture amounts to shared cognitive categories that exist in abstraction and submerge the diversity of everyday life. Rather than beliefs, values, attitudes, or "knowledge" (the traditional centerpieces of many conceptualizations of culture; see, e.g., Leeds-Hurwitz, 1995; Lustig & Koester, 1996) I propose that premises are a more appropriate focal point for an approach to culture centered around language use. I use "premises" in the rhetorical sense, consistent with other linguistic metaphors that reinforce the notion of ideology as constructed in, and visible through, language use (e.g., vocabularies of motives, cf. Burke, 1950; language games, Wittgenstein, 1953). The premises that constitute particular interpersonal ideologies are based on ideas of what is warranted and what is not between people in relationships, in certain circumstances, and in understandings of when talk does (and does not) come into play. They are bases for using talk in particular ways to reach certain objectives, and for discerning others' objectives from their talk. Premises are thus the basis for making sense of action (both formulating lines of action to reach particular goals and interpreting the actions of others, when they act in expected ways and when they do not).

Further, premise captures more fully the taken-for-granted, usually invisible sense in which culture operates as an influence on everyday interaction. This notion of ideology as a set of premises rejects the radical constructivist position that cultural ideals have no power or meaning until they are constructed between individuals in interaction, a perspective that obviates the importance of past experience, cross-situational patterns of use and meaning and that privileges (in my view, to a conceptually unproductive extreme for purposes of most personal relationships research) the particular and the local over the communal. Defining interpersonal ideology as a system of resources drawn upon to make sense of action, hearable in everyday language use, suggests a further point of connection between personal relationships and social context. To the extent that relationships are understood as processes that unfold through talk, it makes sense to study the talk practices through which relationships and identities are constructed. The kinds of communication phenomena focused on here provide useful starting points for such inquiry. The examination of conversation between relational partners, such as the one offered as part of this analysis, when combined with investigation of patterns and meanings of culturally infused communicative phenomena, provide a way of tacking between local particulars and the communal resources from which they are created.

Having emphasized the power-laden nature of interpersonal ideology, it is just as important to note that both hegemony and social accountability are culturally situated.

Gender role expectations are obviously rooted in culture, as are communal understandings of class, ethnicity, sexuality, and a host of relational configurations, among them notions of family, marriage, friendship, romantic relationships, and so forth. More importantly, the means of resistance and change (and, indeed, understandings of the possibilities for change) are grounded in community-specific symbolic systems. It is those communal understandings that infuse the interactions and relational histories of partners. Often (though not always) traditional critical theory downplays the cultural symbolic context of institutionalized power imbalances. Oppression is examined solely in terms of the social structural factors that create and sustain it, with little attention to its community-specific symbolic contours, perhaps because of a sense that "merely" symbolic aspects of power pale in significance compared to the material ones. The sturdiest accounts of power may be those that situate members' understandings of who has power and why, and when and how it is being exercised, against a background of critical theory. Willis (1977) provides a classic example of this type of work. Comparison of the Colombian data to other case studies may further illuminate this point.

A COMPARATIVE GLANCE AT POWER IN INTERPERSONAL IDEOLOGY

Given the conceptual commitment to power inherent in the term "interpersonal ideology," some attention to macrosocial structures of power and how they may be linked to personal relationships is necessary to illuminate the term. I proposed in Chapter 6 that parallel sources of authority in Colombia constitute a system that is pervasively hierarchical and oriented toward preserving status differences. The bases of power that constitute and sustain these parallel hierarchies are significantly different and carry quite different connotations. The power of the family hierarchy, for example, is derived from social agreement that members are connected by blood and ***confianza*** and connotes positive affect. The power of the military is derived from high in-group cohesion and a great deal of fear, among the general populace, of their coercive capabilities, thus connoting a negative affect. Authority is an important symbol to Colombians because of the perception that, however fragile or untrustworthy these parallel hierarchies might seem, they are the only enduring forces of order in a potentially chaotic world. Thus, although the aims and directives of superiors in any of these hierarchies may be subverted or evaded, legitimacy of the structures themselves is very rarely questioned.

Keshavarz (1988) describes forms of address in postrevolutionary Iran in terms of only two structures of authority, but the cultural ideology of hierarchy suggested in that account provides an enlightening comparison to the Colombian system. The author notes that the massive demonstrations during the revolution of 1978–1979, which brought an end to a centuries-old monarchy, also "brought different strata and sections of society close together and narrowed the wide gaps previously existing among different social classes" (Keshavarz, 1988, p. 566). Because the revolution was as much religious as it was social, however, respect borne of fear for the nobility was transformed into renewed reverence for the religious hierarchy. This is evidenced by the respectful terms reserved for those who have made the pilgrimage to Mecca. The traditional values of self-abasement, humility, and extreme politeness are still reflected in personal address, such as the common honorific term for self-reference, *bænde* (slave, servant). Terms used to address and refer to the royal family, aristocracy, and high officials have been eradicated, and the terms *bæradær* (brother) and *xahær* (sister) are now used in ways parallel to "comrade" after the Russian and Chinese revolutions. Unlike "comrade," however, *bæradær* and *xahær* carry overtones of religious association, as well as revolutionary solidarity.

The Iranian revolution showed an obvious willingness to challenge, and even abolish, an authority structure. An underlying belief in the idea of hierarchy seems to have remained, however, as evidenced in the renewed and expanded power of the *mullahs*. By contrast, civil war has been far more frequent than revolution in Colombian history. Negotiation of power exerted by the government as opposed to the Catholic Church is occasionally a public dilemma, in Colombia as in much of Latin America. The norms and goals of the two hierarchies do not, however, clash so strongly that allegiance to one rules out obedience to the other, which may be the most significant difference between Iranian and Colombian experiences of multiple sources of authority. Both cultures thus seem to place a fundamental importance on authority as a social governing force. They differ, however, in their preference for direct, overt challenge to an oppressive authority as opposed to more indirect subversion of it.

This example suggests that a fundamental question that may be raised in examinations of interpersonal ideology is

1. What bases of power are recognized within the speech community, and what institutionalized imbalances of power exist within and between speech communities?

A second fundamental question focuses on power at the level of social accountability and the communicative means available for exercising influence in a given speech community.

2. What are the recognized and preferred means of exerting personal influence in the speech community?

A common understanding of *personal* influence is that it is located within, or exerted by, individuals. Description of this urban Colombian speech community makes apparent that, in this culture, personal influence is often exercised by way of a third party. This is a case in which power is more clearly relational than in some others; but, plainly, urban Colombians are not unique in this regard. Philipsen's (1975, 1976, 1992) descriptions of U.S. working-class males notes the importance, in that community, of connections with higher-status people to accomplish a wide range of objectives. Because Philipsen's account concentrates primarily on males and on public objectives (getting a job, seeking a political favor, etc.), it is difficult to know whether the premise of connections extends into personal relationships in Teamsterville as pervasively as it does among these urban Colombians. In both cases, however, there is clearly a communal understanding that the most effective way for an individual to pursue certain objectives is by way of connections to others. An adequate account of personal relationships in these and other communities, then, would require consideration of the power derived from connections between persons, above and beyond that exertable by individuals.

By contrast, there are speech communities in which personal influence seems to flow from engaging with others in a style of interaction particularly valued by the members of the group. For example, an interactional style that creates and sustains interpersonal involvement by way of disagreement, criticism, and complaint has been described as characteristic of American Jews, particularly those of European descent, by several authors (Heilman, 1976, 1982; Myerhoff, 1978; Schiffrin, 1984; Tannen, 1981, 1984). In this speech community, disagreement is a valued resource for sociability and the display of relational stability. Evident from the consistency of the findings across such studies is that, within this speech community, personal influence might rest on willingness to engage in the kinds of verbal disputes valued by the members, as well as agility in conducting them. Against a backdrop of premises that attach connotations of involvement to conversational activities such as fighting, overlap, and interruption, personal relationships are revealed, rather than diminished, by those activities.

By contrast, the verbal artistry extensively described as valued and meaningful within some African American speech communities rests on assertive self-expression that often happens at the expense of others' dignity and self-esteem (see Abrahams, 1976; Kochman, 1981, 1990; McCollough,

1992; Smitherman, 1977; Stanback, 1985, 1989). Confrontation and ridicule are poetic arts in such communities, and probably figure in construction and maintenance of personal relationships in ways that are not yet understood. It is a style with clear historical roots, both in the oral patterns and in the forceful rejection of passivity that characterized Blacks' traditional position of oppression within U.S. society.

A final pair of interrelated questions that may be raised in comparative investigations of interpersonal ideology is

3a. What identities, relational configurations, and ways of speaking are salient and contestable within the dialectics of personal relationships and in interface with society specific to this speech community?

3b. Within those dialectics, how (if at all) are certain categories of participants and forms of participation legitimated over others?

These questions have been raised in some postmodernist efforts to deconstruct traditional understandings of personal relationships, and in some critical approaches to culture and interpersonal communication as well. For example, some U.S. researchers have problematized the notion of the family. Stacey (1991) describes contemporary family practices in the United States as unpredictable and contested, and argues that during the past 20 years so much has changed in the ways Americans create and live their family lives that fundamental shifts are required in understandings of what constitutes family. McDaniel (1995) and Weston (1991) make similar arguments in their discussions of gay and lesbian couples and families, making the point that traditional understandings of family privilege forms of relating that do not fit the lived experiences of significant proportions of the population.

What is curiously absent in these ethnographic accounts of social change is consideration of the cultural aspects of both the changes in family life and the enterprise of deconstructing the notion of family itself. A reasonable prior question is, in what cultural context is it even sensible to problematize the notion of family? It is reasonable to assume that notions of family (and other kinds of personal relationships) are more readily challenged and changed within a social structure that incorporates cultural ideals of uniqueness and self-determination (as in the United States) into a legal apparatus that allows for (some of) those changes to be officially legitimated by the state (sometimes). As noted in the example of Iran above, cultural change happens in distinctive ways according to social structure, among other factors. This is likely to be at least as true with regard to personal relationships as with political and economic systems.

Some discussions of friendship and marriage, although conceding that certain forms of those important relationships are privileged within particular cultural contexts, are nonetheless vague about what cultural context is being referred to and how, in interactive and relational terms, that privilege is enacted. Rawlins (1992), for example, notes that the scope of his research on friendship is middle-class Americans and that the patterns of friendship he describes are framed within cultural beliefs, such as free choice and voluntary action as the definitive qualities of friendship. Yet, there are issues discussed as having enormous impact on friendship (such as balancing a work relationship with friendship, time constraints that "can make developing or cultivating friendships resemble another job, requiring scheduling and effort to make them 'work'"—1992, p. 203) that are not examined for their cultural underpinnings. A useful question to ask might be, what is it about work (in the understandings of the U.S. respondents that were the focus of his study) that it constructs identity in a way that friendship does not?

Carroll (1988) suggests other symbolic dimensions of friendship among middle-class Americans that privilege certain configurations over others. She notes that American friendships tend to be dyadic in nature and suggests that the notion of a single "best friend" may be a culturally bound phenomenon: "For an American, the word 'friend' is a title one must constantly merit, of which one must constantly prove oneself worthy, and which therefore demands vigilance and effort" (p. 82). She notes that most Americans have a much wider group of people whose company they enjoy and with whom they get along well, and that there may be a great deal of fluctuation in the membership of that group. Being "friendly," defined as presenting oneself as open, sociable, and largely agreeable, is thus highly valued as an interactional style within this group. Because "true friendship" is a connection reserved for a very few people, however, requiring "work" and investment of scarce time resources, many relationships viewed by these North Americans as adequately friendly and sociable may seem superficial to members of other cultures. Similarly, Moffatt (1989) draws on an ethnographic study of Rutgers students in the late 1970s to describe this "friendly" demeanor as one displayed primarily by middle-class whites, a practice vastly at odds with African Americans' practices and thus problematic in intercultural contact between the two groups.

These four questions have been posed as a basis for research that examines personal relationships from a cultural perspective. Other applications of this notion of interpersonal ideology may also be noted. The framework sketched here can be utilized to approach a variety of communication and relational processes. Accounts and other narratives, as suggested in Chapter 4, may be interrogated for their cultural symbolism. The kinds of stories told about relational development, turning points, and dissolution are likely to reveal premises about personhood and communication that underlie dialectical tensions that shape social life in a particular speech community. Likewise, communal patterns of social support may be examined to discover the relational configurations that are significant by investigating the ways of speaking (such as advice, gossip, complaints) through which these configurations are constructed and maintained.

Finally, the value-laden nature of interpersonal ideology suggests its usefulness as a perspective on interpersonal persuasion processes. Culture may be understood as (among other things) a range of what can be made sensible. Members of a given culture can only be persuaded to (or away

from) ideas and actions that fall within that range of sensi-
bility. Examination on a case-by-case basis of what is per-
suadable (and comparison across cases to discern what
persuadables may be present in some cultures and not in
others) is likely to reveal ideological premises that serve as
the bases for particular persuasive attempts, and for the
broader contours of social life in that community as well.

At the beginning of this book, I confessed that one of
my objectives in studying interpersonal communication in
Colombia was to show that there was more to social life in
that culture than violence. In focusing on these other aspects of urban Colombian life, the very real and pervasive
influence of violence on the lives of the people I worked
with there has largely disappeared. To capture some part
of that influence requires a shift in perspective and in form,
and leads to ending on a rather different note than those I
have played so far.

EPILOGUE

CONNECTIONS

A Death Foretold

There has been considerable discussion in recent years of traditional ethnographic research, calling into question fundamental aspects of both its practices and the status of its claims. Particular attention has been devoted to conventions of writing ethnography and the issues of representation of culture implied in following those conventions (see, e.g., Clifford & Marcus, 1986; Hammersley, 1992; Rosaldo, 1989; Van Maanen, 1995). Calls for closer attention to the position and involvement of ethnographers in the cultural "scenes" they describe have been accompanied by numerous discussions of the value of narratives (e.g., Bochner & Ellis, 1995; Richardson, 1990, 1995) and performance (e.g., Conquergood, 1991; Jones, 1996; Paget, 1995) in presenting ethnographic findings. For the most part, as is obvious from the rest of this book, I have listened to these discussions from the sideline, generally choosing to follow the conventions of traditional ethnographic practice and writing. I have gotten less comfortable with those decisions during the process, seeing all too clearly the impact of my presence, my relationships with the people I "studied," and my inevitable value judgments on events and my interpretations of them. I have also become more uneasy with the absence, in virtually all of this discussion of "Colombian culture," of an all-too-pervasive aspect of everyday life and personal relationships in that speech community. There is no question that public violence is an inescapable parameter for existence there; yet it is invisible in these pages because I have found it to be undefinable. A narrative that seeks to begin to address these issues thus seemed the most appropriate way to close.

I came home from choir practice that night humming and glowing and at peace with a world filled with music. It was the first week in November, the leaves were gone from the trees, not many Christmas lights up yet. A time of gathering darkness, made brighter by the people, the harmonies, the song. Gabe was at the door by the time I was halfway through it. His words mixed in with Jairo's, who was talking loudly into the phone on the other side of the living room.

"They killed Anto—"

"Pero donde fue es—"

"Auro—"

"Y que pa—"

"What?" Was this a TV show they'd been watching, that Gabe was trying to tell me about? Who the hell was Jairo screaming into the phone to?

"Mataron a—a—Auxilio." Gabe's Spanish was not foolproof, but this message was not getting across in either language. I hung my purse on the doorknob, unwound my muffler, took off my coat. "What, sweetie? what happened? what were you watching?" He couldn't *really* be telling me about someone who was *killed*. This was a translation problem, or a report on a movie presented as real life.

Jairo turned to look at me, his eyes large in a still, shocked face. Something *was* wrong, maybe somebody died—he had many elderly or sickly relatives in Colombia. He told the person on the phone that we would be here, they should call back, he would try to get hold of Melba in New York. *"Chao"*—bye—as he hung up the phone. Gabe was still trying to string the right syllables together.

"They killed Absten—*mataron a Arber—Aure—Artemio—...*"

Finally, Jairo finished the sentence. *"Mataron a Aurelio."* *They killed Aurelio.*

The carpet was rubbery where I stood, in the middle of the room, Gabe hanging onto me, Jairo in a foggy plastic bubble ten feet further. The sofa registered behind me, and I wished vaguely I were on it.

"Aurelio—" There was something in that sequence of words I couldn't understand, my Spanish wasn't foolproof either. That couldn't mean—

"Aurelio Muñoz. Lo mataron." *They killed him.* A strange choice of words—they killed him. "They?" If something killed Aurelio, it was a heart attack, predicted by a lifetime of heavy smoking, heavy eating, heavy drinking. . . . "They who?"

"Todavia no saben quién fue." *They don't know yet who it was.*

"What? *Who* it was? Some*body*. . . " I was really confused now. Was it a car accident? crazy drivers being the norm all over Colombia—sadness started seeping in. Aurelio was dead, that much I was pretty sure of.

"Cinco balazos en la cabeza. Alguien lo mató." *Five gunshots to the head. Someone murdered him.*

The whole room turned foggy and rubbery, I saw only Jairo's wide dark eyes.

I thought very seriously: I'm going to turn around and go back outside the door, come back in, and start this moment over, and it will compose itself entirely differently.

The room was full of crashing, jangling sound. I found my way to the couch and sat down.

My first trip to Colombia, in 1983, was a spin through a neverending crowded room—endless friends and relatives to meet, endless repetitions of the same conversation.

"Where in the States are you from?"

"From Houston."

"Oh, you met Jairo there, of course." I perfected a shy smile, feeling like a lottery winner meeting the press to field questions about what she'll do with the millions. Sometimes that's what I felt like.

"Your Spanish is very good."

"Oh, thank you. Jairo is an excellent teacher." The fact was I understood a third to a half of what was going on. Enough to know I was similar to Jairo's mother in ways that would make Freud proud, and to know that she and I would have to work hard to like each other. Not enough to follow the story of how Josefina came to know his mother for 20 years and "help out in the house." But I saw her cooking, cleaning, washing clothes by hand, ironing my blouses before we went out on our numerous shopping trips and visits. I didn't know yet where his father and brother disappeared to in the evenings, greeted by icy stares yet buttery smooth tones from his mother when they came back, ebullient, an hour or so later.

"You're very tall." Until I went to Colombia, I lived my life as a woman of medium height. Jairo was a shade taller than I was, so it was a surprise to suddenly have people looking up at me and commenting on my immensity. There were stares on the street, remarks about my blue eyes. I had never seen so many varieties of lush dark hair and rich black eyes, and I stared right back.

Nobody who marries into a large family can really keep the members and connections straight in the early days (or years). Asking who was on whose side, who was married to whom, what connection made it imperative that a visit be arranged made lots of conversational opportunities. I did know when we ran into women Jairo had dated; the hushed attentiveness when we were introduced, the brief civilities we exchanged, the intense interest in what we wore, how our hair was fixed, how sweet we could make our tones. I quickly learned to act well-acquainted, even affectionate, with my future mother-in-law, Mariela. She really *was* an excellent teacher. She may have had romantic ideas about forging motherly/daughterly bonds with me, unaware of my struggles to come to terms with my own mother. We enacted connection, and hoped the acting would make it so.

From Bogotá we went to Cali, and I met the steely-eyed five-foot dynamo that was *her* mother. Leaning down to shake her hand felt like a Japanese bow, and utterly appropriate for her stiff dignity. Her children and grandchildren fussed over her constantly and teased her energetically, and I was glad to be offstage. Cali was a sweating inferno, and I suffered in every direction: intestinal distress, away from home on Christmas day (where it was 12 degrees in south Texas, and all the pipes froze and broke), between the heat and the nerves never feeling quite dry or clean. I knew just what to say sometimes: "Oh, my, this is *delicious,* I really must take some back with me." "The palm trees are lovely, we don't have those in my part of Texas." A lie, but everyone beamed at me. "What a nice place for a swimming pool!" Nothing was too inane to try to be a part of the conversation.

Most of the real questions went unasked, of course: "Do you people *always* drink this much, or only around the holidays?" "Don't you think that dress is a little revealing for a family Christmas party?" "Why do you keep parading Jairo's old girlfriends in front of me?" "Why do we have to go have lunch at these peoples' house when you said yourself you don't like them? and they're the loudest, pushiest ones of the bunch?"

After several days in Cali we drove further south, to cool, foggy Pasto. I sighed to be away from the crowds and the heat and the rivers of **aguardiente** —firewater—they pickled themselves in day and night. When I told Jairo of my relief, he looked at me sideways. "You thought these people drank a lot?" Did I hear a little more emphasis on *these*?

"Don't they?"

"At least they put it in a glass first."

Aurelio was a very successful sales manager for Bavaria, a national brewery. He was so good at it that they moved him to a bigger market: Duitama, in Boyacá. The transfer was later reconstructed as the beginning of a road that led to his death. His irrepressible humor would not go over well with the dour **boyacenses**; appointment of a **pastuso** to such a visible post would gall them. Aurelio complained that they had no sense of humor; there was no way to connect with people who took things so deadly seriously. He pined to be back in Pasto—"There I was *somebody,*" he lamented.

There was a vendor who paid Bavaria with a bad check. It was up to Aurelio to tell him that the rest of his contract would not be honored. The vendor took him to dinner to try to convince him to give him another week to cover the check. Aurelio said no: he had no connection to this person, no way of knowing if he really was good for the debt or would string him along for months. He tried smoothing the man's feelings with his silky charm, changing the subject to something they could laugh about, but the answer was still no. "I'll kill that sonofabitch **pastuso**" (native of Pasto), the man said loudly as he left the restaurant. A dozen people had to have heard him, but they were **boyacenses** too: tough, clannish, silent. Even by Colombian standards they are quick to anger and violent by nature.

We got to Pasto on December 28, **Día de los Inocentes** —the equivalent of April Fool's Day. The ride was punctuated with stories of tricks and mayhem from other years: the kitten imprisoned in an air duct so it screamed in terror until located and retrieved hours later; the alarm clocks set for 3 A.M; the group of amateur actors who dressed up as guerrillas and burst into a crowded cafeteria, brandishing all-too-realistic-looking machine guns. The countrywide tradition had expanded to a week of revelry in Pasto, in keeping (I was told) with the natives' simplemindedness. Much of it sounded too close to the bone for me. On **Día de las Aguas,** the trick was to throw water on people, strangers, friends, enemies, family members. You had to be on guard as you walked under a balcony, or rounded the corner of a building, or drove down the street, watching out for people with buckets, hoses, Dixie cups. The temperature hovered damply in the mid-40s, a bone-chilling ambience as unchangeable as Cali's muggy heat.

The biggest prankster of them all, I was warned, was our host. He was my father-in-law's cousin, they grew up together somewhere near Pasto, they were as close as brothers. He was *terrible*. "In what way?" I kept asking, etching a new phrase into my mind that I used a lot when I did ethnography. Shaking heads, "you'll have to see for yourself," were the only answers I got. I wondered how bad a businessman, father of teenaged sons, could be, and wished they would stop telling me so much about people before I met them.

The family's house was spacious and airy. Instead of a garage separated from the house, there was a kind of well adjacent to the living room. A very garage-like door slid up into the ceiling, the car was driven into the house, and the door slid back down. I knew by then that cars couldn't really be parked on the street overnight in most parts of Colombia, even in smaller, relatively tranquil places ("out in the boonies," Jairo said) like Pasto. I focused hard on the logic of keeping your cars—there was room for two—inside the house, the safest possible place, rather than adding on a room that would have to be secured as elaborately as the house was. Still, it took a long time not to be distracted by the sight of cars parked a few yards from the crystal figurines on the marble-topped coffee table.

We got there in late afternoon and met his wife first, before Aurelio got home from the office. Small and round and sweet-voiced, Libia was the calmest person I'd laid eyes on since we landed in Colombia.

"So, you've been taking the whirlwind tour?" she asked. I liked how she took my hand instead of kissing my cheek when we were introduced. "Lots of relatives to keep straight?"

"Oh, and such wonderful people," I started my litany of praise.

"Oh, and haven't they all loved giving you the once-over," she laughed, and something in the way she said it made me want to sit on the sofa all evening and tell her stories about the past two weeks.

An aunt said they had overcome strong resistance from both families to get married. Although she wasn't quite sure what the reasons for this opposition were, their fathers had the same last name, not unheard of with a common name like Muñoz. Someone else insisted they were cousins, perhaps distant ones but surely related more closely than kinship ideals would allow. Much later I asked Libia if that were the case, and she laughed out loud. No, they were no relation; both families insisted that Aurelio finish college before they got married, a command they ignored. They were married for 30 years, and Libia was beside him in the passenger seat of the car when Aurelio was shot.

By the time she told of the night he was murdered, I had heard several versions of the events. She was teaching me how to make a stuffed roasting hen, an elaborate dish that involved deboning the chicken while keeping nearly all the meat and skin intact.

I was chopping onions more finely than I'd ever done, to prolong the task she'd found for me. A really good cook like Libia is often hard to "help"—at best you do the minor tasks, stay out of the way, enjoy the excuse to be there in the kitchen.

"Aurelio always said he felt sorry for the chicken when I made this," she said, sliding the knife inside a drumstick and wiggling the bone from side to side. "He used to say, what if her friends saw her like this? all limp and discouraged and then filled up with nuts and onions like a Christmas cake." She laughed softly, warmed with the memory.

I diced more slowly, retrieving every sliver, subdividing it into precise pungent cubes. "The guy who did it is in prison now?" No need to spell out what guy, who did what.

"Well, yes, the one who pulled the trigger. Poor man, he's not the one they should be punishing, of course."

I knew it was obvious from the beginning that it was a hired killer. "How did they catch him?"

"Oh, someone saw him drinking at a bar across the street just before it happened. It wasn't hard to find him, really."

"This was very near your apartment, wasn't it, that it happened?"—my voice got more elaborately casual with every question, I was down to trimming edges on the onion pieces to make them symmetrical in size and shape.

Libia nodded, never looking up. The knife flashed along one side of the breast bone as she neatly separated away the ribs. "We were just pulling up to the gate and Aurelio honked for the doorman to come and open it. Instead of Tomás though, out comes this guy in a ruana, his hands underneath like this, and he came over to the side. Aurelio rolled down the window and said, *¿qué pasa maestro?— what's up buddy?—*those were his last words ever, *¿qué pasa maestro?*" I sneaked a furtive look at the corner of her eyes, but they were focused on the knife, the task. The delicate sawing and separating never slowed. "The guy just stood there, white as this countertop, stuck his hand through the window and started firing. Five shots. Aurelio slumped over on my side, on top of me, in my lap, and the guy leaned in and pointed the gun at him, to shoot him some more. I said *¡Ya no más! Ya lo mató, ¡ya no más! No more, you've already killed him, no more!* and he pointed the gun at me. I thought, well, he's going to kill me too so I can't identify him." I had heard more emotion in her telling about the misadventures of their string of household help. "But he just kind of looked at me, and at Aurelio, and ran away."

"Did he—live for a while?" Kitchens make questions possible that would hurt too much anywhere else, as long as you don't run out of onions.

"No, not really. There was blood everywhere, you can imagine, and I screamed for the neighbors to come. They came out right away and helped me get him into a taxi, but really he was dead before we ever got in. I knew he was dead, five bullets from two feet away? Four in his head, one in his chest." Finally the knife was still. "He never had a chance, but we went to the hospital as though maybe . . ." Her voice thinned. Wordlessly, she handed me a bowl. I slid the macerated onions in slowly.

"The killer finally told who hired him?"

"No." A firm shake of her head, the knife moving again, trimming away some fat. "That kind never do. He knows he won't be in prison for long, someone will take care of his family while he's there. If he ever told who was responsible, he would be dead." Matter of fact. "Really I'm not sure he should be in prison at all. All he did was pull the trigger, he had no reason to be killing Aurelio. We all knew that from the start."

"So they could never prove who was behind it."

A sigh. "No. The police said they could investigate further, try to get more evidence, but then we had that bomb outside our house New Year's Eve"—two months after the murder, a trash can exploded 25 feet from their front door, minutes after Libia's sons and several nephews and nieces came in from running an errand. They understood it as a warning against further efforts to prove who was responsible. "What's the point, really? We know who did it, the man who arranged it has that to live with all his life. Prison wouldn't change anything."

She sounded so resigned—so calm, as always. I tried to imagine what this must have been like for her. At seven o'clock she met Aurelio at his office, and waited while he called each of their sons in Bogotá. He called them, or they called him, almost every day, just to say hello, how's it going, what are you up to? The webs of their daily routines intersected at dozens of points, even from hundreds of miles apart. Around 7:30 they left in the company car, a Mazda, and Aurelio drove slowly through the congested streets of Duitama toward their apartment. Did they hold hands? He always had stories of the day to make Libia laugh. After 30 years, they had less than 15 minutes left together.

He came home from the office that first day in Pasto and stepped out of the car, already shouting. "What's this about a ***gringa,*** Jairo? What will Teresita say?"

We all stood up from where we'd been chatting in the living room as the door rattled noisily down behind the car.

"Aurelio, *respetico,* she's company." I stared at Mariela; that was the first time I'd ever heard her giggle.

I always think of Aurelio and his sons as tall, but the pictures in our album show them to be about my height. He had a way of filling a room, though, with a luxuriant black mustache and a voice that boomed. He was barrel-chested and elegantly dressed, and my father-in-law to be beamed at him like I'd never seen him do.

"Luis Alfonso, how's life treating you? Mariela, what a delight to have all of you with us. Beloved Libia, the hours have been endless. Don Jairo, always an honor." He passed out hugs and greetings, and I waited my turn.

"So you are the *gringa.* " He paused and looked me up and down, and everyone snickered at his frank apprais-ing gaze. I stared at him coolly and stuck out my hand; no hugs from me for this loudmouth. He grabbed my hand and kissed it with an elaborate courtly flourish, and the others roared as though this were fine humor. "Kristine, do sit down. Let me get you a whisky and tell you alllllllll about this guy you think you want to marry."

"Aurelio," my mother-in-law cautioned him.

"There's a lot you should know about him while there's time to back out," he began. I glared at the floor, wonder-ing why his very obvious jokes seemed to amuse the oth-ers so thoroughly, wishing he would center his attention on someone else.

The evening passed more slowly than most, and I was glad to go to bed early. Jairo and his father stayed down-stairs talking to Aurelio, their laughter loud and frequent, until long after midnight. I huddled under the rough wool blankets that weighed several pounds but didn't quite keep me warm, and wondered how often we would have to visit Pasto. For that matter, who knew whether we would end up living in Colombia permanently someday? Jairo was in graduate school, studying engineering. If he had trouble finding work in the States and got a great offer in Colom-bia, I couldn't very well refuse to go. Could I deal with all of this on a permanent basis? I wondered. Could I learn to laugh at the jokes, could I live with being stared at (or would people someday stop staring), could I learn to enjoy Aurelio's sense of humor as much as everyone else apparently did? Was it always this way when people became a couple and intertwined their lives, or were cultural differences making this harder than it would otherwise be?

A few days later was New Year's Eve, full of action, and as always, full of sound. Mariela had us up early to drive all over town collecting a mysterious array of ingredients: several dozen red roses, a particular brand of men's after-shave that was almost unknown, molasses, eucalyptus branches, saffron. I couldn't quite understand what all this was for, except that the recipe had come from a **curandero** —a faith healer—in Cali and Mariela was ever so pleased to have gotten hold of it. After lunch she flew between the kitchen and an upstairs bathroom to mix and chop and boil and strain things, humming.

Meanwhile the sons, Oscar and Ivan, and their friends were putting together an **año viejo**—an "old year"—which turned out to be a life-sized doll made of newspaper, dressed in old clothes. All week as we drove around town there had been groups of children, sometimes teenagers, rattling cans at us as we stopped at stoplights, collecting donations for these often elaborately constructed scarecrows. I wasn't sure what the money was for—the secondhand clothes? the small pieces of felt sewn on for eyes and mouths? All of them wore hats of some kind—maybe it was the hats that cost money? Late that afternoon I found out. Eleven of us wedged into Aurelio's jeep (he and my father-in-law were just beginning to toast the sunset) and careened around congested streets to a fireworks stand in the center of town. Oscar got out and waited in line while the rest of us waited in the jeep, a few of the friends smoking cigarettes. There were lots of giggles and excitement and a flirtation going on between Ivan and one of the girls, a chorus of commentary and encouragement from the rest of the group. I listened to this, fascinated; earlier in the week we had met Ivan's girlfriend, and this one wasn't her. Why all this egging him on to "square off" with her (evidently this meant romance, not a

fight) when presumably he was going steady with someone else?

Finally Oscar came back with several brown paper
bundles. "Careful with this, it's kind of spilling," he pointed
out as he handed it back. "What is it?" it finally occurred to
me to wonder. "Gunpowder—hey, put out the cigarettes!"
They were hastily snuffed out amid guffaws, as I gulped
and looked over at Jairo, who just smiled and shook his
head.

Back at home, the teenagers laced the newspaper-
stuffed doll with the gunpowder. Mariela had an evil-look-
ing mixture in several large plastic bottles lined up near the
bathroom door. Libia had taken over the kitchen, and along
with the maid, a narrow-eyed girl who looked to be around
12, was bustling around enough food for half of Pasto. I
shuddered to think what the evening might hold. My offer
to help in the kitchen was greeted with polite, somewhat
embarrassed confusion, as though a child had suddenly
asked where babies came from in the middle of an adult
conversation about politics.

"Kristine, your bath is ready. You can go first." My
mother-in-law beamed at me and pointed at one of the
plastic bottles near the bathroom. "This one is yours, see?
You pour it over your head and rub it in all over your body
real well. It's important not to rinse any of it off, just kind
of rub it in and let it stay."

I stared at Jairo, terrified, waiting for him to save me
from this. The stuff in the bottle was brown and lumpy, it
was 50 degrees outside and permanently chilly inside the
house, I was supposed to pour this over myself and not rinse
it off? This couldn't be happening. "What's this all about?" I
murmured to him in English.

"Just a good luck thing you do on New Year's Eve."

"I think I've had all the luck I need, thanks." Mariela
pressed the bottle at me; there seemed to be no choice. I
hunched miserably in the bathroom, making whatever
would sound like appropriate splashing noises and fighting back tears. Maybe this cross-cultural marriage wasn't
such a good idea. Maybe Mariela was just a weirdo; Libia

was so pleasant, sweet, and normal—but those sons of hers, apart from being mere teenagers, seemed also to be jerks like their father. There was no connection between me and these people, there never would be. I wanted badly to get on a plane and fly home to Texas.

Downstairs Aurelio had dance music blasting on the stereo. As I came into the living room I heard an explosion down the street. This was not firecrackers; it sounded like it might have been a shotgun. I gripped the railing and fought cold, mute terror.

"They're after you, *gringa*!" Aurelio shouted, and grabbed my hand. "C'mon, dance with me so they'll think you're Colombian!" My father-in-law grinned fuzzily from the sofa—haha, they'll think she's Colombian—instead of telling him to leave me alone. Where the hell was Jairo? Why wasn't he here to tell me what to do? Was there a polite way to tell your host to bug off in this culture? I hated how close Aurelio held me, hated the cigarette and *aguardiente* smell of his breath, hated feeling so helpless and clueless.

The doorbell rang and Aurelio let me go so he could answer it. "We'll have another dance later, OK *gringa*?" I shrank upstairs.

The evening lasted for weeks. People came and went, all dressed in satin and soft wool and emeralds, all of them brothers or sisters or cousins or aunts' husbands (who were not uncles, nor were uncles' wives aunts), all of them laughing and hugging and talking loudly over the music. The explosions outside got more frequent, and some seemed to be right outside the window. I looked out through the lace curtain at the street and saw small fires here and there on the street, consuming remains of *año viejos,* who sprawled eerily alone on the pavement. After a while it was too cold to stay in my room, and I went down hoping I could hang on the fringes of the merriment and watch, listen, learn what to do before somebody thrust me onstage again. I would have loved to get drunk on *aguardiente* —surely an effective strategy for blending in to any number of cultural groups—but the bitter licorice taste gave me a headache and seemed not to blur the tension at all.

I went to the kitchen hoping to find a beer. The thin brown child maid sat hunched on a tall stool, immobile, and stared at me as I came in. "Is there beer in here?" I stood near the refrigerator, wondering whether it was polite to help myself. She didn't understand me. "Beer?" I couldn't decipher the look in her dull black eyes—amusement? fear? curiosity? Yes, she said, there's beer in there. So . . . what do I do? I wanted to ask her. In your culture, am I expected to tell you to get it for me, or do I get it myself, or should I go through the hostess? The knot grew tighter in my stomach as we stared at each other.

Finally, I opened the refrigerator and grabbed a beer, trying to ignore her and the nervous feeling that I might be committing some horrible faux pas. The opener was carefully hidden in a drawer, of course, instead of being stuck with a magnet to the refrigerator door, and I had to rummage in several before I found it. Yes, in the States it's perfectly acceptable to ransack the kitchen at a party. I started out with my hard-won beer, and at that point the child came to life. *"No no no señora,"* she waved her hands and hopped off the stool. I stood in the doorway, blushing— what had I screwed up now? She scrambled to the freezer and took out a thick, frosty mug, muttering something I couldn't understand, took the beer from my hand and sloshed it in. Way too much foam—I nearly groaned—and a frozen mug in this frigid climate seemed to me remarkable overkill. I silently took the beer from her and left the room.

The party was in full swing, people dancing, laughing, shouting, and I had never felt so alone and tired. Another explosion went off outside—would this ever end? It sounded like a war zone out there.

The explosion in the trash can outside their house, that New Year's after Aurelio was killed, was a bomb, not an *año viejo.* I wondered how they could tell the difference? Pretend violence, real violence. Stuffed scarecrows in the street, dead husbands and fathers in taxis on the way to the hospital. Too much a part of life to be surprised, if you're Colombian.

Aurelio, standing between Jairo and his father, caught sight of me.

"C'mon, ***gringa,*** time for us to dance again! Let's go, it's nearly midnight!" I shrank against the wall and tried not to grimace. Why wouldn't Jairo step in and do something about this? Why didn't Libia? Why did no one realize that the last thing I wanted was to be pressed up against this big-bellied man with his flowing mustache and his bitter-licorice breath?

The nightmare went on, and it was like being strapped into a chair and forced to watch slasher movies. The crowd seemed a whirling mass of elegantly dressed birds, fluttering and lighting and chattering noisily in the brightly lit living room. As it got later their tongues got fuzzier, their steps unsteadier, and I yearned to join them. Something, anything to connect me to them. The beer I'd worked so hard for was the only one. In the house of a man who worked his whole life for the largest brewery in Colombia, Chivas, Coca-Cola, and ***aguardiente*** were the only drinks that could be served on an important occasion like New Year's Eve. At midnight someone turned off the lights, and Jairo hugged me; for once we were allowed to focus on each other, instead of him attending to his mother, his father, the gallery of unknown faces swirling just beyond my reach. The explosions outside paused, then a wave of cracking, booming sound began, a mad crescendo of violent sound to celebrate a moment designated by humans (arbitrarily, I mused, in this land of human-constructed meanings—you can get drunk on ideas if you don't like ***aguardiente***) as the end of one year and the beginning of another.

When the lights came on I looked around. Jairo's father was semiconscious in an armchair, and his mother was stroking his hair, looking stolidly ahead of her, enduring the moment and waiting, somewhat sternly, for it to pass. One of the younger cousins was weeping quietly in a corner, her brother (was it a brother? was she a cousin?) with a languid arm around her. Apparently she was yet another of Jairo's earlier conquests, her heart forever broken to see him lost to this pale blue-eyed stranger who danced so poorly. I wondered if he would really be better off with her than with me.

In the middle of the room were Aurelio, Libia, and their two sons. The four of them stood with their arms around each other, heads down, a tight silent circle. They were still there, motionless, long after others had moved on to distribute more casual hugs around the room. I looked at Aurelio, the loud playful bear, at how closely he gathered his family to him, holding them in fiercely loving embrace, for once not shouting or laughing or hoisting a bottle. All four of them dabbed at their eyes when they moved apart, and a tiny crack formed in the wall of disapproval and dislike I'd built against him.

The party died down around 3 A.M, though the explosions still happened here and there. Jairo was putting his father to bed when I shut the door behind me and crawled gratefully under the covers. It was over; I had survived; I was alone.

I was deep in a dream about exploding clowns when, after a loud chorus of knocking and unintelligible shouts, the door burst open. Aurelio lumbered in, my father-in-law behind him, both of them in bathrobes. "Wake up, *gringa,* time for the grapes!" He plopped onto the side of the bed, and I could tell he was still drunk. I recoiled inside and tried to pretend I could sleep through this maniacal scene. Aurelio held a bunch of grapes under my nose. "You have to eat these, quick! It's good luck! If you don't eat the grapes who knows what will happen this year!" I tried harder to ignore him, my stomach churning. "Here!! Eat them, twelve of them!" He started stuffing grapes into my mouth, one at a time. Helplessly, I loosened my clenched jaws and chewed listlessly at the grapes, wondering if he would stop if I choked on them. Mariela came in then, yelling as loudly as he was: *"Aurelio, qué grosero! Cómo se le occurre entrar a la pieza de uno, escándaloso! Déjela en paz!"* (How dare you come barging into someone's bedroom, you bad-mannered thing! Leave her alone!) Her scolding was lost in a chorus of chuckles from the door, the rest of the family gathered around to enjoy the spectacle of Aurelio being his hilarious self. When they finally dragged him away and shut the door, I huddled under the covers, sobbing and screaming how much I hated this horrible Colombian boor, how much I hated Colombia and Colombians, and how impossible the whole idea of joining my life to them seemed.

It was easier to avoid Aurelio during the rest of that visit. He and Luis Alfonso alternated between drinking and sleeping it off, while the sons took Jairo and me around Pasto. We rode to the top of the volcanic mountain that dominated the landscape, crawling over boulders and through ruts in the road as big as the Jeep. Along with the respective girlfriends, we went dancing one night at a discothèque that got so dark during the slow songs that you bumped into other couples on the dance floor and had to feel your way along the booths to find where you'd been sitting. One day the sun came out, a glorious relief from endless drizzle and fog, and we all drove to a jewel of a lake that sparkled under a velvet blue sky. There were motorboats there with drivers that you paid a dollar for a ride out around an emerald island in the middle of the lake. I wished they would let me off there, let me stay all alone among the evergreens where it was quiet and smelled good and no one had a bottle under their arm.

On the last day Aurelio emerged from his festive semi-coma, and we went in two cars to what he described as the best place in Colombia to eat *cuy.* I didn't ask what this delicacy was, so I wouldn't have to see his eyes twinkle as he teased me. He'd say it was tiger, or elephant, or human flesh, and think I was gullible enough to believe him; no thanks. I'd figure out what it was when I saw it.

The "restaurant" was a long drive out into the still, lush countryside. It was one of a group of small houses made of mud and straw, leaning against the years, more dirt than rustic charm. We parked in the dusty yard near a pen made of sticks and corrugated metal.

"Here we go." Aurelio peered into the pen, rubbing his hands in anticipation. "Here, Kristine, I'll pick you out a nice tasty one."

These must be the *cuy.* I looked down, my face carefully set in a smile, ready to voice enthusiasm over whatever local custom was about to be revealed. Inside were a dozen guinea pigs, coated with the same dust of the yard, some running in circles and others lounging on the ground. I stared at them, telling myself I was much too culturally sophisticated to be horrified. I listened to Aurelio negotiating with the proprietor; we needed four *cuy* for the seven of us, "with all the fixings." Whole or cut up? I heard the owner/cook ask. Cut up they cost twice as much as having them whole.

We went to an inner patio of the house to wait, passing through dim rooms with a sagging bed, some carefully hung clothes, a faded couch. The patio had a wooden table and some chairs, and here the cold beer was plentiful. Soon we could smell the roasting *cuy*—I was pleased we hadn't heard the slaughter. For once, the sunshine was bright and the air was dry; for once, the chatting seemed easy.

"Jairo, we need to run that errand after lunch," Aurelio said.

Errand? Jairo just grinned at him.

"*You* know Jairo, the *errand.* " There was no wink, the tone seemed completely serious, but I heard a note of music in his voice.

"C'mon Jairo, they'll be waiting for you at Teresita's house."

Understanding snuck up on me. The name Teresita had come up at odd moments, everyone laughed but me, now a light was beginning to dawn. A smile tugged at my mouth. Jairo was someone I could tease.

"Is that the phone I hear? Yes Tere we're on our way, don't you worry." Aurelio mimed hanging up a telephone. If there was one in this village at all, it was at the police station. He widened his eyes meaningfully at Jairo. "The *errand,* Jairo."

"The *errand,* Jairo," I mimicked, and was terribly pleased at the chuckle that produced.

"What can we get you from the supermarket, Kristine? Come on, we'll be back before the *cuy* is done, or if we're not you all just start without us."

"The closest supermarket is an hour from here," I intoned, my face serious.

"Ohhhhhhhhh, but we'll hurry. We won't take long, will we Jairo? Look at poor Jairo, how pale he is."

"Aren't you feeling well, dear?" Visions of the parade of old girlfriends. This was well worth needling him about. There were more chuckles around the table. I couldn't believe it; this was so smooth, so easy.

Aurelio directed himself to my mother-in-law. "Mariela. How are you going to manage two daughters-in-law?" I giggled. "Ask Luis Alfonso, he knows what it's like to try to keep two women happy."

"He'll tell you all about it," I chimed in. I loved needling her, too.

"Kristine, you have your list ready for the supermarket? Jairo, you go put on some smell-good—quick, they'll close up on us. Is that the phone again?"

"I'll bet they're calling from the supermarket."

"Teresita's there and boy, is she mad at Jairo."

"Here he is, late *again.*"

"See you later, Kristine; now, don't take it into your head to go for a stroll in El Saladito"—a small town near Pasto, whether fictional or real I never knew, but the home of any number of Teresitas.

The conversation moved on after a while, and I glowed from the exchange. The first time you get someone's jokes— a person's or a culture's—you're on your way to connecting. Aurelio had been giving me chances all along, with the shouts of *gringa* and the dancing and the grapes. All I really needed was some time to watch, listen, see how it was done: a slow-paced cloudless day, a wooden table with beer bottles glinting in the sun, and the savory smell of roasting *cuy* and wood smoke to soften around the edges a little.

We left Pasto the next day to drive back to Bogotá. Oscar and Ivan got up to see us off; Aurelio held off going into the office. Libia had made us some *empanadas* for the road, and they smelled rich and inviting from the brown paper bag. "Here, Kristine, you might get thirsty"—Aurelio handed a six pack of *Costeñita*, the lighter, less foamy beer I'd come to like a lot, in through the window. Nothing was ever said about that New Year's Eve, but every time I went back to his house there was beer there. I even learned which drawer they kept the opener in, and Libia let me help in the kitchen after a while.

"Take care."

"Thanks so much for everything."

"It's been great to meet you."

"Come back anytime, the house is at your service."

"Bring us back your *gringuitos*!" yelled Aurelio as we backed down the driveway, and I saw Libia playfully slap his arm. This was the most direct reference yet made to the idea that Jairo and I were getting married. For all the jokes and introducing around to the family, the subject had been carefully avoided. Naturally, Aurelio was the one to break the ice. He specialized in outrageous behavior, just beyond the boundaries of the expected, and he was the one most able to extend the web of family around a partner they never anticipated for Jairo.

The day after we stuffed the hen, Libia and I talked about her giving my daughter a haircut. She'd done it before, in Bogotá, in the backyard. "I have the hair scissors with me," she agreed.

"Always prepared."

"You never know when you'll find someone needing a haircut." We laughed together; she was so easy to laugh with.

We put newspapers on the floor, and I went to get a chair, while Erica dragged herself away from the Saturday morning cartoons. Libia pulled out a small pair of scissors smaller than my hand.

"That's all you need? I thought you had bigger ones."

"Well, at home I do. I brought these because they're easier to take on a trip." As she clipped away at the hair over Erica's ear, meticulously evening out the ends, she had a faraway look. "These are the scissors Aurelio used to trim his mustache."

"Really?" I remembered the flowing black walrus, how over the years I got used to him scratching it along my cheek when he said hello. "Did you ever trim it for him? I trim Jairo's." I brushed the hair busily off of Erica's neck, suddenly shy.

"No, he did it himself, every Sunday. He'd stand there in the living room where the light was best and put on good music, of course, and trim that mustache. You know that first year you came to Pasto?" She stopped and looked over at me. "You all left on a Friday. Well, that Sunday he was trimming his mustache, and I was keeping him company, and he said he thought you and Jairo made a very good match."

"Did he say that?" I couldn't quite look at her, the woman who loved that bear of a man for 30 years and then held him while he died a senseless death.

"Sure. He thought you were just what Jairo needed." She clipped on for a while in silence, then we talked of other, lighter things. When the haircut was over and Erica scampered away, she touched my arm. "Here. You keep the scissors to trim Jairo's mustache with." She said it simply, a smile in her eyes.

I hugged her, fighting away a grip in my stomach. "I'll do it on Sundays, and I'll put on good music."

She hugged me back, hard. "That sounds like the best possible use for those scissors."

The argument I have with grad students about writing like this is, how can this be science? How do you know if any of it is true? Along with a novelistic style could come novelistic license to stretch the real events, make some up if you need them to advance the plot. At that point they ask, well, what's truth anyway? Are statistics truth, are field notes truth, are "glosses" or "categories" truth? Now having written this, I find myself wishing less of it were true. I wish I hadn't seen so much loveliness in Aurelio's marriage, in his dedication (despite all the Teresita jokes and hangovers and holding women tight when he danced with them) to his family. I wish it had been a heart attack or cirrhosis that got him instead of a hired killer. Sad as that would have been, I could have understood that better, a cause-and-effect kind of thing. You smoke, you drink, you die—it fits more easily into my head than "you move someplace where the people are very different from you, and you don't have any connection to them except business, and they get mad at you and hire a man with no way to support his family except to shoot you." I wish Libia had been spared seeing it, that her sons hadn't been three hours away when it happened so that she waited alone in a strange hospital for them to get there. *I wish I'd made all this up* —but it's all too true, all too real, and in the Colombia of today it is all too common.

The day after Aurelio was murdered I had to teach my graduate seminar in ethnography. It was brutal pain to drag myself into school, clench my teeth against the screams of rage that I wanted to bounce off the walls, and look around the conference room table at bland, unknowing faces that had no reason to realize that anything was wrong. The whole project of ethnography seemed ironic that day: I had spent most of a decade explaining what I called "Colombian culture" to mostly middle-class, mostly North American (like me) audiences. To explain and describe that culture—not my own—was to make sense of it. Maybe not the sense the natives would make of it, but *my* sense, that could all be *non*sense. All the neat patterns I'd seen in the data and called "premises," "values," "beliefs," suddenly seemed convenient, meaningless fictions. "Colombian culture" was nothing but pain and blood and darkness now, a widow, a hired gun, a vendor with a bad check and a worse temper. There was no "sense" to be made of that, and I realized I didn't want to look for any, didn't want to find *sense* in what was senseless. To find *a cultural explanation* for something so tragic would be obscene and dehumanizing, a set of lies that would tell nothing of Aurelio's life or family or his wicked sense of humor. I knew I would write about it someday, but I hope never to *make sense* of it.

MASTER LIST
OF ADDRESS TERMS

negro/a
moreno/a
negrito
doctor/a
patrón
jefo
profesor
doctor/a + first name
doctor/a + last name
señor/a
mi don/doña
last name
first name
first name diminu-
    tive
señora/ita last name
señora/ita first name
last name diminutive
'ñora
'ña + first name (r)
first name + middle
    name
jefecito
misia

costeño
gringo/a
isleño
boludo
pendejo/a
hijueputa
maricon
huevón
llave, llavecita (r)
lanza, lancita (r)
socio
maestro
cuadro
amigo
campeón
tira (r)
tombo (r)
grosero/a
atrevido/a
ingrata
gordo
viejo
caballero
mi linda

Papá
Mamá
Padre
mamita
madre
mamacita
madrecita
mi mami
mi madre
madrina
hermano/a
mano
mi'amá
mamasota
mijo/a
mijito/a
chico/a
niña/o
muchacho/a
jóven
mi amor
hijo mío
bebé
mi niña

tú	sinvergüenza	china
usted	vagabunda	mi vida
su merced	mugre	cucho/a, cuchito/a
vos	preciosura	abuelita
tío/a (+ first name)	camarada/camarita	compañero/a,
papá + first name	cochino	compa (r)
(to grandfather)	bruto	muñeca
mamá + first name	indio/a	comadre
(to grandmother)	indiacito/a	esposo/a
su persona	señor agente	marido
mi + title (e.g.,	mi gente (r)	mujer
doctor, general)	me raza	abuelo/a
teniente		primo/a

(r), reported but never observed.

REFERENCES

Abrahams, R. (1976). *Talking black*. Rowley, MA: Newbury.

Ahern, E. (1979). The problem of efficacy: Strong and weak illocutionary acts. *Man, 14,* 1–17.

Allan, G. (1993). Social structure and relationships. In S. W. Duck (Ed.), *Social context and relationships* (pp. 1–25). Newbury Park, CA: Sage.

Altman, I., & Taylor, D. (1973). *Social penetration: The development of interpersonal relationships*. New York: Holt, Rinehart & Winston.

Austin, J. L. (1962). *How to do things with words*. Cambridge, MA: Harvard University Press.

Bakhtin, M. M. (1929/1984). *Problems of Dostoevsky's poetics* (C. Emerson, Trans.). Minneapolis: University of Minnesota Press.

Bakhtin, M. M. (1981). *The dialogic imagination: Four essays by M. M. Bakhtin* (C. Emerson, M. Holquist, Trans.). Austin, TX: University of Texas Press.

Basso, K. (1979). *Portraits of "the whiteman": Linguistic play and cultural symbols among the Western Apache*. New York: Cambridge University Press.

Baxter, L. A. (1987). Symbols of relationship identity in relationship cultures. *Journal of Social and Personal Relationships, 4,* 261–280.

Baxter, L. A. (1988). A dialectical perspective on communication strategies in relationship development. In S. W. Duck (Ed.), *Handbook of personal relationships* (pp. 257–273). New York: Wiley.

Baxter, L. A. (1990). Dialectical contradictions in relationship development. *Journal of Social and Personal Relationships, 7,* 69–88.

Baxter, L. A. (1992). Interpersonal communication as dialogue: A response to the "Social Approaches" forum. *Communication Theory, 2,* 330–337.

Baxter, L. A. (1993). The social and the personal of close relationships: A dialectical perspective. In S. Duck (Ed.), *Social contexts of relationships* (pp. 139–165). Newbury Park, CA: Sage.

Baxter, L. A., Mazanec, M., Nicholson, J., Pittman, G., Smith, K., & West, L. (1997). Everyday loyalties and betrayals in personal relationships. *Journal of Social and Personal Relationships, 14,* 655–678.

Baxter, L. A., & Montgomery, B. (1996). *Relating: Dialogues and dialectics.* New York: Guilford Press.

Baxter, L. A., & Wilmot, W. (1985). Taboo topics in close relationships. *Journal of Social and Personal Relationships, 2,* 253–269.

Bell, R., Buerkel-Rothfuss, N., & Gore, K. (1987). The idiomatic communication of young lovers. *Human Communication Research, 14,* 47–67.

Bergmann, J. R. (1993). *Discreet indiscretions: The social organization of gossip.* New York: Aldine de Gruyter.

Billig, M. (1995). *Banal nationalism.* London: Sage.

Bilmes, J. (1976). Rules and rhetoric: Negotiating the social order in a Thai village. *Journal of Anthropological Research, 32,* 44–57.

Blum-Kulka, S. (1990). You don't eat lettuce with your fingers: Parental politeness in family discourse. *Journal of Pragmatics, 14,* 259–288.

Bochner, A. (1994). Perspectives on inquiry II: Theories and stories. In M. Knapp & G. Miller (Eds.), *Handbook of interpersonal communication* (pp. 21–41). Thousand Oaks, CA: Sage.

Bochner, A., & Ellis, C. (1995). Telling and living: Narrative co-construction and the practices of interpersonal relationships. In W. Leeds-Hurwitz (Ed.), *Social approaches to communication* (pp. 201–216). New York: Guilford Press.

Boden, D., & Zimmerman, D. H. (Eds.). (1991). *Talk and social structure: Studies in ethnomethodology and conversation analysis.* Berkeley, CA: University of California Press.

Brown, P., & Levinson, S. (1987). *Politeness: Some universals in language usage.* New York: Cambridge University Press.

Brown, R., & Gilman, A. (1960). The pronouns of power and solidarity. In T. A. Sebeok (Ed.), *Style in language.* Cambridge, MA: MIT Press.

Burke, K. (1950). *A rhetoric of motives.* Berkeley: University of California Press.

Canfield, D. L. (1981). *Spanish pronunciation in the Americas.* Chicago: University of Chicago Press.

Carbaugh, D. (1988). *Talking American: Cultural discourses on Donahue.* Norwood, NJ: Ablex.

Carbaugh, D. (1989). Fifty terms for talk: A cross-cultural study. In S. Ting-Toomey & F. Korzenny (Eds.), *Language, culture and communication: Current directions* (pp. 93–120). Newbury Park, CA: Sage.

Carbaugh, D. (1996). *Situating selves: The communication of social identities in American scenes.* Albany, NY: SUNY Press.

Carroll, R. (1988). *Cultural misunderstandings: The French-American experience.* Chicago: University of Chicago Press.

Chang, J. (1992). *Wild swans: Three daughters of China.* New York: Doubleday.

Clark, H. H., & Lucy, P. (1975). Understanding what is meant from what is said: A study in conversationally conveyed requests. *Journal of Verbal Learning and Verbal Behavior, 14,* 56–72.

Clifford, J., & Marcus, G. (Eds.). (1986). *Writing culture: The poetics and politics of ethnography.* Berkeley, CA: University of California Press.

Conquergood, D. (1991). Rethinking ethnography: Towards a critical cultural politics. *Communication Monographs, 58,* 179–194.

Craig, R. B. (1981). *Domestic implications of illicit drug cultivation, processing, and trafficking in Colombia.* Washington, DC: U.S. State Department Conference on Colombia.

Cronen, V., Chen, V., & Pearce, W. B. (1988). Coordinated management of meaning: A critical theory. *International and Intercultural Communication Annual, 12,* 66–98.

Davis, K. E., & Todd, M. J. (1985). Assessing friendship: Prototypes, paradigm cases and relationship description. In S. W. Duck & D. Perlman (Eds.), *Understanding personal relationships* (pp. 17–38). London: Sage.

de Certeau, M. (1984). *The practice of everyday life* (S. Rendall, Trans.). Berkeley, CA: University of California Press.

Duck, S. (Ed.). (1993). *Social context and relationships.* Newbury Park, CA: Sage.

Duck, S. (1994). *Meaningful relationships: Talking, sense, and relating.* Thousand Oaks, CA: Sage.

Duck, S., West, D. L., & Acitelli, L. (1997). Sewing the field: The tapestry of relationships in life and research. In S. W. Duck (Ed.), *Handbook of personal relationships* (2nd ed.). New York: Wiley.

Ervin-Tripp, S. (1972). On sociolinguistic rules: Alternation and co-occurence. In J. Gumperz & D. Hymes (Eds.), *Directions in sociolinguistics* (pp. 300–324). New York: Holt, Rinehart & Winston.

Ervin-Tripp, S. (1976). Is Sybil there? The structure of some American English directives. *Language in Society, 5,* 25–66.

Fairclough, N. (1992). *Discourse and social change.* Cambridge, UK: Polity Press.

Fincham, F. D., & Bradbury, T. N. (Eds.) (1990). *The psychology of marriage.* New York: Guilford Press.

Fisher, W. R. (1984). Narration as a human communication paradigm: The case of public moral argument. *Communication Monographs, 51,* 1–22.

Fisher, W. R. (1985). The narrative paradigm: An elaboration. *Communication Monographs, 52,* 347–367.

Fisher, W. R. (1987). *Human communication as narration: Toward a philosophy of reason, value, and action.* Columbia, SC: University of South Carolina Press.

Fiske, J. (1991). Writing ethnographies: Contribution to a dialogue. *Quarterly Journal of Speech, 77,* 330–335.

Fitch, K. (1991a). The interplay of linguistic universals and cultural knowledge in personal address: Colombian *madre* terms. *Communication Monographs, 58,* 254–272.

Fitch, K. (1991b). *Salsipuedes* : Attempting leave-taking in Colombia. *Research on Language and Social Interaction, 24,* 209–224.

Fitch, K. (1994). A cross-cultural study of directive sequences and some implications for compliance-gaining research. *Communication Monographs, 61,* 185–209.

Fitch, K., & Sanders, R. (1994). Culture, communication, and preferences for directness in expression of directives. *Communication Theory, 4,* 219–245.

Franco Isaza, E. (1959). *Las guerrillas del Llano.* Bogotá, Colombia: Distribuidores Librería Mundial.

Friedrich, P. (1972). Social context and semantic feature: The Russian prominal usage. In J. Gumperz & D. Hymes (Eds.), *Directions in sociolinguistics* (pp. 35–71). New York: Holt, Rinehart & Winston.

Goffman, E. (1971). *Relations in public: Microstudies of the public order.* New York: Harper & Row.

Goodman, R. F., & Ben Ze'ev, A. (Eds.). (1994). *Good gossip.* Lawrence, KA: University of Kansas Press.

Gottman, J. (1979). *Marital interaction: Experimental investigations.* New York: Academic Press.

Gudykunst, W., & Ting-Toomey, S. (1988). *Culture and interpersonal communication.* Newbury Park, CA: Sage.

Gudykunst, W. B., & Kim, Y. Y. (1992). *Communicating with strangers* (2nd ed.). New York: McGraw-Hill.

Guzmán Campos, G., Fals Borda, O. Umaña Luna, E. (1986). *La violencia en Colomiba* (vol. I.). Bogatá: Carlos Valencia Editores.

Hamblen, C. (1979). The married woman's name: A metaphor of oppression. *Et Cetera: A Review of General Semantics, 36,* 248–256.

Hammersley, M. (1992). *What's wrong with ethnography?* London: Routledge.

Harris, T. (1982). *From mammies to militants: Domestics in Black American literature.* Philadelphia: Temple University Press.

Harvey, J. H., Orbuch, T. L., & Weber, A. L. (1990). *Interpersonal accounts: A social psychological perspective.* Oxford: Basil Blackwell.

Heath, S. B. (1983). *Ways with words.* New York: Cambridge University Press.

Heilman, S. (1976). *Synagogue life.* Chicago: University of Chicago Press.

Heilman, S. (1982). Prayer in the Orthodox synagogue: An analysis of ritual display. *Contemporary Jewry, 6.*

Hodge, R., & Kress, G. (1993). *Language as ideology* (2nd ed.). London: Routledge.

Hollos, M., & Beeman, W. (1974). The development of directives among Norwegian and Hungarian children: An example of communicative style in culture. *Language in Society, 7,* 345–355.

Hopper, R. (1992). *Telephone conversation.* Bloomington, IN: Indiana University Press.

Hopper, R., Knapp, M., & Scott, L. (1981). Couples' personal idioms: Exploring intimate talk. *Journal of Communication, 31,* 23–33.

Hymes, D. (1962). The ethnography of speaking. In T. Gladwin & W. C. Sturtevant (Eds.), *Anthropology and human behavior.* Washington, DC: Anthropological Society of Washington.

Hymes, D. (1972). Models of the interaction of language and social life. In J. Gumperz & D. Hymes (Eds.), *Directions in sociolinguistics: The ethnography of communication* (pp. 35–71). New York: Holt, Rinehart & Winston.

Hymes, D. (1986). Discourse: Scope without depth. *International Journal of the Sociology of Language, 57,* 49–89.

Jones, J. (1996). The self as other: Creating the role of Joni the ethnographer for Broken Circles. *Text and Performance Quarterly, 16,* 131–145.

Katriel, T. (1986). *Talking straight: Dugri speech in Israeli Sabra culture.* New York: Cambridge University Press.

Katriel, T. (1992). *Communal webs: Communication and culture in contemporary Israel.* Albany, NY: SUNY Press.

Katriel, T., & Philipsen, G. (1981). "What we need is communication":

"Communication" as a cultural term in some American speech. *Communication Monographs, 48,* 301–317.

Keshavarz, M. H. (1988). Forms of address in post-revolutionary Iranian Persian: A sociolinguistic analysis. *Language in Society, 17,* 565–575.

Kim, Y. Y. (1988). *Communication and cross-cultural adaptation: An integrative theory.* Clevedon, UK: Multilingual Matters.

Kochman, T. (1981). *Black and white styles in conflict.* Chicago: University of Chicago Press.

Kochman, T. (1990). Cultural pluralism. In D. Carbaugh (Ed.), *Cultural communication and intercultural contact* (pp. 219–224). Hillsdale, NJ: Erlbaum.

Kuiper, K. (1996). *Smooth talkers: The linguistic performance of auctioneers and sportscasters.* Mahwah, NJ: Erlbaum.

Labov, W., & Fanshel, D. (1977). *Therapeutic discourse: Psychotherapy as conversation.* Orlando, FL: Academic Press.

Lannaman, J. (1991). Interpersonal communication research as ideological practice. *Communication Theory, 1,* 179–203.

Lannaman, J. W. (1994). The problem with disempowering ideology. In S. Deetz (Ed.), *Communication yearbook 17* (pp. 136–147). Thousand Oaks, CA: Sage.

Leeds-Hurwitz, W. (1995). *Social approaches to communication.* New York: Guilford Press.

Levinson, S. (1983). *Pragmatics.* New York: Cambridge University Press.

Lustig, M., & Koester, J. (1996). *Intercultural competence: Interpersonal communication across cultures.* New York: HarperCollins.

Markova, I., & Foppa, K. (1991). *Asymmetries in dialogue.* Savage, MD: Barnes & Noble Books.

McAdams, D. (1993). *Stories we live by: Personal myths and the making of the self.* New York: William Morrow.

McCollough, M. (1992). *Black and white women's friendships: Claiming the margins.* Philadelphia: Temple University Press.

McDaniel, J. (1995). *The lesbian couples' guide.* New York: HarperCollins.

Mishler, E. (1986). *Research interviewing: Context and narrative.* Cambridge, MA: Harvard University Press.

Moffatt, M. (1989). *Coming of age in New Jersey: College and American culture.* New Brunswick, NJ: Rutgers University Press.

Molano, F. (1992). *Un beso de Dick (A kiss from Dick).* Medellín, Colombia: Fundación Cámara de Comercio de Medellín para la Investigación y la Cultura.

Montgomery, B. (1988). Quality communication in personal relation-

ships. In S. W. Duck (Ed.), *Handbook of personal relationships* (pp. 343–359). New York: Wiley.

Montgomery, B. (1992). Communication as the interface between couples and culture. *Communication Yearbook, 15,* 476–508.

Myerhoff, B. (1978). *Number our days.* New York: Simon & Schuster.

Pacificon Productions. (1981). *Friends can be good medicine.* Sacramento, CA: California Department of Mental Health.

Paget, M. (1995). Performing the text. In J. V. Maanen (Ed.), *Representation in ethnography* (pp. 222–244). Thousand Oaks, CA: Sage.

Philipsen, G. (1975). Speaking "like a man" in Teamsterville: Culture patterns of role enactment in an urban neighborhood. *Quarterly Journal of Speech, 61,* 13–22.

Philipsen, G. (1976). Places for speaking in Teamsterville. *Quarterly Journal of Speech, 62,* 15–25.

Philipsen, G. (1987). The prospect for cultural communication. In L. Kinckaid (Ed.), *Communication theory: Eastern and Western perspectives* (pp. 245–253). New York: Academic Press.

Philipsen, G. (1992). *Speaking culturally.* Albany, NY: SUNY Press.

Philipsen, G., & Huspek, M. (1985). A bibliography of sociolinguistic studies of personal address. *Anthropological Linguistics, 27,* 94–101.

Rawlins, W. (1992). *Friendship matters: Communication, dialectics, and the life course.* New York: Aldine.

Richardson, L. (1990). *Writing matters.* Newbury Park, CA: Sage.

Richardson, L. (1995). Narrative and sociology. In J. Van Maanen (Ed.), *Representation in ethnography* (pp. 198–221). Thousand Oaks, CA: Sage.

Rheingold, H. (1988). *They have a word for it.* Los Angeles: Tarcher/St. Martin's.

Rosaldo, M. (1982). The things we do with words: Ilongot speech acts and speech act theory in philosophy. *Language in Society, 11,* 203–237.

Rosaldo, R. (1989). *Culture and truth: The remaking of social analysis.* Boston: Beacon Press.

Rushforth, S. (1981). Speaking to "relatives-through-marriage": Aspects of communication among Bear Lake Athapaskan. *Journal of Anthropological Research, 37,* 28–45.

Sacks, H., Schegloff, E., & Jefferson, G. (1974). A simplest systematics for the organization of turn-taking for conversation. *Language, 50,* 696–735.

Sanders, R., & Sigman, S. (1994). An editorial caveat. *Research on Language and Social Interaction, 27,* 419–421.

Schiffrin, D. (1984). Jewish argument as sociability. *Language in Society, 13,* 311–334.

Schneider, D. (1976). Notes toward a theory of culture. In K. Basso & H. Selby (Eds.), *Meaning in anthropology* (pp. 197–220). Albuquerque, NM: University of New Mexico Press.

Scollon, R., & Scollon, S. (1981). *Narrative, literacy and face in interethnic communication.* Norwood, NJ: Ablex.

Scotton, C., & Zhu, W. (1983). *Tongzhi* in China: Language change and its conversational consequences. *Language in Society, 12,* 477–494.

Searle, J. (1969). *Speech acts.* New York: Cambridge University Press.

Searle, J. (1979). *Expression and meaning.* New York: Cambridge University Press.

Sequeira, D. (1993). Personal address as negotiated meaning in an American church community. *Research on Language and Social Interaction, 26,* 259–285.

Sequeira, D. (1994). Gifts of tongues and healing: The performance of charismatic renewal. *Text and Performance Quarterly, 14,* 126–143.

Silverstein, M. (1976). Shifters, linguistic categories, and cultural description. In K. Basso & H. Selby (Eds.), *Meaning in anthropology.* Albuquerque, NM: University of New Mexico Press.

Smitherman, G. (1977). *Talkin' and testifyin': The language of Black America.* Boston: Houghton Mifflin.

Spradley, J. P. (1979). *The ethnographic interview.* New York: Holt, Rinehart & Winston.

Spradley, J. P. (1980). *Participant observation.* New York: Holt, Rinehart & Winston.

Stacey, J. (1991). *Brave new families.* New York: Basic Books.

Stanback, M. H. (1985). Language and Black women's place: Evidence from the Black middle class. In P. Treichler, C. Kramarae, & B. Stafford (Eds.), *For alma mater: Theory and practice in feminist scholarship* (pp. 177–191). Urbana, IL: University of Illinois Press.

Stanback, M. H. (1989). Feminist theory and Black women's talk. *The Howard Journal of Communication, 1,* 187–19.

Tannen, D. (1981). New York Jewish conversational style. *International Journal of the Sociology of Language, 30,* 133–149.

Tannen, D. (1984). *Conversational style: Analyzing talk among friends.* Norwood, NJ: Ablex.

Ting-Toomey, S. (1988). Intercultural conflict styles: A face-negotiation theory. In Y. Y. Kim & W. B. Gudykunst (Eds.), *Theories in intercultural communication* (pp. 213–238). Newbury Park, CA: Sage.

Ting-Toomey, S. (1991). Intimacy expressions in three cultures: France, Japan, and the United States. *International Journal of Intercultural Relations, 15,* 29–46.

Tucker, S. (1988). *Telling memories among Southern women: Domestic workers and their employers in the segregated South.* New York: Schocken Books.

Turner, V. (1980). Social dramas and stories about them. *Critical Inquiry, 7,* 141–168.

van Dijk, T. (1993). Principles of critical discourse analysis. *Discourse in Society, 4,* 249–283.

Van Maanen, J. (Ed.). (1995). *Representation in ethnography.* Thousand Oaks, CA: Sage.

Varenne, H. (Ed.). (1986). *Symbolizing America.* Lincoln, NE: University of Nebraska Press.

Weeden, C. (1987). *Feminist practices and poststructuralist theory.* Oxford: Basil Blackwell.

Weigel, M., & Weigel, R. (1985). Directive use in a migrant agricultural community: A test of Ervin-Tripp's hypotheses. *Language in Society, 14,* 63–79.

Weiss, L., & Lowenthal, M. F. (1975). Life-course perspective on friendship. In M. Thurnher & D. Chiriboga (Eds.), *Four stages of life* (pp. 48–61). San Francisco: Jossey-Bass.

Werner, C., Brown, B., Altman, I., & Staples, B. (1992). Close relationships in their physical and social contexts: A transactional perspective. *Journal of Social and Personal Relationships, 9,* 411–431.

Weston, K. (1991). *Families we choose: Lesbians, gays, and kinship.* New York: Columbia University Press.

White, H. (1980). The value of narrativity in the representation of reality. *Critical Inquiry, 7,* 5–27.

Willis, P. (1977). Learning to labor: How working class kids get working class jobs. New York: Columbia University Press.

Wittgenstein, L. (1953). *Philosophical investigations.* Oxford: Blackwell.

Wood, J. T. (1982). Communication and relational culture: Bases for the study of human relationships. *Communication Quarterly, 30,* 75–83.

Wood, J. T. (1993). *Gendered lives: Communication, gender and culture.* Pacific Grove, CA: Wadsworth.

Zimmer, T. (1986). Premarital anxieties. *Journal of Social and Personal Relationships, 3,* 149–160.

AUTHOR INDEX

SUBJECT INDEX